The Bristol and Gloucestershire Archaeological Society
Gloucestershire Record Series

Hon. General Editor
C. R. Elrington, M.A., F.S.A., F.R.Hist.S.

Volume 21

Gloucester Cathedral Chapter Act Book 1616–1687

GLOUCESTER CATHEDRAL
CHAPTER ACT BOOK
1616–1687

Edited by Suzanne Eward

The Bristol and Gloucestershire Archaeological Society

2007

The Bristol and Gloucestershire Archaeological Society
Gloucestershire Record Series

© The Bristol and Gloucestershire Archaeological Society 2007

ISBN 978 0 900197 69 7

British Library Cataloguing in Publication Data.
A catalogue record for this book is available from the British Library.

Printed in Great Britain by 4word Ltd., Bristol

CONTENTS

ACKNOWLEDGEMENTS

Thanks are offered to the Dean and Chapter of Gloucester, the owners of the Chapter Act Book, for permission to publish the edition; to Mr. Lowinger Maddison, the cathedral librarian, for making the manuscript available; to Miss Pamela Stewart for advice on the Latin of the manuscript; to Sir John Sainty for help with the identification of government office-holders; to Mr. Brian Frith for help with other identification; and to Dr. Martin Crossley Evans for contributions to the introduction.

The drawing on the title-page is taken from an engraving by J. Kip published in R. Atkyns, *The Ancient and Present State of Glocestershire* (1712).

LIST OF ABBREVIATIONS

A.M.	Artis Magister (i.e. Master of Arts)
Alumni Cantab.	*Alumni Cantabrigienses, A Biographical Register*, Part 1, to 1751, ed. John and J. A. Venn, 4 vols. (1922–7)
Alumni Oxon.	*Alumni Oxonienses, 1500–1714*, ed. Joseph Foster (1891–2)
Bigland, *Glos.*	Ralph Bigland, *Historical, Monumental and Genealogical Collections relative to the County of Gloucester*, 4 vols., ed. Brian Frith, Bristol and Gloucestershire Archaeological Society, Gloucestershire Record Series vols. 2, 3, 5, 8 (1989–95)
Bonnor, *Gloucester Cathedral*	T. Bonnor, *Ten Views of the Interior of Gloucester Cathedral* (1799)
D.N.B. (orig. edn.)	*The Dictionary of National Biography* (1885–1900)
D.Th.	Doctor Theologiae (the equivalent of Doctor of Divinity)
Fasti	John Le Neve, *Fasti Ecclesiae Anglicanae, 1541–1857*, viii, ed. J. M. Horn (1996), 40–64
Freemen of Gloucester	*Calendar of the Registers of the Freemen of the City of Gloucester*, ed. John Juřica, Bristol and Gloucestershire Archaeological Society, Gloucestershire Record Series vol. 4 (1991)
G.B.R.	Gloucester Borough Records, in Gloucestershire Archives
G.D.R.	Gloucester Diocesan Records, in Gloucestershire Archives
Laud's *Troubles and Tryal*	*History of the Troubles and Tryal of . . . William Laud, wrote by himself* (1695)
O.D.N.B.	*The Oxford Dictionary of National Biography* (2004)
Parsons	*Notes on the Diocese of Gloucester by Chancellor Richard Parsons c. 1700*, ed. John Fendley, Bristol and Gloucestershire Archaeological Society, Gloucestershire Record Series vol. 19 (2005)
Rudder, *Gloucester*	Samuel Rudder, *The History and Antiquities of Gloucester* (1781)
S.T.B., S.T.P.	Sacrae Theologiae Baccalaureus, Professor (the equivalent of Bachelor of Theology and Doctor of Divinity)
Th.B.	Theologiae Baccalaureus (i.e. Bachelor of Theology)
Trans. B.G.A.S.	*Transactions of the Bristol and Gloucestershire Archaeological Society*
V.C.H. Glos.	*Victoria History of the Counties of England: Gloucestershire*, in progress; vol. iv (1988), the City of Gloucester; vol. vii (1981), Brightwells Barrow and Rapsgate Hundreds
Walker Revised	*Walker Revised, being a Revision of John Walker's Sufferings of the Clergy during the Grand Rebellion 1642–60*, ed. A. G. Matthews (1948)
Wood, *Athenae*	Anthony à Wood, *Athenae Oxonienses*, 3 vols. (1813–17)
Wood, *Hist. et Antiq.*	Anthony à Wood, *Historia et Antiquitates Universitatis Oxoniensis* (1674)

INTRODUCTION

The Act Book which is here edited covers the period from December 1616 to November 1687. It is the earliest surviving Act Book of the chapter of Gloucester cathedral, and it may well be that no earlier record was kept.[1] It records the business transacted by the dean and chapter at their formal meetings or by the dean or one of the canons acting on behalf of the chapter. There are also copies of letters addressed to the chapter, notably from the Crown for the election of the bishop (the *congé d'élire*, the king's licence to the chapter to elect the man nominated by the Crown), for the admission of those appointed by the Crown to the deanery or to prebends and for the dispensation from the observance of statutes or from royal ordinances. The Act Book begins with a record of the installation of William Laud as dean and ends seven months after James II's first Declaration of Indulgence. It spans the periods of the Civil War and the Commonwealth, but there is a gap between 1641 and 1660: the only entries for the years 1642–59 are three relating to the appointment of William Brough as dean, and of them at least one was made after the Restoration.

The picture which the Act Book gives of the cathedral community, known as the college, in the 17th century is enhanced by the cathedral accounts for the same period,[2] and the activities of the dean and chapter are to be understood in the context of the statutes[3] which governed them.

THE CATHEDRAL ESTABLISHMENT

The great Benedictine abbey of St. Peter at Gloucester, with all its vast possessions, was surrendered to the king's commissioners on 2 January 1540 by the prior Gabriel Moreton and the monks.[4] Then, by letters patent dated 3 September 1541, Henry VIII founded the diocese of Gloucester, taken out of the former huge diocese of Worcester, and established the town of Gloucester as a city.[5] The new diocese contained the whole of Gloucestershire, the county and city of Gloucester, and that part of Bristol which had formerly been in the diocese of Worcester. The former abbey was refounded as the cathedral of the new diocese, and was newly dedicated to the Holy and Undivided Trinity. In place of the abbot, prior, and monks, there were now a bishop, dean, and six canons or prebendaries, all of whom were priests.[6]

The Dean and Chapter

The dean and canons were to be a body corporate known as the Dean and Chapter of the Holy and Undivided Trinity of Gloucester. The statutes promulgated in 1544 specified the officers who were to make up the cathedral establishment. As the head of the chapter

---

[1] The reference to a Chapter Book in the list below, at **316**, appears to be to the book in which it is written rather than to an earlier Act Book. Cf. below, p. 1 n. 3.

[2] The accounts are preserved in Gloucester Cathedral Library. They are the principal source for the present editor's book *No Fine but a Glass of Wine: Cathedral Life at Gloucester in Stuart Times* (1985), and are used freely in this introduction.

[3] Printed in translation in R. Atkyns, *The Ancient and Present State of Glostershire* (1712, reprinted 1974), p. 44, and in Latin and English as *The Statutes of Gloucester Cathedral* (1918).

[4] The last abbot, William Malvern, had died in 1539.

[5] William Dugdale, *Monasticon Anglicanum* (1836), i. 553–6.

[6] Rudder, *Gloucester*, appendix, p. xxxvii.

the dean had ultimate authority. The dean, or in his absence the subdean, and the six canons or prebendaries, all of whom were appointed by the Crown, were the decision-making body which governed the cathedral. The Act Book records that each new member of chapter, at his installation, laid his hand on the gospels and took an oath to observe the cathedral statutes, to renounce the bishop of Rome and to acknowledge the king as supreme head. The subdean was elected from among the canons annually at the general audit on 30 November, the feast of St. Andrew, when he took the oaths required of his office. Deans were frequently absent in the 16th and 17th centuries, by virtue of being royal chaplains or holding university appointments, with the result that the subdean's authority was almost as great as the dean's. The dean was allowed to be absent from the cathedral no more than one hundred days a year, and each canon was allowed an absence of no more than eighty days a year, in order that they might visit their cures, carry out their other duties, or 'mind their own private concerns'. If, however, by reason of being a royal chaplain or engaged on other royal service, or attending convocation, the dean or a canon was absent on more days than those allowed by statute, that absence was not counted against him.

The statutes specified the stipends to be paid to the dean, canons and various officers. The stipends were augmented by the sharing out of the surplus income accruing to the dean and chapter after various annual expenditures and obligations had been met. The stipends or salaries were paid quarterly. For every day that the dean was absent beyond the number allowed, 4*s*. was deducted, and for every such day that a canon was absent 8*d*. The money thus collected was divided at Michaelmas between the dean and the canons who were then resident, the dean receiving twice as much as a canon.

The accounts for 1624–5 (a year taken at random, since no accounts survive for the earliest years covered by the Act Book) show that the dean received an annual stipend of £100, while that of each canon was £20. The subdean received an extra £6 (though in 1609–10 he had received only £2), but in 1666 the extra payment was raised to £10 (**178**).[1] The statutes provided for a receiver, who was to collect all moneys, rents and debts owing to the dean and chapter, and a treasurer, who was to pay to the minor canons and those singing in the choir their monthly diet and commons, as well as the quarterly payments due. The treasurer was also responsible for making sure that the church buildings, and the houses of the dean and canons, were kept in good repair, and he had to supply building materials for their repair when needed. In addition, it was he who had the task of keeping the chapter accounts and writing them up every year in the account book.[2] Although the statutes indicate that the offices of receiver and treasurer were distinct, throughout the period of the Act Book here edited a single canon was elected to both offices at the annual audit. The heading to each set of surviving annual accounts, 'Compotus . . . Receptoris generalis sive Thesaurarii', shows that by 1609 that was the practice. For his reponsibilities the treasurer received £10 in addition to his canon's stipend.

Each of the six canons had a numbered prebendal stall, and in the earlier 17th century a newly appointed canon took the numbered stall of his predecessor. Apparently after 1665, when Thomas Vyner resigned the prebend which he already held in order to be presented

---

[1] References in the introduction to the text of the Act Book are in bold figures in brackets.

[2] Painted at the beginning of the second and third volumes of accounts, along with the coat-of-arms of the dean and chapter (granted in March 1542), are the personal arms of William Loe and Richard Harwood, treasurers in 1635 and 1664 respectively when those volumes were begun.

to that made vacant by the death of Thomas Warmestry (**196**), it became the practice that when a stall became vacant the canons in the stalls of a higher number moved up one and the sixth stall was assigned to the canon who filled the vacancy.

The Choral Foundation

The largest single group of people were those who made up the choral establishment of the cathedral, for to sing the praises of God daily was the reason for the cathedral's existence. The statutes ordained that six priests were to be appointed as minor canons, with six lay clerks, and eight choristers.[1] The minor canons were musical men who could sing well, each with a stipend of £10 a year in the period of the Act Book. At the bishop's visitation in 1613, however, the dean and two of the canons presented that there were in fact four minor canons, only two of whom were in priests' orders, and eight singing men or lay clerks, the explanation being that two of the minor canons were then carrying out the duties of lay clerks. The number of minor canons was officially reduced to four at the Restoration,[2] but the accounts show that immediately after the Restoration there was only one minor canon; in 1664–5 there were two, by 1667–8 there were three, and by 1670–1 there were the statutory four. One of the minor canons, 'older than the rest, and more eminent both for his behaviour and for his learning', was appointed precentor, for which he received an extra £1 6s. 8d. a year. The same minor canon served as precentor for many years in succession.[3] Among other duties the precentor was to lead the other men in their singing, keep the absentee-book and report any defaulters at the fortnightly chapter meeting, and make sure that music books were ready for the use of the choir. The election of the precentor took place at the annual audit, and was duly recorded in the Act Book. In 1616 on William Laud's arrival as dean the precentor was Thomas Tomkins, who 'was of a family that produced more musicians than any other family in England'.[4] In addition to his stipends as minor canon and precentor, Thomas Tomkins received another £10 13s. 4d. as vicar of St. Mary de Lode, to which the dean and chapter had the right of presentation.

Another of the minor canons, 'being a careful and honest man', was chosen by the dean and chapter as sacrist. He was responsible for preparing the altar for communion services, for the chapels, vestments, altar books, chalices and ornaments such as candle-sticks. The statutes also entrusted him with care of the muniments, a responsibility which in 1617 had been neglected, as is shown by Laud's order that the 'evidences' should be set in order (**7**). The sacrist had, furthermore, to take care that there was no lack of communion wine, water, or wax candles, and he had responsibility for visiting the sick. Although his was a statutory position, we have no knowledge of any sacrist during Laud's time at the cathedral, and the earliest mention of a sacrist in the Act Book does not occur until December 1666 when Edward Jackson (who had been a minor canon since October 1664) was elected (**180**). That evidently resulted from a decree of Bishop Nicholson,

---

[1] Today, when the number of choristers at any one time is about sixteen boys, the eight most senior are known as the foundation choristers.

[2] Dugdale, *Monasticon*, i. 540.

[3] Thomas Tomkins from 1609 or earlier to 1625, Richard Marwood 1625–40, Francis Hanslape 1661–7 [no record of election 1662–4 inclusive], Edward Jackson 1667–78, John Deighton 1678–88.

[4] *D.N.B.* (orig. edn.). He was father of the famous composer Thomas Tomkins, then organist of Worcester cathedral, of John, organist of King's College, Cambridge, and of Giles, organist of King's College, Cambridge, and later of Salisbury cathedral.

following his visitation the previous year, when he ordered that 'there be a Sachrist to doe the dutie required in the Statute'.[1] The record in the accounts for 1666–7 of a payment to Edward Jackson of £1 6s. 8d. is the earliest of any payment to a sacrist at Gloucester, but it was not until 1671 that it became the norm for a sacrist as well as a precentor to be elected annually at the audit (227). Under the sacrist were two subsacrists, each receiving £6 a year. Their tasks were to 'lay up the vestments, light the candles, keep the altars, take care that the church be swept and kept clean, toll the bells, or see that they be tolled'.

The six lay clerks, or singing men, were each paid £6 13s. 4d. a year, and the eight choristers ('youths who have good voices and are inclined to singing, who may serve, minister and sing in the choir') £3 6s. 8d. each. The master of the choristers, who also acted as organist, received £10 in the 1620s, but after the Restoration his salary was raised significantly. The minor canons and lay clerks were naturally expected to be musical and have good voices; that they were not always of the required standard is shown by the chapter's efforts in 1620 and 1626 to improve the singing of some of the lay clerks (27, 66).

The minor canons were permitted to hold one near-by benefice with their cathedral appointment. In 1616 the minor canons were Thomas Tomkins, John Phelps (who at the 1613 visitation had been described as a lay clerk), John Johnson and Richard Marwood. John Sandy and Peter Brooke were among those named as lay clerks in 1616, though in 1613 Sandy had been described as a minor canon and received a salary as one from 1609 or earlier until 1641. Both minor canons and lay clerks were often in trouble: in 1618 Richard White, lay clerk, was accused of frequenting alehouses and 'slouthfulnesse in performing his service' (12); Rowland Smyth, lay clerk, was accused of beating a tailor as he sat at work (14) and being drunk in church in the time of divine prayer (21); the minor canon Richard Marwood was accused of cruelly whipping a child (48). The condition and behaviour of the minor canons and lay clerks were paralleled at other cathedrals.[2]

Of the choristers, some who were the sons of lay clerks later became in their turn lay clerks at Gloucester. Among these 'choir families' were the Brodgates, the Dobbses and the Smiths, the adult members of the latter family being often in trouble with the dean and chapter (14, 21, 25, 41, 42, 45). The choristers too were occasionally unruly, notably Richard and Thomas Longe: they were presented as incorrigible boys at William Laud's metropolitical visitation in 1635, and on his orders were expelled from the choir (Richard having by then already been removed by the dean) (130, 132).

The stipends earned by choristers and lay clerks were not enough to provide them with a livelihood, and the lay clerks presumably followed a trade. Christopher Hayes, a lay clerk from 1620 to 1641, may be the glazier of that name.[3] Richard Elliott the elder, a chorister from 1636 to 1641 and a lay clerk from 1660 to 1684, was a barber. There were three Richard Brodgates connected with the cathedral in the 17th century. One was a chorister from 1618 to 1630, a lay clerk from 1639 to 1641 and 1660 to 1667, who may be identical with a bedesman of that name from 1660 to 1667; by trade he was a barber surgeon. He seems to have been the very paradigm of someone whose whole existence was centred on Gloucester cathedral. For a genuinely musical person, the lay clerk may be thought to have had a reasonably satisfying life, for much of the music they

[1] Glos. Archives, D 936 X 15.

[2] e.g. Chester and Norwich: *Journal of Chester Archaeological Soc.* vol. 68, pp. 97–123; *Minute Books of Dean and Chapter of Norwich Cathedral, 1566–1649*, Norfolk Record Soc. vol. 24.

[3] *Gloucester Apprenticeship Registers, 1595–1700* (Bristol and Gloucestershire Archaeological Society, Gloucestershire Record Series vol. 14), p. 63.

were called upon to sing (some of which still survives in the 17th-century music part-books in the cathedral library) is today considered among the great glories of the English cathedral musical repertoire. There were occasional perks for the lay clerks, as at Christmas in 1667 when they were given an extra £10 between them. The accounts show that in some years after the Restoration the lay clerks received a gratuity, following a petition sent to the bishop *c.* 1664 and signed by the lay clerks, in which they expressed their hope that, when the cathedral's revenues had improved, their 'salaryes would be augmented to such a competency as might render their lives comfortable unto them.'

There is no evidence that in the 16th and 17th centuries the choristers attended the college school. A presentment at the bishop's visitation in 1613, when it was reported that 'the choristers are not well ordered and that there is none appointed to catechise them', certainly implies they were not being educated there, as indeed does a chapter order in 1628 that one day a week Philip Hosier, the master of the choristers, was to teach the choristers the principles of Christian religion (**83**). Besides being taught to sing, the choristers were, it seems, taught to play the viols, for in 1629 the chapter paid the lay clerk John Merroe ten shillings 'for a rome which he rented of John Beames to teache the children to play upon the vialls'.[1] The accounts show that in the 1630s Richard Brodgate junior and others were paid for playing on the sackbut, while at various times others were paid for playing on the cornet. In 1638–9 Abraham Blackleech and Richard Machin each gave a sackbut to the cathedral. At the bishop's visitation in 1663 it was presented that 'according to custome theire ought to be two sackbutts & two cornetts for the use of our singinge service & anthems.' There is no evidence that the choristers learned either instrument, but they were taught to play the organ.

The College School and the Schoolmasters

Before the Dissolution there had been a school attached to the abbey, and it was refounded by Henry VIII as the college school. Although it is not known for sure where the earlier school had been situated, it was probably in the undercroft of the building later called the Parliament Room,[2] to which the Commonwealth survey of cathedral property in 1649 referred as the old workhouse and the old schoolhouse.[3] Be that as it may, the new cathedral statutes ordained that the annual sum of £20, intended to be spent on repairing bridges, should for the next three years go instead towards the repair of the grammar school and 'almost all the buildings, in which we would that the minor canons and other officers . . . should lodge.'

The school was throughout the period of the Act Book kept in the long room on the upper floor between the north transept and the chapter house, which had been the abbey library and was later the cathedral library. The room had been put in good repair and made suitable for a school at the expense of Mrs. Elizabeth Wiltshire, widow, a member of a large Gloucestershire family which in the late 16th and early 17th centuries gained a reputation for charitable and educational works.[4] The school remained there until 1849

---

[1] Ian Payne, 'The Will and Probate Inventory of John Holmes (d. 1629): Instrumental Music at Salisbury and Winchester Cathedrals revisited', in *Antiquaries Journal*, vol. 83 (2003), gives information about the playing of viols by choristers in the early 17th century.

[2] In the early 17th century the building stretched as far west as the archway linking Millers Green and Lower College Green.

[3] 'Oliver's Survey', Glos. Archives, D 936 E 1, p. 281.

[4] F. Hannam-Clark, *Memories of the College School, Gloucester, during 1859–67* (1890), p. 19.

when, following a fire, a new schoolroom was built and the old schoolroom became the cathedral library.[1] The school day began at 6 a.m. and ended at 5 p.m.

The dean and chapter chose two schoolmasters: the headmaster or 'archididascalus' was paid £16 13s. 4d. a year, and the undermaster, usher or 'hypodidascalus' £8. According to the statutes the headmaster was to be skilled in both Latin and Greek, the usher only in Latin. The headmaster taught the older boys, the usher (usually a young man just down from the university and waiting to be ordained) the younger boys, giving them a grounding in grammar. The dispute in September 1686 between the headmaster and the usher concerning the transfer of boys from the lower to the upper school (**305**) sheds some light on the method of teaching at the time. The dates of admission of the schoolmasters seem to suggest that when a headmaster left there was generally a change of usher.[2]

Known as the college school, the name emphasising the collegiate nature of the cathedral establishment, until the late nineteenth century, it then came to be called the King's School, acknowledging Henry VIII as founder. When John Langley appeared at the bishop's visitation in 1616, he was described as usher of the free school, and the school was referred to as the free school twice in the Act Book (**9, 124**). The earliest known instance of the name the King's School seems to be in 1685 when the new forward-thinking headmaster, Maurice Wheeler, began a register of the names of the boys at the school.[3]

Almsmen or Bedesmen

The cathedral establishment included four bedesmen or almsmen, 'poor men, oppressed with want and poverty, maimed in the wars, weakened with age, or any other ways disabled, and reduced to want and misery.' Many of the almsmen's duties, such as serving and helping the priests in preparing for services, were those which today are performed by the vergers. The almsmen had also, if they were able, to keep the cathedral clean and to help the subsacrists in lighting the candles and in ringing the bells. How many of the statutory duties they actually carried out is uncertain, for many of them seem to have been genuinely infirm. Each almsman received £6 13s. 4d. a year, the same as the lay clerks. In addition, they were given simple accommodation in the precinct, in the large building called Babylon, along with the lay clerks and various poor widows. They were nominated by royal letters patent, recorded in the registers of leases and stating why each man was deserving. On several occasions when a prospective almsman appeared with his letters patent and requested admission, there was some doubt whether his predecessor was in fact dead (**17, 51, 61, 62, 76, 81, 95**); the proviso that his admission should be void if his predecessor was found to be still living suggests that some almsmen were not active in the life of the cathedral.

Of the admissions of almsmen recorded in the Act Book only two are matched by entries in the registers of leases. James Evans, admitted as an almsman in December 1669 (**218**), had, according to his letters patent dated 16 March 1669, served Charles I in the

---

[1] Cf. *Gloucester Journal*, 3 March 1849.

[2] J. N. Langston, 'Headmasters and Ushers of the King's (College) School, Gloucester, 1541–1841', in *Records of Gloucester Cathedral,* vol. iii (2) (1927), p. 176.

[3] 'Scholæ Regis Glocestriensis Liber Censualis, sive Matricula Alumnorum,' i.e. Census Book of the King's School, Gloucester, or Register of Pupils. Wheeler also used the name the King's School for the benefactors' book which he compiled.

wars under the command of Colonel Mynn at the siege of Gloucester.[1] In June 1674 he received his first monition for neglecting his duty and not coming to prayers (**247**). Robert Stagg had letters patent dated 5 July 1676 which stated that he had served Charles I in the companies of the earl of Lindsey and the earl of Bath and had received wounds which rendered him almost helpless and unable to maintain himself or his family. He was not admitted as an almsman until February 1687, presumably having to wait until there was a vacancy (**307**). The Act Book does not record the admission of all those whom the accounts show to have been paid as almsmen year by year.

Other Officers

The cathedral establishment included a number of 'inferior officers'. Two doorkeepers, known variously as porters or janitors, were each paid £6 a year. They were to 'do the office of virgerers', look after the gates of the precinct, keeping the keys and not letting the gates be open at night unless with the express permission of the dean or the subdean. Other inferior officers were the butler or manciple (£6), the cook (£6), and the undercook (£3 6s. 8d.), who were to supply the provisions and prepare meals for those of the community who dined in the common hall. Archbishop Laud at his metropolitical visitation in 1635 ordered that the offices of butler and cooks should be discontinued (**136**), since the common hall had gone out of use. The order was reiterated by Bishop Nicholson in 1669 (**221**), but whereas the accounts show the last payment to a cook in the year 1663–4 Charles Pitfeild received a salary as butler from 1661 until 1681.

The chapter clerk or registrar received no salary but was entitled to fees for writing out indentures and patents, sealing documents and writing letters. In 1627 the chapter ordered that he should receive 26s. 8d. a year until further notice (**77**), a payment which appears in the accounts not as a salary but rather as a payment for attending the annual audit with his servant. He also received £10 yearly as collector of the chapter's rents from the city of Gloucester.

The cathedral's accounts record annual payments in the early 17th century to people who performed functions for which the statutes did not provide, £6 to the plumber, £5 to the glazier, £1 6s. 8d. to the barber,[2] £2 to the water-supplier (*aquaeductor*). There were also payments to a doctor (apparently not mentioned in the accounts after 1613), an auditor and legal advisers, besides those to men looking after or collecting rents from the chapter's estates outside Gloucester.

THE CATHEDRAL AND ITS PRECINCT

Henry VIII granted to the dean and chapter the whole of the former monastic precinct. Gradually the existing buildings were adapted from monastic to domestic use, though being no longer required the monks' dormitory north of the chapter house was demolished. The former abbot's house on the north side of the precinct was granted to the bishop as his palace, the prior's lodging became the deanery, while other buildings were allocated to the six canons as their dwelling-houses. When a canon died or resigned his successor took the house assigned to his canonry. Other buildings, converted to dwelling-houses, were assigned to lesser cathedral officers; only the choristers did not necessarily

---

[1] Glos. Archives, D 936 E 12/4.

[2] Apart from the Commonwealth period, Samuel Sisemore received a salary as barber from 1633 until 1665 when, at his death, Richard Elliott, the lay clerk, subsequently received the barber's salary.

live in the precinct. Some houses and plots of ground were gradually let to lay people who might not have any particular connection with the cathedral.

In the 17th century the cathedral and its precinct was entirely surrounded by a wall which had been built in the days of Abbot Peter (1104–13), with access by means of three gateways; a fourth entrance to the east of the infirmary was added later. The part of the

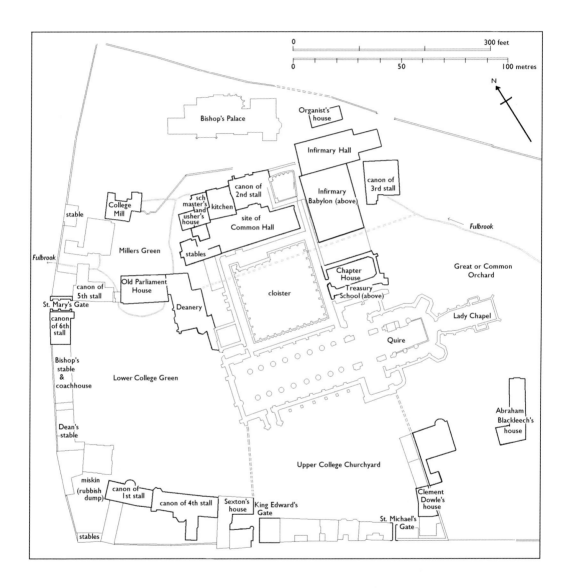

THE CATHEDRAL PRECINCT IN THE EARLIER 17TH CENTURY
The outlines of the buildings are largely taken from 19th-century Ordnance Survey plans.

precinct south and west of the cathedral and the former conventual buildings was divided then as now into two, College Green, which had been the large outer courtyard of the monastery, and Millers Green, the inner courtyard, containing the service buildings of the abbey. Millers Green took its name from the abbey mill on the north side of the courtyard.[1]

College Green was itself divided into two by a wall extending southwards towards King Edward's Gate from the south-west corner of the cathedral. The area east of the wall was Upper College Churchyard (where the lay people were buried), while to the west was Lower College Green. King Edward's Gate gave the laity access to the burial ground.[2] There were in the early days of the cathedral no houses in Upper College Churchyard, but by 1616 a small house had been built on the site of the later no. 20, and during the Commonwealth period Clement Dowle built a house on the site of the later no. 19 (**296**). Another wall extended southwards from the south transept, and east of it was the former monks' graveyard. Beyond that graveyard was a great orchard,[3] which in the early 17th century was divided into separate parcels of ground which were let. In 1626 it was the subject of a chapter order forbidding the removal of earth (**65**). On one plot William Blackleech, chancellor to the bishop of Gloucester, had by 1597 built a new house (later King's School House). That was the property for which in 1626 the dean and chapter allowed William's son Abraham to put a door through the college wall (**67**). An enormous cross stood in the Upper College Churchyard until 1647, when six men took more than a week to demolish it and 124 cartloads of stone were hauled away.[4]

St. Michael's Gate, at the south-east corner of College Green, was then known as the upper or over college gate. Stretching westwards from it to King Edward's Gate was a long strip of garden ground on which in 1616 was a dwelling-house newly built by John Elbridge, cordwainer, and which by the Commonwealth period had three houses built on it. Over King Edward's Gate was a great gatehouse which belonged to one of the porters, but which had long been let to private tenants as a separate dwelling-house (**244**). The tenants, until 1649, also leased the strip of garden ground between the two gates. Presumably the porters had the use of some rooms over the gate. In 1673 Samuel King paid rent for the gatehouse, but the porter Walter Allard lived over the gate; that was the last time that the gatehouse was recorded as let, and it may be that it fell down or was demolished soon after.

West of King Edward's Gate was an old house known as the sexton's house or chamber (later no. 6 College Green), and there in the early 17th century lived members of the Penny family. The next two houses (later nos. 7 and 8), which were assigned to the canons holding the 4th and 1st prebendal stalls, were also part of the former abbey buildings. Adjoining the house of the canon of the 1st stall was his stable. The south-west corner of Lower College Green contained no buildings, and was the miskin ground, the cathedral rubbish-dump and dung heap. It was let in 1607 to Roger Nicholson, locksmith, at a rent of 3s. 4d.; he probably made a profit by charging members of the college who wished to make use of it. The location of the miskin is probably explained by its nearness

---

[1] W. H. St. John Hope, *Notes on the Benedictine Abbey of St. Peter at Gloucester* (1897), p. 127.

[2] The lich gate was so called in 1223: *Historia Monasterii S. Petri Gloucestriæ* (Rolls Series), i, p. 26. It was rebuilt by Edward I and called after him.

[3] By the time that Maurice Wheeler became master of the college school in 1684 the orchard was nothing but a rubbish-dump. With the help of the schoolboys, Wheeler managed to transform it into an academic garden called the Grove.

[4] G.B.R., Minute Books, 11 Feb. 1647.

to several stables. The canons of the 2nd, 4th and 5th stalls had stables there, and in 1626 the canon of the 6th stall, Thomas Iles, having complained that there was no stable for his prebendal house, was allowed to build one in the miskin (**68**). The dean's stable was on the site of the later nos. 10 and 11. Between it and St. Mary's Gate were the bishop's stables and coach-house. During the Commonwealth period part of the bishop's 'great Stable roome' was inhabited by poor people put in by the mayor of the city.

At the end of the row was the house of the canon of the 6th stall (later no. 14), thought to have been the abbey almonry. Alongside, in the centre of the precinct's west wall, was St. Mary's Gate, which had been the main entrance to the abbey. Over the great gateway were rooms which from 1587 or earlier were assigned to the chapter clerk for keeping his records. They were the rooms which were in dispute early in the 17th century (**126**). In 1636 the very first clause in Archbishop Laud's injunctions following his metropolitical visitation ordered that the muniments were to be kept in the room which anciently was assigned to them (**132**).

The house assigned to the canon of the 5th stall stood between St. Mary's Gate and the 14th-century archway leading from Lower College Green into Millers Green. East of the archway was a single long building known as the old workhouse and old schoolhouse, later called the Parliament Room. In Laud's time at Gloucester the building was let to Alderman John Jones, the bishop's registrar. Thomas Pury junior, the tenant in 1649, then repaired it and shortened its length. South-east of the old schoolhouse, adjoining the west side of the cathedral cloisters, was the deanery, formerly the prior's lodging. During Laud's tenure of the deanery a new floor was put in the dining room (**29**). The panelling in what was later called the Laud Room may have been put in at the same time.

On the west side of Millers Green were several small tenements on the site of the later deanery. In Laud's time as dean they were in the tenure of Robert Oldisworthe, gent. Adjoining them on the north was the stable of the canon of the 3rd stall. North-east of the tenements, opposite the archway into Millers Green, was the college mill, in Laud's time occupied, at a rent of 20s., by William Mason, described as a cutler. Mason may have been the person of the same name who was the cathedral clerk of works and who deputised for some of the minor office-holders. On the east side of Millers Green was the house assigned to the schoolmasters, comprising two separate tenements, the upper and the lower schoolmaster's house. South of it was a piece of waste ground on which, in the later 17th century, three stables were built, two of them used by canons Abraham Gregory and Ralph Cudworth; an inventory of Gregory's possessions, made after his death in 1690, shows that he had three horses.[1] In 1666 a mounting block was erected in Millers Green.

Adjoining the schoolmasters' houses on the east was the building known in the 17th century as the common kitchen, on the north side of the common hall, formerly the monks' refectory, where in the early days of the cathedral the junior staff were expected to eat communally. The hall[2] was still standing in 1605, though in a dilapidated state, when Bishop Ravis at his visitation said that it needed immediate repair,[3] but soon after, and certainly by 1612, it had fallen down. By then the kitchen had been made into a

---

[1] Eward, *No Fine but a Glass of Wine*, 332.

[2] The belief that the hall was burned down shortly after the Dissolution derives from a note added to a survey of monastic property (Augmentation Office Book 494), but the note was added long after the survey was made: cf. S. J. A. Evans, 'Cathedral Life at Gloucester in the early 17th century,' in *Trans. B.G.A.S.* vol. 80 (1961).

[3] 'Episcopal Visitations', TS. in Gloucester Cathedral Library, pp. 98, 108.

dwelling-house (later no. 3 Millers Green) for which Simeon Wrench paid a rent of 2*s.* a year.[1] Adjoining the kitchen on the east was the house (later Little Cloister House) assigned to the canon of the 2nd stall, then held by Simeon's father, Elias, who 'when the hall fell, . . . made a garden on the cellar arch'.[2]

Little Cloister House, together with a large house east of the little cloister itself (which until the 1640s retained the roofs over all four walks), had been part of the abbey infirmary. The large house (on the site that became the King's School playground) contained a collection of rooms where the elderly and infirm monks had lived. The upper floor of the building in Laud's day still retained its ancient title of Babylon, while the lower floor was known as the Firmary. The Firmary was divided into various dwellings, but above, the congeries of cramped little rooms which made up Babylon was given over to the singing men and almsmen to live in, as well as sundry poor widows. In 1620 the building was thought to be at risk from fire (**28**). The minor canons and singing men complained about their accommodation at the metropolitical visitation in 1635, and Laud ordered that they should 'have all right done to them concerning their houses' (**132**). The infirmary hall, north-east of the little cloister, was a great room with arches (the arches survived the hall's demolition) and at its east end a chapel. The hall was evidently what was known as the fencing school, for which Richard Parker paid a rent of 3*s.* 4*d.* in 1609–10, and which in 1630 was in danger of collapse and ordered to be taken down (**96**).

North of the common kitchen was the bishop's palace, formerly the abbot's lodging. The bishops in the early 17th century seem to have lived at the Vineyard, their house in Over, and in 1647 the palace was in such a poor condition that it could not be let at a proper rent.[3] East of the palace was the cathedral organist's house (demolished in the 1860s), and east of the infirmary was the house (later Dulverton House) assigned to the canon of the 3rd stall. In the precinct wall nearby was an opening, the infirmary gate, which had been made by 1673.[4]

Across the east and north sides of the precinct ran an ancient watercourse, the Fulbrook, providing water for drinking and washing, working the mill and leaving the precinct near St. Mary's Gate. In 1605 Thomas Field, a Gloucester brewer, held the office of cathedral *aquaeductor* and a lease of the watercourse. At the visitation that year he was ordered by Bishop Ravis to repair it, as obliged by his lease, and to cause enough water to be brought into the cloisters,[5] where the ancient washing-place in the north walk was evidently still in use. The tenant of the college mill was bound to scour, dig and cleanse the brook running to the mill, which apparently remained largely open to the air; from 1661 Stephen Halford, gent., then tenant, had to cover over part of it. College Green and Millers Green then each had a pump, and there were also wells.

In the Commonwealth period five of the canons' houses were assigned to puritan ministers of the city, that of the 5th stall being used as a debtors' prison, and the deanery was let to Thomas Pury junior. The schoolmasters continued to occupy their houses, but other houses were sold.

[1] Glos. Archives, D 936 A 22.
[2] Ibid. D 936 E 16, p. 11.
[3] Ibid. G 3/19.
[4] *V.C.H. Glos.* iv. 286.
[5] 'Episcopal Visitations', TS. in Gloucester Cathedral Library, pp. 98, 108.

THE ESTATES OF THE DEAN AND CHAPTER

In 1541 the dean and chapter had been generously endowed with lands, manors, rectories, tithes, meadows, woods and rents, most of which had belonged to Gloucester abbey; a few had belonged to Tewkesbury abbey. In Gloucestershire were the manors of Abload and Sandhurst, Barnwood, Bulley, Churcham, Coln Rogers, Cotes, Cranham, Eastleach Martin, Matson, Rudford, Taynton, Tibberton, Tuffley, and Wotton, the rectories of Barnwood, Brookthorpe, Churcham, Coln St. Aldwyn, Eastleach Martin, Fairford, and St. Mary de Lode, Gloucester, meadows and woods including Archdeacon's Meadow and half of Woolridge Wood and the Perch in St. Mary de Lode parish (the other half of the woods going to the bishop), and a very large number of properties in the city of Gloucester and its suburbs: in 1649 it was said that the chapter owned almost a third of all the houses of the city.[1] The endowment also included manors, rectories, lands and tithes in neighbouring and distant counties in England and in Wales, and there were annual payments from the churches of St. Peter Mancroft, Norwich, and St. Martin le Vintry, London. The chapter was charged with an annual rent to the Crown of £90 14s. 0½d.

The greater part of the cathedral's revenues came from rents and particularly from entry-fines for property leased to tenants. The statutes ordained that houses in cities or villages could be leased for up to sixty years. The chapter's leases were for varying terms either of lives or years: the Act Book records attempts by the Crown to restrict the granting of leases for lives (**119, 123**): a lease for lives enabled the chapter to demand a larger entry-fine than one for a term of years, but potentially lengthened the time until another entry-fine became payable. The chapter nevertheless decided (**284**) that tenants who already had leases for lives should be allowed to renew them for lives, and on occasion the king instructed the chapter to do so either for that reason (**291**) or because of the tenant's good service (**294**). According to the statutes, either the dean or the receiver had to make an annual inspection of all the chapter's manors, tenements, lands and woods and to make a written report of necessary repairs. That the inspection was not always made is suggested by Bishop Nicholson's decree, following his visitation in 1665, that the chapter's lands be visited as they ought.[2]

Following the recovery of its estates at the Restoration the chapter experienced difficulty in collecting rents from the tenants (**217**), who may have been unwilling to pay for a variety of reasons. In the end, just after the period covered by the Act Book here edited, the chapter decided at the audit of 1688 to write off arrears that were utterly lost.[3]

Many estates were relet at fines much smaller than could have been obtained, as the chapter acknowledged in 1681, citing two reasons: 'The first was to gratifie Dr. Frampton, who was then passing from the deanery to the bishoprick: the second was the very bad face of things which lookt with a dismal aspect towards the Church, and made severall of the prebendaries very willing to make money at any tolerable rate'.[4] In 1672 Giles Fettiplace paid £170 as an entry fine for the rectory of Coln St. Aldwyn, which was considered to be low but was accepted because his father Sir John had in the worst of times paid his rent constantly and been good to members of the college, and also because Giles made a gift of ten guineas to the library. In 1673 the chapter accepted an entry-fine of £75 for a messuage in Sandhurst from Charles Underhill, whose principles and

---

[1] Rudder, *Gloucester*, p. 332.
[2] Glos. Archives, D 936 X 15.
[3] Gloucester Cathedral Library, TR 4.
[4] Glos. Archives, D 936 E 16.

practices it disliked, because Dean Vyner, then lying on his death bed, wished it. The chapter seems generally to have given preference to tenants who supported the established Church and the monarchy, and the tenants seem to have paid less than they would have to another landlord.

ADMINISTRATION OF THE CATHEDRAL

Henry VIII's statutes prescribed how the cathedral was to operate in all its departments, how it was to be staffed, and how its personnel were to be ordered and disciplined. They were written into each of the two earliest Act Books, so that they were easily to hand should any point need to be checked. Though the statutes are now missing from the first Act Book, the fact that they were originally there is evident from the index at the end of the volume (**315**).

Chapter Meetings

The statutes required the chapter to hold two general meetings each year, on 30 November and 23 June, but by 1616 the general meeting in June was no longer held. At the November meeting the chapter elected the subdean and the treasurer and receiver for the year, and the dean chose the precentor for the year.[1] That meeting was also the annual audit when the treasurer presented his accounts. On occasion the king allowed the date of the audit to be varied because the dean was unable to be present on 30 November (**8, 114, 161**). In addition to the general meetings the chapter was to meet, according to the statutes, at least once every two weeks, and more often if business required, but either there were often longer gaps between meetings or some meetings went unrecorded: up to 1640, apart from the annual audit, two or more members were recorded as acting together (as distinct from the dean or a single canon acting alone) between one and seven times a year. If the dean or a canon was unable to attend a meeting in person he could be represented by another as his proxy.

Meetings were usually held in the chapter house, but some took place in the deanery, sometimes with only the dean and no canon present. A single meeting in the period 1616–87 was held in the vestry (**92**). Members of the choir attended at least some of the meetings (**96**), but perhaps only when a singing man or a chorister was to be admonished.

The Treasury

The treasury, in what later became the minor canons' vestry, was divided into two. The inner room held a large chest in which £40 was kept for emergencies. Inside this chest was a smaller chest containing the common seal. The seal used in the 17th century bore a depiction of the Holy Trinity.[2] That it depicted the Trinity was used as an argument in the

---

[1] In 1617 and until 1640 the dean chose the precentor except in the nine years (1622 and 1625 to 1632) when the dean was absent from the audit and the prebendaries who were present elected the precentor. In 1661, 1665 and 1666 the prebendaries present at the audit elected the precentor, subject to the dean's approval. Thereafter the dean chose the precentor except when he was absent from the audit: in 1683 and 1686 the subdean chose the precentor, and in 1684 the subdean and chapter were said to elect both the precentor and the sacrist, the dean's consent to each choice being mentioned apparently as an afterthought.

[2] Rudder, *Gloucester*, 339–40, says that the earliest seal also bore the arms of Dean William Jennings and the initial letters of his name, together with the words SIGILLV COMVNE DECANI ET CAPITULI ECCLESIÆ CATHEDRAL. SCTE ET INDIVIDUÆ TRINITAT. GLOU.'

controversy which raged at the cathedral in 1679 (**270**, **271**, App. I). Another chest in the inner room contained the statutes, the foundation charter and other muniments. Each chest had three locks, the keys being held by the dean, the subdean and the treasurer respectively. In the outer room were kept the rentals, court rolls, inventories of cathedral goods and of lands, account books and an iron chest containing money for daily expenses. In 1617 it was agreed that the chapter clerk and one or more of the canons should spend one afternoon each week to put the untidy muniments in order (**7**).

The Library

The chapter seems to have looked with favour on a tenant renewing his lease if he also gave a book to the library. In 1672 when Robert Hill paid £34 as an entry-fine for a messuage in Sandhurst he also gave a copy of Heylyn's *Cosmography*. The library had been founded by Thomas Pury junior in 1648,[1] and following an Act of Parliament in 1656 settling the cathedral on the mayor and burgesses of Gloucester the library became the city's responsibility.[2] At the Restoration the chapter appointed a librarian to look after the books which they found in the chapter house, but in 1680 when the librarian was the poet-vicar of Naunton, Clement Barksdale, it was ordered that one of the porters should be paid to look after the library (**275**).

Patents

The chapter increased its income by selling patents of office, that is to say it granted the right to an office in the cathedral for a term of years or for life to someone who paid a premium for it. A patent-holder was usually a well-to-do citizen or a member of a canon's family, and in most instances he did not intend to perform the office himself but to pay someone else less than the salary to perform it. Among the offices so exploited were those of porter, sexton or subsacrist, butler, cook, under-cook, bailiff or rent-collector, registrar or chapter clerk, plumber, woodward, surveyor or clerk of works, glazier, *aquaeductor*, attorney and auditor. In October 1620 Simeon and William, sons of canon Elias Wrench, were jointly granted 'the office of one porter', the patent stating that the salary of £6 was to come 'from our lands and tenements in our manor of Abload and Sandhurst or from lands and tenements in Gloucester.' When in 1629 Simeon Wrench wanted to resign the patent he was roundly told that he could not as William Mason, who was doing the work on his behalf, was doing it satisfactorily. Likewise, on the same day his brother Barkeley Wrench wanted to dispose of his patent for the office of subsacrist, granted in 1617, and for the same reason was told he could not (**87**). The Wrench family seems to have profited from patents, and even after the Restoration Barkeley Wrench continued as a subsacrist until 1691, while William, an attorney, was in 1662 granted one of the porter's offices for life, and in 1673 acquired the patent for the other sub-sacrist's office (**242**). A patent could pass through several generations of a family: the glazier's office was granted to successive members of the Wager family. In 1669 Bishop Nicholson strongly deplored the use of such patents, for which there was no authority in the statutes (**221**).

Monitions and Punishments

If the dean was thought to be scandalous or covetous his correction lay with the bishop. If a canon offended, he was to be admonished by the dean, or in his absence by the subdean, and if he did not amend his behaviour he was to be called before the bishop as

---

[1] Gloucester Cathedral Library MS. 71, Library Benefactors' Book.
[2] G.B.R., Minute Books, 1658.

visitor. A minor canon or lay clerk guilty of a lesser infringement was to be punished at the dean's discretion, and for a more serious offence was to be expelled from the cathedral. In 1667 the dean only suspended Francis Hanslape, minor canon and precentor, though he might have expelled him (**208**). It was left to the bishop and the chancellor to censure him, and as Hanslape received no stipend from the chapter after 1667 he was evidently dismissed. Lesser cathedral officers who transgressed in any way were subject to a monition or formal warning by the dean. Such monitions took place publicly in the chapter house at chapter meetings and were formally recorded in the Act Book. On his third monition the miscreant was expelled, i.e. dismissed from office. A third monition was a rare occurrence. Ely Smith, a lay clerk, was dismissed in 1623 not only for being absent without leave for very long periods but also for insolence to members of the chapter (**41, 42, 45**).

Episcopal Visitations

At the bishop's visitation of the cathedral all the members of the chapter, the minor canons, lay clerks, all other officers, and even the choristers were expected to be present, their attendance emphasising the collegiate nature of the cathedral foundation. A visitation gave members good opportunities to air grievances and tell tales. There were several reports of incontinent behaviour by minor canons and lay clerks, and even by canons, of choristers' misconduct and having no-one to catechise them, of encroachments on land in the cathedral precinct, of lack of necessary service books, and of various misdemeanours. Although visitations were meant to take place every three years, throughout the period of the Act Book (55 years, allowing for the gap 1646–60) only eleven seem to have taken place,[1] and the only one mentioned in the Act Book is that of Bishop Nicholson in 1669 (**213, 221**).

The cathedral statutes required the dean and chapter to spend £20 a year on the relief of the poor and another £20 a year on repairing bridges and mending highways. The statutes made the bishop responsible, at his triennial visitation, to enquire whether those obligations had been carried out. In 1640–1 the dean and chapter were indicted at Quarter Sessions for not repairing a bridge.

Upkeep of the Cathedral and Buildings

The chapter's responsibility for keeping the cathedral and the buildings in the precinct in good repair was in effect delegated to the cathedral treasurer (**3, 7, 182, 186**). After the Restoration very large amounts of money were spent, in particular on repairing windows both in the cathedral and in people's houses. The chapter employed a large work-force on routine maintenance and on extraordinary repairs.

The Act Book records, though in an inconclusive way, the chapter's concern for the organ (**10**) and the font (**187**).

LAUD'S INNOVATIONS AT GLOUCESTER

When in 1616 James I appointed William Laud as dean of Gloucester he told him there was 'scarce ever a Church in England so ill govern'd, and so much out of order' as Gloucester cathedral, and instructed him to reform what he found amiss there.[2] Bishop Miles Smith's visitation just three years earlier had certainly shown failings in many aspects of cathedral life. The statutory chapter meetings were not held every fifteen

---

[1] 'Episcopal Visitations', TS. in Gloucester Cathedral Library.
[2] William Prynne, *Canterburies Doome* (1646), p. 77.

day; a certain amount of incontinence was reported (even canon William Loe was suspected of adultery with his servant, who had been sent away with child);[1] encroachments were made in the churchyard with the result that gardens were being created on ground where burials had taken place; two people were said to sell drink within the precincts; the choristers were not well ordered and there was no-one appointed to catechise them. Though there were sufficient books and 'ornaments' with which to celebrate holy communion, the monthly communions were not held monthly, and there were no copes for the priests celebrating.[2] There was no copy of the latest translation of the Bible (though the bishop himself was one of the main translators of the 1611 Authorised Version, and had written the preface). Dean Field and canons Aisgill and Wrench reported that even though much was spent every year on repairs, 'by reason of former neglect' the cathedral was not in good repair. Laud obviously had many and various problems to tackle when he took up his duties as dean.

The dispassionate recording of decisions in the Act Book gives no indication of the upheaval that the high-church Laud's arrival caused in puritan Gloucester. Peter Heylyn, contemporary theologian and historian, described how on his arrival Laud found the building in great decay and the communion table placed in the middle of the quire. He immediately called a chapter meeting, informed the canons of the king's instructions, and got their consent to carry out the most necessary repairs to the cathedral and to move the communion table to the east end of the quire against the wall.[3] It may be that, if indeed it was Laud who initiated the series of Chapter Act Books, one reason for so doing was to defend himself from accusations of high-handed actions, for the fact that the canons present at those two meetings subscribed their names to those acts seems to indicate their approval (2, 3).

The upset caused by the moving of the communion table (2) was to reverberate for many years, and would be one of the depositions made against Laud at his trial in 1644. To the puritans the communion table, which had stood east–west in the body of the quire, was just that, a table to be used for a commemorative meal. Those of a high church persuasion regarded the service of holy communion as a sacrament, the climax of the liturgy, and putting the table north–south at the east end of the quire (with suitable altar-furnishings set thereon)[4] made it an altar, which Laud railed in to keep it from profanation.[5] Laud also insisted that the canons, choirmen, choristers and the under-officers should make their 'humble reverence to Almighty God'[6] both on coming into the quire and when they approached the holy table. The Calvinist bishop Miles Smith disliked bowing and ceremonial in worship, and strongly protested at what had been done. Almost the whole of the population of puritan Gloucester was offended at the moving of the communion table, and a libellous paper was placed in the pulpit of St. Michael's church accusing the canons of not having spirit enough to resist the dean or to

---

[1] It may be that Loe became pastor of the Merchant Adventurers in 1619 because it was thought expedient for him to be absent from Gloucester for a while, though an attestation from the chapter then described him as having carried out his duties at Gloucester 'without impeachment' (16).

[2] Article 24 of the Canons of 1604 stated that copes were to be worn 'in Cathedral Churches by those that administer the Communion'.

[3] Peter Heylyn, *Cyprianus Anglicus* (1668), p. 69.

[4] Since no accounts survive from Laud's time we do not know what purchases were made in order to embellish the quire.

[5] The Laudian altar-rails are now in the Lady Chapel.

[6] Heylyn, *Cyprianus Anglicus*, p. 69.

tell him what harm the move might do. It was also said that the papists would rejoice that popery was coming in.[1]

Having not even attempted to win his opponents over to his way of thinking by persuasion, and at the height of the upset, Laud wrote letters to bishops Miles Smith of Gloucester and Richard Neile of Lincoln justifying his actions and claiming that he had authority for them from the king. He also claimed that communion tables in other cathedrals, as well as in the king's own chapel, were placed at the east end. His statement about cathedrals William Prynne later wrote was 'a grosse untruth'.[2]

The ruinous state of the fabric was certainly one of the most urgent of the problems which Laud set himself to address, for since little money was available for repairs proper maintenance had been difficult. Means had to be found to raise the necessary sums. Laud got the chapter to agree that £60 a year should be spent for the purpose until the necessary repairs were finished (3). In addition, no-one was allowed to have their dead buried in the cathedral until 40 shillings had been paid for each such burial, the money being earmarked towards the cost of the fabric repairs, nor was the treasurer to authorise any particular repairs to the cathedral unless he had first obtained permission from the dean (7).

One reason behind the order for the 'evidences' to be sorted (7) may have been the need to raise money. The documents and title-deeds were in confusion, and until they were properly sorted it was not possible to discover what rents and other income were due to the chapter from the lands and property which they owned. Although the work of putting the documents in order was begun in 1617 it seems, from the very first injunction laid on the chapter following Laud's metropolitical visitation in 1635 (132), that the task was not completed in his time as dean.

The organ was also in decay, and the chapter had recourse to a public appeal to raise money either for its repair or for making a new one (10). To accompany the services with fine music was part of the 'beauty of holiness' for which Laud was striving (and which was so much a part of the Laudian movement), as opposed to the plainness of the regime of prayer, preaching and the singing of psalms of which the puritans approved. The result of the organ appeal of 1617 is not known, but it seems that it was unsuccessful since in 1640–1 the organ-builder Robert Dallam was to build a new organ for Gloucester cathedral, while after the Restoration a magnificent new instrument was built (177). The smaller choir organ, however, has a case which has not been precisely dated but, to judge from its fine craftsmanship and the style of the woodwork, may be either the case made for Dallam's organ or a result of Laud's organ appeal.[3]

The conduct of services also had to be regulated. In 1618 Laud and two canons ordered that morning prayer at 6 a.m. in the lady chapel, which had long been in abeyance, should again be held during part of the year and the chapel cleaned. Attempts to preserve orderliness in time of divine service are evidenced by Laud's decrees (subscribed in the Act Book by himself alone) that, to prevent running around during services, certain choristers should be appointed to lay out the correct music beforehand; penalties were also laid on any lay clerk or minor canon who was often absent from services (28). During Laud's time as dean are recorded some eight cases of discipline that had to be dealt with for various specified lapses of conduct. He also made an attempt to abolish sinecure offices and to put the money saved to better use by increasing the choirmen's salaries (15).

---

[1] Prynne, *Canterburies Doome*, pp. 75–6.

[2] Ibid. p. 77.

[3] Michael Gillingham, in *The Organs and Organists of Gloucester Cathedral* (1971), p. 25.

Laud's continuing concern for the state of Gloucester cathedral was apparent in his supervision as archbishop. He is likely also to have influenced the appointment of the dean and canons. Among them were Accepted Frewen and Gilbert Sheldon, later to be leaders in the post-Restoration church.

That Laud, as archbishop of Canterbury, intended to change the statutes of Gloucester cathedral is suggested by a list, which he wrote in his diary, of 'Things which I have Projected to do, if God Bless me in them.' Project number VIII reads, 'To settle the Statutes of all the Cathedral Churches of the new Foundations; whose Statutes are imperfect, and not confirmed. Done for Canterbury.'[1] At his trial in 1644 Laud had to answer for his 'popish innovations'[2] at Gloucester and elsewhere, one of the main accusers of his innovations at Gloucester being the puritan schoolmaster John Langley.[3] Little more than twenty years after Laud left Gloucester his liturgical reforms at the cathedral were, during the 1640s, swept away. The table was then put back in the middle of the quire; the choir, choral music, and Book of Common Prayer were done away with; Dallam's organ was sold (though repurchased at the Restoration); chapter lands were sequestrated; instead of a bishop, dean and canons an 'orthodox divine' was appointed preacher at the college; and the cathedral once more fell into such decay that it was said to be in danger of falling.[4]

THE MANUSCRIPT

The manuscript is a book of 160 paper folios measuring 33 cm. by 22 cm., with six folios of modern paper inserted as fly-leaves, three at the beginning and three at the end, when the book was rebound in 1998. The blank folios 5–19 are also of modern paper, replacing original folios which contained, according to the index at the end of the book, a copy of the cathedral statutes and were removed presumably when they were copied into the second Chapter Act Book.[5] The original folios, of which many have a fool's cap as a watermark, were numbered with arabic figures in the top right-hand corner of the rectos in what appears a 17th-century hand. In the mid 19th century, at an earlier rebinding of the book,[6] an attempt seems to have been made to put the earlier folios in chronological order: a modern hand had added dates in the margin of entries **1–5** and **8–10**, misdating those between 1 Jan. and 24 March by failing to allow for the fact that in the 17th century the year was reckoned to begin on 25 March.[7] Some at least of the folios were given new numbers in pencil, which have since been erased; the versos were numbered in pencil in the top left-hand corner. By the late 20th century many of the folios had become loose, and the book was rebound in 1998 by Desmond Shaw of Cambridge, with the folios

---

[1] Laud's *Troubles and Tryal*, p. 68.

[2] Prynne, *Canterburies Doome*, p. 78.

[3] Ibid. p. 75.

[4] G.B.R., Minute Book 1632–56, p. 873, quoted in Eward, *No Fine but a Glass of Wine*, 110. Laud is commemorated every year at Gloucester cathedral on 10 Jan., the anniversary of his execution.

[5] The accounts for 1686–7 record the payment of £1 to Mr. Palmer, stationer, for two folio paper books, and of £1 to Mr. Pike for transcribing the statutes into one of them, evidently the second Chapter Act Book.

[6] Probably in 1858 or 1860: in those two years 100 MS. volumes were sent to Oxford for rebinding: notebook in the cathedral library begun in 1849 by C. Y. Crawley.

[7] The error was noted in 1920 by Henry Gee, dean 1917–38, on a loose sheet formerly inserted in the book.

ordered according to the inked folio-numbers and the 'abstract', or outline index (**315**), which was added in the 17th century on fos. 156–7.

Before the book was rebound in 1998 a leaf one centimetre shorter than the other leaves followed folio 77, where it had been pasted in; it also was numbered in pencil as 77, in a modern hand. It contains the record (**171**) of William Brough's installation as dean, which at Brough's request the chapter clerk, William Lamb, compiled and inserted in the book, where it followed the king's letter nominating Brough as dean (**159**). William Lamb was appointed as chapter clerk in November 1665 (**170**). Presumably William Brough wanted the leaf added to avoid any doubt that he had been installed as dean, in the troubled times of 1644. When the MS. was rebound the leaf was moved to become folio 82, there having been no folio so numbered immediately before the 19th-century rebinding. The leaf may originally have been folio 82, the correct place in the book for a date of compilation soon after Lamb's appointment, and may have been moved (and trimmed so that the folio-number was lost) to come after folio 77, the correct place for the date of the installation which it records; that possibility is the more likely since on the verso is what appears to be the blotted impression of the number of folio 83.

On folio 157, in the lower right-hand corner are the letters GHF, in a later hand, probably that of the cathedral librarian, Canon George Harold Fendick, who died 24 Dec. 1962. Before the volume was rebound in 1998 that was the last page to contain any writing: Canon Fendick presumably wished to record the fact that he had read through to the end of the book.

Up to 1640 the entries are largely in chronological order. From 1660 onwards they are less methodical: they are far from chronological in order before 1668, the records of the annual audit (**166-9**) and of admissions to prebends (**190–9**) being grouped together, the names of canons present are seldom given and spaces that had been left blank seem to have been used for entries which would otherwise have come later.

Some of the entries in the book are in English, others in Latin. The more formal entries tend to be in Latin, and a large proportion of the book is devoted to recording the installation of the dean, the admission of canons, the election of the subdean and the treasurer and receiver, the election of the precentor, the admission of the schoolmaster and the assistant schoolmaster, of the organist and master of choristers, of minor canons, of lay singers and choristers and of almsmen, and the election of the sacrist. Such entries are mostly repetitive, and it seems that an entry was often copied from an earlier entry of the same sort. A few entries record the chapter's involvement in the appointment of diocesan officers, such as the archdeacon of Gloucester (**266**) and the diocesan registrar (**54**).

A comparison of the entries recording the admission of canons shows the evolution of the form. The form in **37** is followed closely in **60**, but in **107** there are various changes, including the way the prebend is defined, the substitution of 'quibus perlectis' for 'eisdemque perlectis' and the omission from 'Et immediate venerabilis vir' of one 'm' from 'immediate' and of the word 'vir', changes which (with the exception in **117** and **151** of the omission of 'vir') are repeated in later entries of the same kind. In **107** the record begins with the name of the man being admitted, but later entries (other than the anomalous **190**) begin either with the date and the names of those of the dean and chapter who were present, as in **37**, or with 'In domo capitulari' ('In the chapter house'). In **111** and the later entries (except for **117**) the title 'fidei defensor' is added to the king's title. In **226** the clause stating that the prebendary being admitted had taken his oath is enclosed in parentheses, and all the later entries of the same kind include the opening but not the closing parenthesis, a clear indication that each was copied from the preceding entry. That indication is corroborated in the incomplete entry **256** by the repetition of the erroneous 'professoris' (for 'possessoris') from **255**. The records of the installation of deans show a similar repetition of scribal peccadilloes: in **241** the statement that the new dean had taken the oath omits the phrase about observing the statutes, while in **286** the phrase is included but the closing bracket which should follow it is omitted, an omission that is repeated in **301**.

Up to November 1665 (**174**, on folio 84), the month in which William Lamb was appointed as chapter clerk, each entry, except for the first on folio 76 (**157**), has a marginal heading. From April 1666 (**175**), however, nearly a quarter of the entries have no marginal heading, and some of the headings are written at the foot rather than the head of the entry. By contrast there are five marginal headings for entries that were never written into the book (**184, 187, 192–3, 195**).]

The handwriting of the manuscript

The variety of hands suggests that the book was not kept solely in the care of the chapter clerk and makes it clear that in stating that all acts and orders of the dean and chapter had to be entered in the act book either by the dean or by the chapter clerk as soon as they were made (below, pp. 157–8) Abraham Gregory, a canon from 1671 to 1690, was not strictly accurate. Either when an entry was written or at a later meeting the canons present subscribed their names. In the early part of the book about 70 of the first 157 entries are written in the rather crabbed hand of the chapter clerk, Anthony Robinson. The rest of the main text is in other, unidentified hands, which suggests that he left the writing of the entries to assistants. In places Robinson subscribed as a witness to the more formal proceedings, and most of the marginal headings are in his hand.

After the Restoration the tall sloping hand of the chapter clerk, William Lamb, is more frequent than any other. From 1669 (**221**) a neat hand which may be that of an assistant employed by Lamb occurs frequently. Entries in the hands of Dean Brough, Thomas Washbourne, Thomas Vyner, Abraham Gregory (a very neat hand), Robert Frampton and Nathaniel Hodges can be identified from their signatures. In 1667 the record of the election of officers (**206**) is written in five sections in three different hands, Brough, Lamb, Vyner, Brough, Vyner. Many of the entries towards the end of the book are in unidentified hands. Lamb, who frequently subscribed the entries, wrote most of the marginal headings, though some are in the untidy hand of Dean Brough and that of Thomas Vyner.

Up to folio 57 many of the more formal documents have the opening words in large capitals or in enlarged lower-case letters, sometimes in intensely black ink. Sometimes intermediate words, usually names, are similarly treated, for example the words Miles, Frederick, Rheine and Canterbury in (**23**) and the name Marburye at the end of (**19**).

EDITORIAL METHOD

In this edition serial numbers in bold type have been added for ease of reference, a separate number being given to each act, or group of acts done on the same day, and each document copied into the Act Book. The text is given mostly in full transcript. The date and the place, however, of an act or group of acts, whether done at a meeting of the chapter or by the dean or a canon on behalf of the chapter, and the names of those stated as being present are given in calendared form. Appointments and similar documents in common form are given in full on the first occasion and thereafter in many instances, particularly in longer entries, only in summary, with a reference back to the full form.

Documents in Latin have a summary in English added as editorial comment. Phrases in Latin in the middle of a document in English are translated or summarised in English as editorial comment, with the exception of some recurrent words and phrases which are explained below. In the transcripts the edition retains the spelling of the manuscript (except that the thorn in 'ye' is transcribed as 'th' and the accents which are sometimes used in the manuscript are ignored), but it greatly reduces the number of initial capitals and modernises the punctuation, while retaining the manuscript's occasional use of a hyphen (often written there as =). Abbreviated words that are represented in the manuscript by more than a single letter are extended silently in the edition, where that can be done with confidence; in the signatures appended to entries, as also in names occurring in the headings to entries, the extensions are enclosed in square brackets. Words and letters omitted from the manuscript, apparently by mistake, are enclosed in square brackets. Spaces left blank between words in the manuscript and words that are illegible are represented by ellipses in square brackets.

LATIN WORDS AND PHRASES COMMONLY USED
and not always translated in the edition

acta: acts (things done)

decanus: dean

eodem die et loco et anno: on the same day and in the same place and year

imprimis: first of all

in domo capitulari: in the chapter house

Ita testor: As I am witness

quibus (or *quo*) *die*, etc.: on which day, etc.

registrarius: registrar

subdecanus: subdean

LISTS OF BISHOPS, DEANS AND CANONS IN THE PERIOD OF THE ACT BOOK

Deans

1616–21	William Laud
1621–4	Richard Senhouse
1624–31	Thomas Winniffe
1631	George Warburton
1631–43	Accepted Frewen
1644–71	William Brough
1671–3	Thomas Vyner
1673–81	Robert Frampton
1681–5	Thomas Marshall
1685–1707	William Jane

Bishops

1612–24	Miles Smith
1624–56	Godfrey Goodman
1660–72	William Nicolson
1672–81	John Pritchett
1681–90	Robert Frampton

Canons

1st stall	1612–32	Thomas Prior
	1632–58	George Palmer
2nd stall	1599–1633	Elias Wrench
	1634–47	John English
3rd stall	1580–1625	Laurence Bridger
	1625–40	John Wood
	1640–57	Gilbert Osborne
4th stall	*c.* 1612–1633	Thomas Anyan
	1633–60	Gilbert Sheldon
5th stall	1602–45	William Loe
	c. 1645–60	Thomas Washbourne
6th stall	1597–1622	Henry Aisgill
	1622–49	Thomas Iles
	1660–5	Walter Blandford, *vice* George Palmer
	1660–2	Robert Harris, *vice* Thomas Iles in 6th stall
	1660–87	Thomas Washbourne, admitted to 3rd stall 1660
	1660–9	Richard Harwood, *vice* Gilbert Sheldon in 4th stall
	1660–75	Hugh Naish, *vice* Thomas Washbourne in 5th stall
	1660–5	Thomas Warmestry, *vice* John English in 2nd stall
	1662–5	Francis Jacob, *vice* Robert Harris
	1665	Thomas Vyner, *vice* Francis Jacob
	1665–71	Thomas Vyner, *vice* Thomas Warmestry
	1665–78	Anthony Andrewes, *vice* Thomas Vyner in stall held by Francis Jacob
	1666–72	Henry Savage, *vice* Walter Blandford
	1669–75	William Washbourne, *vice* Richard Harwood
	1671–90	Abraham Gregory, *vice* Thomas Vyner
	1672–3	Robert Frampton, *vice* Henry Savage
	1673–1700	Nathaniel Hodges, *vice* Robert Frampton
	1676–91	Edward Fowler, *vice* William Washbourne
	1676–8	Asahel King, *vice* Hugh Naish
	1678–88	Ralph Cudworth, *vice* Asahel King
	1678–1705	George Bull, *vice* Anthony Andrewes
	1687–1723	Luke Beaulieu, *vice* Thomas Washbourne

GLOUCESTER CATHEDRAL
CHAPTER ACT BOOK
1616–1687

[Gloucester Cathedral Library, Chapter Act Book 1]

[*Title page, fo. 2*[1]] ECCLESIA CATHEDRALIS GLOUCESTRIAE. ACTA[2] habita et facta in domo capitulari vel in aedibus decani vel alibi infra ambitum et precinctum ecclesiae cathedralis Gloucestriae, incepta[3] tempore Gulielmi Laud, sacre theologie professoris, dictae ecclesie decani, Laurentii Bridger, Henrici Aisgill, Elie Wrenche, Willelmi Loe, Thome Anyan, sacre theologie professoris, et Thome Prior, prebendariorum ecclesie praedicte, meique Anthonii Robinson, dicte ecclesie amanuensis sive registrarii. 1616. [*Cathedral church of Gloucester. Acts had and done in the chapter house or in the deanery or elsewhere within the ambit and precinct of the cathedral church of Gloucester, begun in the time of William Laud, S.T.P., dean of the said church, and of Laurence Bridger, Henry Aisgill, Elias Wrench, William Loe, Thomas Anyan, S.T.P., and Thomas Prior, prebendaries of the said church, and of me, Anthony Robinson, clerk or registrar of the said church.*]

[*fo. 2v. blank*]

1. [*fo. 3*] Friday 20 December 1616. Chapter House.
(Thomas Prior, subdean; Henry Aisgill; Elias Wrench; Anthony Robinson, registrar.)[4]

[**Instal**]*lacio ve*[*nerabilis*][5] *viri Gulielmi Laud Decani Gloucestriae.* [*Installation of the venerable man William Laud as dean of Gloucester. Theophilus Tuer, B.D., fellow of St. John's College, Oxford, appeared in person and exhibited his proxy for William Laud, S.T.P., appointed as dean of the cathedral church of the Holy and Undivided Trinity of Gloucester, and made himself party for the same and presented the royal mandate, dated 6 December 1616, addressed to the chapter and prebendaries, to assign to the dean a stall in the choir and a place and voice in the chapter. And Theophilus Tuer exhibited the dean's letters of proxy, dated 15 December 1616, appointing Henry Aisgill, M.A., his proxy for the installation etc., which Mr. Aisgill accepted. Afterwards on the same day the*

---

[1] Folio 1 is blank except for the words 'Quer[y] if Dr. Moreton was deane of Gloster' written on the recto in a 17th-century hand. Thomas Morton (1564–1659), later bishop successively of Chester, of Coventry and Lichfield and of Durham, was dean of Gloucester 1606–9: *O.D.N.B.*

[2] The first four words and the date 1616 at the end of the entry are written very ornately.

[3] The word, which has been inserted above the line in an abbreviated form, may imply that it was William Laud who, on his appointment as dean, began the series of Chapter Act Books.

[4] The preamble to the entry states 'In presentia mei Anthonii Robinson, dictae ecclesiae amanuensis sive registrarii', so the early entries are evidently in Robinson's hand.

[5] The top of the folio is damaged.

chapter and prebendaries with due solemnity brought Mr. Aisgill to the dean's customary stall in the choir and installed him and put him in possession, and led him thence to the chapter house and assigned him his place and voice. All which the prebendaries required to be enacted, and all these things were done in the presence of William Sutton, clerk,[1] *Thomas Philpotts, clerk, Tobias Bullock, gent., Arnold Cellwall, notary public, John Hoare, M.A., John Langley, B.A., Thomas Tomkins, precentor,*[2] *and other servants of the said church. Witnessed by Anthony Robinson, registrar of the dean and chapter, and by Arnold Celwall.*] Quibus die et loco comparuit personaliter quidam Theophilus Tuer, sacrae theologie baccalaureus, socius collegii Sancti Johannis Baptiste infra universitate Oxoniensis, ac exhibuit procuratorium pro venerabili viro Gulielmo Laud, sacrae theologie professore, constituto et ordinato in decanum ecclesie cathedralis Sancte et Individue Trinitatis Gloucestriae, ac fecit se partem pro eodem, et ex parte eiusdem venerabilis viri prefatis capitulo et prebendariis ecclesie cathedralis predicte presentavit literas mandatorias regias, gerentes datas sexto die mensis Decembris anno regni domini nostri regis Jacobi Anglie, Frauncie et Hibernie decimo quarto et Scotie quinquagessimo, eisdem capitulo et prebendariis antedictis directas, per quas mandatum fuit capitulo et prebendariis supranominatis ad assignandum sive assignari faciendum venerabili viro decano ordinato predicto stallum in choro et locum et vocem in capitulo in ecclesia cathedrali Gloucestriae predicta ut moris est. Ac insuper dictus Theophilus Tuer ex parte dicti domini decani ordinati exhibuit supranominatis capitulo et prebendariis litteras quasdam procuratorias, a prefato venerabili viro Gulielmo Laud, sacre theologie professore, decano ordinato et constituto ut supra, per quas discretum virum Magistrum Henricum Aisgill, in artibus magistrum, unum prebendariorum ecclesie cathedralis Gloucestriae predicte, inter alios suum verum, certum, legitimum et indubitum procuratorem nominavit, fecit et constituit, pro se ac loco, vice et nomine suis, stallum in choro, ac locum et vocem in capitulo in dicta ecclesia cathedrali Gloucestriae sibi assignari et limitari petendi et obtinendi, necnon realem, corporalem et actualem possessionem, installacionem et inthronizacionem huiusmodi ingrediendi et [*fo. 3v.*] adipiscendi illasque sic adeptas ad usum dicti venerabilis viri custodiendi, conservandi [et] omnia et singula alia perimplenda faciendi que in huiusmodi installacionis negotio necessaria fuerint seu quomodolibet oportuna, prout per easdem litteras procuratorias gerentes datas decimo quinto die Decembris 1616 plenius liquet et apparet. Quas litteras procuratorias dictus Magister Henricus Aisgill debite recepit ac onus earundem in se acceptavit. Postea vero eodem die prefati capitulum et prebendarii ecclesie cathedralis Gloucestriae predicte, omni cum solemnitate qua in hac parte fieri potuerit, prefatum Henricum Aisgill ad stallum in choro ecclesie cathedralis Gloucestriae hactenus decano eiusdem ecclesiae cathedralis Gloucestriae pro tempore existente solitum et consuetum attulerunt, eumque in realem, actualem et corporalem possessionem eiusdem stalli et dignitatis [*MS.* dignitate] decanatus ibidem cum suis membris, juribus, et pertinentiis universis loco, vice et nomine ac pro prefato decano ut prefertur ordinato installarunt et inthronizarunt, ac pacificam possessionem eorundem premissorum ei dederunt. Ac ex inde

---

[1] Presumably he whose patent for the office of chancellor of the diocese was confirmed in 1623: below, **42**.

[2] For Hoare, Langley and Tomkins, below, pp. 165–6, 169.

dictum Henricum [*MS.* dictus Henricus] Aisgill in domum capitularem dicte ecclesie cathedralis simili cum solemnitate attulerunt eique locum et vocem in capitulo eiusdem cathedralis ecclesie prefato decano, racione decanatus sui huiusmodi debitum, solitum et consuetum assignaverunt, possessionemque eorundem prefato Henrico Aisgill loco, vice et nomine dicti domini decani dederunt et tradiderunt. Que omnia et singula dictum capitulum et prebendarii inactitari requisiverunt et omnia hec antedicta facta fuerunt in presentia Willielmi Sutton, clerici, Thomae Philpotts, clerici, Tobie Bullocke, generosi, Arnoldi Cellwall, notarii publici, Johannis Hore, artium magistri, Johannis Langly, artium baccalaurei, Thomae Tomkins, precentoris, aliorumque dicte ecclesie ministrorum.

Testante Anthonio Robinson, decani et capituli registrario.

Iterum teste Arnoldo Celwall.

2. [*fo. 4*]   25 January 1616/17.   Chapter House.
(William Laud, S.T.P., dean; Thomas Prior, subdean; Henry Aisgill; Elias Wrench.)

Decanus iurat.[1] [*The dean takes the oath. The aforesaid dean took the bodily oath on the gospels, touched and kissed by him, to renounce the bishop of Rome, to acknowledge the royal supremacy and to observe the cathedral's statutes.*] Quibus die et anno venerabilis vir decanus antedictus sacramentum prestitit corporale, ad sacrosancta dei evangelia per eum tacta et deosculata, de renuntiando Romano episcopo et de agnoscendo serenissimum dominum nostrum, Dominum Jacobum, Anglie &c. regem &c., supremum &c., fidei defensorem &c., ac de observando ordinaciones et statuta dicte ecclesiae cathedralis quatenus consentiunt verbo dei ac statutis huius regni.

Eodem die post susceptum juramentum. [*On the same day after the oath was taken.*] ***Order for the communion table.*** It was by Mr. Deane and the chapter aforesaid ordered and decreed that the communion table should be place[d][2] altar wise at the upper ende of the quier close und[er the] walle upon the uppermost greeses or steppes acc[ording] as it is used in the king's majestie's chappell and in [all] or the moste parte of the cathedrall churches of [the] realme.

William Laud, deane; Thomas Prior, subd[ean]; Henr[y] Aisgill; Elias Wrenche.

3. [*fo. 4v.*]   27 January 1616/17.

Forasmuch as the fabricke of this church is verry ruinous and in greate decay in many places, so that if speedy care and dew prevention be not used and taken soe goodly an edifice is eyther likely to come to lamentable ruine or else the poore estate of this church to be overcharged with the waighte and burthen of so greate coste and expence which will fall on it at once: It is therfore by Mr. Deane and the chapter now assembled ordered and decreed for the speedy redress hereof that Mr. Threasurer for this yeare, and which

---

[1] Brian Taylor, 'William Laud, Dean of Gloucester, 1616–1621', in *Trans. B.G.A.S.* lxxvii (1958), 86, suggests that the declaration which Laud now made was not the 'Juramentum Decani' as laid down in the cathedral statutes, because he was not instituted by the bishop and so could not declare 'Ego N., qui in decanum . . . electus et institutus sum. . . .'.

[2] The right-hand side of the page has been torn away: some of the words in the entry are missing.

hereafter shalbe chosen from yeare to yeare, shall bestow yearly upon the reparacions of this church the somme of threescore pounds and not exceede one hundred markes [*inserted above the line*: being asmuch as the poore estate of this church can possibly beare]. And allso that the supervisor of the workes from time to time shall carefully enforme the threasurer for the time beinge of the places of greatest neede and dainger, and that they be first taken in hand and repayred, and this order to stand in force till the necessary repayres be ended.

William Laud, dean; Thomas Prior, subde[an]; Henr[y] Aisgill; Elias Wrenche.

[*Folios 5–19 blank*[1]]

4. [*fo. 20*]   Friday 11 April 1617.   Chapter House.
(Thomas Prior, subdean; Laurence Bridger; Henry Aisgill.)

A patent in reversion of a prebendarie's place enrolled. Quibus die et loco venerabiles viri antedicti haec rotulari curaverunt [*On which day and place the said venerable men caused these things to be enrolled*] (viz.). Whereas Thomas Bayly, master of artes, hath obtayned a graunte from the Lord Keeper under the king's highnesse broad seale of England of a prebende in this churche upon the next vacancy and whereas the righte honourable Sir Frauncis Bacon, knighte, Lord Keeper of the Greate Seale, hath testified unto Mr. Prior, now subdeane, his desire to have the same enrolled in the chapter booke of this churche (as the said Mr. Prior doth affirme) and allso at the speciall request of the right worshipfull Sir William Cooke, knight, wee whose names are under written have cawsed the same thus to be enrolled and recorded in the chapter booke.

Tho[mas] Prior, subd[ean]; Laur[ence] Bridger.

A patent graunted to Thomas Bayly, Clerke, Mr. of Artes. Marburye.[2] [*Royal patent of 4 April 1617 granting to Thomas Bayly the appointment to the next vacant canonry in Gloucester cathedral, with the proviso that if the present grant cannot take effect at the next vacancy because of an earlier grant it will extend to later vacancies.*] Jacobus, dei gracia Angliae, Scotie, Frauncie et Hibernie rex, fidei defensor &c., omnibus ad quos presentes litterae pervenerint salutem. Sciant quod nos, de gratia nostra speciali ac ex certa scientia et mero motu nostris, dedimus et concessimus ac per presentes pro nobis heredibus et successoribus nostris damus et concedimus dilecto subdito nostro Thome Bayly, clerico, in artibus magistro, quemcunque canonicatum sive prebendam in ecclesia nostra cathedrali Gloucestriae que primum et proximum per mortem, resignacionem, deprivationem, cessionem, creationem in episcopum aut alio quocunque legali modo vacaverit aut vacare contigerit, habendum, tenendum et gaudendum dictum canonicatum [*fo. 20v.*] sive prebendam prefato Thome Bayly durante vita sua naturali, una cum omnibus et omnimodis domibus, mancionibus, proficuis, comoditatibus, emolumentis, dividentiis, excrescentiis, refeccionibus, quotidianis distribucionibus, ceterisque iuribus et

---

[1] The fifteen folios are modern replacements of leaves which had been removed. They had contained the cathedral statutes, as is evident from the index below, p. 154; cf. above, p. xxviii.

[2] For Bayly and Marbury, below, pp. 161, 167.

preheminentiis quibuscunque dicto canonicatui sive prebendae quovismodo pertinentibus sive imposterum spectantibus. Proviso semper quod si contingit presentem hanc nostram donacionem vacationis prioris alicuius donacionis nostre debitum non sortiri effectum iuxta tenorem harum litterarum nostrarum patentium tunc et in eo casu volumus quod eadem haec presens donatio et concessio nostra valeat et sese extendat ad secundam, tertiam et quartam vacationem cuiuscunque canonicatus sive prebendae in ecclesia nostra cathedrali Gloucestriae predicta, ac ulterius etiam si opus fuit nec ante ad nos revertatur, donec et quousque prefatus Thomas Bayly canonicatum sive prebendam aliquam in eadem ecclesia adeptus fuit ac in eadem plenam institucionem & installacionem optinuit, cum omnibus et singulis juribus et proficuis, emolumentis et preheminentiis quibuscunque eidem canonicatui sive prebendae quovismodo pertinentibus sive spectantibus eo quod expressa mentio de vera valore annuo aut de aliquo alia valore vel certitudine premissorum sive eorum alicuius aut de aliis donis sive concessionibus per nos seu per aliquem progenitorum sive predecessorum nostrorum prefato Thome Bayly ante haec tempora factis in presentibus minime facta existit, aut aliquo statuto, actu, ordinacione, provisione, proclamacione sive restrictione in contrarium inde ante hac habito, facto, edito, ordinato seu proviso, aut aliqua alia re, causa vel materia quacunque in aliquo non obstante. In cuius rei testimonium has litteras nostras fieri fecimus patentes. Teste me ipso apud Westmonasterium quarto die Aprilis anno regni nostri Angliae Frauncie et Hibernie quinto decimo et Scotie quinquagessimo.

Per dominum custodem magni sigilli Anglie &c. Marbury. [*By the lord keeper of the great seal.*]

Examinatur per Anthonium Robinson, decano et capitulo registrarium. [*Examined by Anthony Robinson, registrar of the dean and chapter.*]

[*fo. 21*] **Mandamus ad installandum for Thomas Bayly. Marburye.** [*Royal mandate of 4 April 1617 for installing Thomas Bayly in the next vacant canonry.*] Jacobus, dei gratia Angliae, Scotie, Frauncie & Hibernie rex, fidei defensor, &c., dilectis nobis in Christo decano et capitulo ecclesiae nostrae cathedralis Gloucestriae qui nunc sunt vel qui imposterum futuro tempore erunt sive alii cuicunque in hac parte authoritatem habenti seu habituro salutem. Cum nos quarto instantis mensis Aprilis per litteras nostras patentes de gracia nostra speciali ac ex certa scientia et mero motu nostris dedimus et concessimus dilecto subdito nostro Thome Bayly [*etc., as in the foregoing patent*] quovismodo pertinentibus sive imposterum spectantibus, prout in eisdem litteris nostri patentibus plenius continetur, vobis igitur mandamus quod eidem Thome Bayly stallum in choro et locum et vocem in capitulo cum primum et proximum ut prefertur vacaverit aut vacare contigerit assignetis assignarive faciatis in omnibus diligenter, prout moris est. Teste me ipso apud Westmonasterium quarto die Aprilis anno regni nostri Anglie, Frauncie et Hibernie quinto decimo et Scotie quinquagessimo. Marburye.

Examinatur per Anthonium Robinson, decano et capitulo registrarium. [*Examined by Anthony Robinson, registrar of the dean and chapter.*]

5. [*fo. 21v.*]   31 August 1617.

[***Admissio cho****ristae.*[1] [*Admission of a chorister. Henry Purlewent was admitted by Mr. Thomas Prior, subdean, in the place of Polidore Brodgate.*] Quibus die et anno Henricus Purlewent admissus fuit per Magistrum Thomam Prior subdecanum chorista in loco Polidori Brodgate.

> Per me Anthonium Robinson, decani et capituli amanuensem. [*By me, Anthony Robinson, clerk of the dean and chapter.*]

6.   Thursday 16 October 1617.   Chapter House.

Electio Officiariorum.[2] [*Election of officers. William Laud, dean, Thomas Prior, subdean, Laurence Bridger, Henry Aisgill, Elias Wrench, William Loe, prebendaries, being assembled in the chapter house and solemnly proceeding to the election of officers for the coming year according to ancient custom, the dean and chapter elected these officers, viz. Mr. Henry Aisgill as subdean for the following year and Mr. Elias Wrench as receiver and treasurer, who respectively took the oaths of their offices on the gospels, touched by them.*] Congregatis in domo capitulari ecclesiae cathedralis Gloucestriae venerabilibus viris Gulielmo Laud, sacrae theologiae professore, ecclesiae predictae decano, Thoma Prior, tunc subdecano, Laurentio Bridger, Henrico Aisgill, Elia Wrench, Gulielmo Loe, prebendariis, et ad electionem officiariorum pro anno futuro iuxta morem antiquum solemniter procedentibus, idem decanus et capitulum elegerunt[3] hos officiarios vizt. Magistrum Henricum Aisgill in subdecanum et Magistrum Eliam Wrench in receptorem et thesaurarium eiusdem ecclesiae cathedralis pro hoc anno sequente usque ad finem eiusdem anni, qui quidem respective subierunt iuramenta ad sacrosancta dei evangelia per eos tacta ad eorum officia respective spectantia &c.

> Guiliel[mus] Laud, decanus; Laur[entius] Bridger; Guiliel[mus] Loe; Tho[mas] Prior.

Electio precentoris. [*Election of the precentor. The dean chose as precentor for the coming year Thomas Tomkins, one of the minor canons, the oath having been taken by him.*] Eodem die, loco et anno idem venerabilis decanus antedictus elegit in precentorem dictae ecclesiae pro anno futuro Thomam Tomkins, unum minorum canonicorum eiusdem ecclesiae, juramento per eum suscepto.

> Guiliel[mus] Laud, decanus.

Admissio minoris canonici. [*Admission of a minor canon. Richard Marwood*[4] *was admitted and assigned by the dean a place as a minor canon, for which he had taken the oath.*] Eodem die, loco et anno Richardus Marwood clericus admissus et assignatus est per venerabilem decanum in locum minoris canonici ecclesiae cathedralis Gloucestriae, sumpto juramento &c.

> Guiliel[mus] Laud, decanus.

---

[1] The left-hand edge of the page has been torn away.

[2] Cf. above, pp. xii, xxiii.

[3] The MS. has 'eligerunt', as also in **12** below; it is corrected to 'elegerunt' in later similar entries.

[4] For Marwood, below, p. 167.

7. [*fo. 22*]   20 October 1617.   Chapter House.

Decretum est ut sequitur. [*It is decreed as follows.*]

Order for repairs with consent. That the threasurer himselfe for the time beinge shall [not][1] appoynte any worke of reparacions in or aboute this church ex[cept] he have it first obtayned under the deane's hand. And allso th[at] the said licence so obtayned shalbe shewed at the auditt. [. . .] the title of reparacions shalbe examined, but if the threa[surer] shall doe otherwise then is heare decreed, yt shalbe requi[red] at his handes to make repayment. And that neyther [the] deane himselfe nor any prebendary of this chu[rch] shall cawse any reparacions of leade worke (graunte[d by] an auncient order) to be donne in or aboute his or their howse or howses at the charge of the church withoute the consent of the deane and chapter first hadd and obtayned.

Eodem die.

The mony for burialls to be bestowed upon the repairs of the church. That neyther Mr. Deane nor any other of the chapter shall give leave to any person or persons whatsoever, to bury or interre their dead within the body or quire of the cathedral church of Gloucester, or in any other ile, chappell or walk within the said church unless the partie desiringe shall pay [or] cawse to be paid to the handes of the threasurer for the [time] being for every such buriall the somme of forty shi[llings]. Which said somme of forty shillings for every grave [shall] be bestowed upon the reparacions of the fabricke of the [said] church, and shall not be remitted to any, upon any cawse, but be accounted for by the threasurer at the auditt.

Eodem die.

Orders for placinge and settlinge the evidences. Whereas the evidences and other writings of the church ly in a heape together, and are verry hard to be found when they should be used, a speedy course shalbe taken to bring them in order in manner and forme following.

First that Mr. Aisgill, subdeane, Mr. Lawrence Bridger, Mr. Wrenche, tresurer, Mr. Thomas Prior, prebendaries of the said church, Mr. Anthony Robinson, chapter clarke, or the said Mr. Anthony Robinson with one or more of the aforenamed prebendes,[2] shall spend one afternoone at least every weeke from the date hereof in the th[reasury].[3]

[*fo. 22v.*] That there they shall lay the evidences which they find belonging to any mannor, rectory or other portion of lands, or rent belonging to the said church severall by them selves, that afterwards they may be numbred, according to their dates.

That at all times when the said Anthony Robinson and the prebend or prebends with him shall rise from their sittinges, and come oute of the threasury, they shall shutt all windowes, and leave the heape of evidences as safe as they can, from either weather or moist places.

That the aforenamed shall not desist from this worke, till the trust that is reposed in them be performed.

---

[1] The right-hand edge of the page has been torn away.

[2] The Act Book frequently uses the word 'prebend' for 'prebendary'; in normal usage then and later a prebend is that part of the revenues of a church assigned to a particular canon or prebendary.

[3] Cf. above, pp. xxiii–xxiv, xxvii.

That whereas there are two keyes for the cumming in to the said treasury (which usually lye lockte upp in a chest[1]), it shalbe lawfull, during the time of this worke, for any one of the above named prebends to keepe the one key, and the said Anthony Robinson to keepe the other, and boothe to be answereable for their keyes when the deane and chapter shall call for them. And that the prebend that keepes the key, if hee goe oute of towne, shall leave the key with another prebend, that so the worke be not hindred.

William Laud, dean; Laur[ence] Bridger; Elias Wrenche; Thomas Prior.

8. [*fo. 23*]

A dispensation to keepe the auditt to Dr. Laude. [*15 October 1617.*] James R.: Trustie and welbeloved, wee greete you well. Whereas wee are informed that among other your statutes for the government and ordering of that church, yow have one which binds the deane and chapter to keepe the auditt or chuse the officers of that church precisely upon the last day of November, and that Doctor Laud, your deane, by reason of his attendance boothe upon our person in his turne, and upon the colledge whereof he is president in Oxford,[2] cannot conveniently be there at that presise time, our pleasure is to alter this statute during the time hee shalbe deane there, and to ordayne that from henceforth that clause of your statute which binds yow stricktly to the last day of November yearly shall cease for that time, and that it shalbe lawful for you yearly to keepe your auditt and choose your officers of the said church any day which your selves shall thincke fitt within the moonethes of October or November. And our further pleasure is that this our letter be registred in your statute booke with the rest of your statutes which have hadd their beinge from our worthy progenitors. Given under our signet at our pallace at Westminster the fifteenthe day of October in the fifteenthe yeare of our raigne of England, Fraunce and Ireland and of Scottland the one and fiftithe.

To our trusty and welbeloved the deane and chapter of
our cathedrall church of Glocester.

9. [*fo. 23v.*]   9 March 1617/18.   Chapter House.

Admissio archididascali. [*Admission of the schoolmaster. John Langley, B.A.,*[3] *was admitted to the place of master of the free school*[4] *within the college, after he had subscribed to the Three Articles and had taken the oath to observe the statutes and the oath of allegiance to King James.*] Quibus die & loco Johannes Langley, in artibus baccalaureus, admissus fuit in locum archididascali liberae scholae infra collegium vel ecclesiam cathedralem Gloucestriae, prius subscribens articulis tribus in ea parte requisitis ac praestito prius per eum iuramento de observandis statutis & ordinationibus dictae ecclesiae et suscepto simul iuramento allegeantiae regi Jacobo sicut cautum est.

Guiliel[mus] Laud, decanus.

---

[1] Possibly one of the two ancient chests which in 1970 were moved for safety from the lady chapel to the cathedral library. They were later in the triforium exhibition.

[2] i.e. St. John's College.

[3] For Langley, below, p. 166.

[4] In the Act Book it is called the free school only here and in **124**, below.

Eodem die.

Morninge prayer in the Lady Chappel. Whereas the morninge prayer at sixe of the clocke hath binne for the sommer time performed in the ladie chappell and now for divers yeares past hath bin altogether discontinued, wee, holdinge it unfitt that soe goodly & faire a buildinge dedicated to the service of God should loose the use and end for which it was founded & consecrated, doe order & decree that the said prayers at sixe of the clocke shalbe sayed & celebrated yearly in the sayd chappell from the feast of the Annunciation of the Blessed Virgin St. Mary unto the feast of St. Michaell tharchangell. And that the sexton of this church doe take care to see this our decree to bee put in execution; and also that the sayd place may bee swept, made cleane & prepared for the congregacion against the time in this decree limited.

William Laud, dean; Elias Wrenche; Thomas Prior.

10.   [*fo. 24*]   13 March 1617/18.

A decree for a presentation to the vicaridge of Faireford. The deane & chapter of this church, conceavinge themselves (upon perusall of their evidences & leidger bookes[1]) to bee patrones and to have the right of presentation to the vicaridge of Faireford in the county of Gloucester, unto which vicaridge their present farmer of the rectory there hath now of late presented, but with what colour or pretext of right they know not, they beinge therefore desirous & carefull that the right of the sayd church may bee in all thinges preserved doe order & decree that if any man capable of the same vicaridge (against whose life & learning no iust exception may bee taken) wilbe at the chardge & expence in the law of triall of the churche's right thereunto, hee shall have a presentation made unto him under the chapter seale for the same vicaridge & also bee strengthened with such evidences & writings as shalbe requisite to sett forth the churche's right & interest in that behalfe. Provided that such presentacion bee soe graunted & accepted of within the five moneths after the death of the last incumbent.

William Laud, deane; Elias Wrench; Thomas Prior.

Eodem die.

Letters for the settinge upp of the new organ. The organs of this church being in greate decay and in short time likely to be of noe use, we desiringe the speedy repaire of the oulde or makinge of a new, eyther of which courses the poore estate of this church is not able to beare, encouraged therefore by the example of our neighbour church of Worcester[2] we have adventured to addresse our letters to the gentry and others of this countie and citty of Gloucester for their aide and assistance therein. The tenor of which letters followeth in these wordes.

'After our harty commendacions remembred unto you, these are to desire your lawful favor in a case that concernes the good and the ornament of our poore church at Gloucester. The organs in that church are verry meane, and beside that verry farr decayed, which is a great blemish to the solemnity of the service of God in that place. The church is many

---

[1] Perhaps in the course or as a result of putting the muniments in order; cf. **7**, above.

[2] The organ at Worcester was built in 1613 at 'unusual expense': *D.N.B.* (orig. edn.), s.v. Thomas Tomkins. Tomkins was organist of Worcester, and that his father and namesake was precentor at Gloucester may explain the desire of the Gloucester chapter to emulate their neighbours.

wayes impoverished and exceedingly in decaye, neyther have we meanes to amende all that is amisse. Wee are at this time repayringe the decayes of [*fo. 24v.*] the church and by that chardge are utterly disinabled to provide a new organe withoute the helpe of such worthye gentlemen and others well disposed as shall approve our indeavour herein within the countie and the citty. Wee are ledd on upon this adventure by the example of our neighbour church of Worcester, which (though it be farr better able than ours is, yett found this burthen to heavye for them) and therefore tooke this course with good successe to the greate honour of the gentrye and other inhabitants of that sheire. The countie of Gloucester is farr larger, and wee have noe cawse to doupte but that this countie and citty wilbe as forward and bountifull as their neighbours have beene. In this hope wee have adventured our letters, and shalbe gladd to heare they finde kinde acceptance. And for our partes oute of the poore estate lefte to the church, wee shalbe willing to give thirty pounds to the worke over and above the other charges which wee must necessarily be att. Thus in hope to receive a kinde and lovinge answere from yow, we leave yow all to God's gracious favour and protection.

Gloucester, Marche 12 1617[/18]. Given under our chapter seale.

To the right worshipfull our verry worthy and loving freindes the gentrey and others of the countie and citty of Gloucester.'

William Laud, dean; Elias Wrenche; Thomas Prior.

11. [*fo. 25*]   22 July 1618.   Chapter House.
(Elias Wrench; Thomas Prior.)

Presentation to the vicaridge of Bruckthropp. Whereas the donation of the vicaridge of Bruckthrop is fallen into the hands of the deane and chapter of this church by the deathe of the last incumbent, James Bradshawe, whoe deceassed the first of Marche last past, the above named Mr. Wrenche and Mr. Prior, being all that were resident at that time, assembled and mett together in the chapter howse the day above mentioned for the passing of a presentation to the vicaridge aforesaid, havinge received severall letters from the right worshipfull Doctor Laud, deane of this churche, to that purpose, at which time and place allso the said Mr. Prior exhibited a proxie under the hand and seale of the said Mr. Deane bearing date the fowerteenthe day of July 1618, in these words followinge: 'Mr. Prior, I doe further authorise and appoynt yow by vertue hereof, as my lawfull proctor and attorney for me and in my name, to give and passe in open chapter my voice for a presentacion to be passed for the vicaridge of Bruckthropp unto Wetherstone Messinger and shall allwayes be ready to ratifie and confirme what yow shall doe herein, desiringe the speedy dispatche thereof (by reason of the shortnesse of time) that the church receive no prejudice by lapse.' The like proxie under the hand and seale of Mr. Lawrence Bridger, one of the prebendaries of the said churche, the said Mr. Prior exhibited. The like proxie under the hand and seale of Mr. Doctor Loe, one other of the prebendaries of the said church, was exhibited by the said Mr. Wrenche. The like proxie allso under the hand and seale of Mr. Doctor Anyan, one other of the prebendaries of the said church, was exhibited by the said Mr. Prior. According to which severall proxies the said Mr. Wrench and Mr. Prior gave the voices of Mr. Deane and the said prebendaries according as they were authorized in the proxies aforesaid, together with their owne voyces allso, for a presentacion to be passed to Wetherston Messinger of the vicaridge of Bruckthropp aforesaid, whoe hadd a presentation under seale graunted accordingly.

Elias Wrenche; Thomas Prior.

12.   [*fo. 25v.*]   Wednesday 14 October 1618.   Chapter House.
(William Laud, S.T.P., dean; Henry Aisgill, subdean; Laurence Bridger; Elias Wrench; Thomas Prior.)

Electio officiariorum. [*Election of officers. The dean and chapter elected Mr. Elias Wrench as subdean and Mr. Henry Aisgill as receiver and treasurer. As in* **6**, *above.*]
    Guiliel[mus] Laud, decanus; Elias Wrenche; Laur[ence] Bridger;
    Henr[y] Aisgill; Tho[mas] Prior.

Electio precentoris. [*Election of the precentor. The dean chose Thomas Tomkins. As in* **6**, *above.*] Eodem die, loco et anno [*etc.*].
    Guil[ielmus] Laud, decanus.

Admissio laicorum cantatorum. [*Admission of lay singers. Guy Knowles*[1] *and Rowland Smith*[2] *were admitted by the dean to the places of two lay clerks* (*singing men*) *in the places of John Phelps and Richard Sandy. Knowles and Smith respectively took the oaths on the gospels touched by them.*] Quibus die, loco et anno Guido Knowles et Rowlandus Smith admissi erant per dominum decanum in locos duorum laicorum cantatorum infra ecclesiam cathedralem Gloucestrensis in locis Johannis Phelps et Richardi Sandy. Qui quidem Guido et Rowlandus subierunt iuramenta respective ad sacrosancta dei evangelia per eos tacta &c.
    Guil[ielmus] Laud, decanus.

Admissio hypodidascali. [*Admission of the usher or assistant schoolmaster. Daniel Williams*[3] *was admitted by the dean to the place of usher within the college, for which he had taken on the gospels the oath of obedience and allegiance to the king.*] Quibus die, loco et anno Daniell Williams admissus fuit in locum hypodidascali infra collegium ecclesiae cathedralis Gloucestrensis per dominum decanum, sumpto prius per eum iuramento ad sacrosancta dei evangelia respective de obedientia et allegiantia domino regi &c.
    Guil[ielmus] Laud, decanus.

White's feirst monition.[4] At which day and place, upon proofe made to Mr. Deane against Richard White,[5] one of the lay singing men of this churche, for frequentinge of alehouses and slouthfulnesse in performing his service and other unseemely courses not befitting this church, Mr. Deane in the presence of the chapter gave unto him, the said Richard White, his first monition or warning to departe this church.
    William Laud, deane.

---

[1] In Oct. 1619 Guy Knowles leased a piece of ground in the common orchard. He was replaced as a lay singer in Oct. 1621: below, **31**.

[2] A Rowland Smith had received a salary as a chorister in 1610. Rowland Smith was later to receive two monitions for bad behaviour and to be expelled from his place: below, **14**, **21**, **24**, **25**.

[3] For Williams, below, p. 170.

[4] Cf. above, p. xiv.

[5] Richard White had received a salary as a lay singer as far back as 1610, and one of that name had earlier been a chorister. He was replaced as a lay singer in March 1620: below, **22**.

13.   [*fo. 26*]   15 October 1618.   Deanery.

Admissio choristarum. [*Admission of choristers. Philip Bermis, John Pink and Richard Brodgate were admitted by the dean to the places of three choristers within this cathedral church, in the places of Thomas Smith, William Morgan and Thomas Brodgate.*] Quibus die et anno Philippus Bermis, Johannes Pinke et Richardus Brodgate admissi erant per dominum decanum in loca trium choristarum infra hanc ecclesiam cathedralem Gloucestrensis in locis Thomae Smith, Gulielmi Morgan et Thomae Brodgate.

   Guil[ielmus] Laud, decanus.

14.   25 February 1618/19.   Chapter House.
(William Laud, S.T.P., dean; Elias Wrench, subdean; Laurence Bridger; Henry Aisgill; Thomas Prior.)

Smith's first monition. At which day and place, upon complaint made to Mr. Deane against Rowland Smyth, one of the lay singingmen of this church, for beatinge a taylor as he sate at his worke, yt is ordered by Mr. Deane that he shall receive noe wages due unto him untill the feast of Sct. Michaell the Archangell next, and that Mr. Threasurer doe keepe and detayne the same in his hands untill the feaste aforesaid. And upon further complaint for breakinge one Rowland Woode's head, Mr. Deane published his first monition or warning to departe the church.

   William Laud, dean.

15.   27 February 1618/19.

An act concerning the under-cooke's office.[1] Whereas John Taylor of the citty of Gloucester, alderman, did the day and yeare above written surrender and yeeld upp into the hands of us, the deane and chapter of the cathedrall church of Gloucester, a joynt patent of the under-cooke's office within this church heretofore made and graunted to John Taylor and Thomas Taylor, sonnes of the aforesaid John Taylor, for terme of their lives and the longest liver of them, for the performance and execution of which office there is yearly paid [*fo. 26v.*] unto the aforesaid John Taylor the father, upon a former patent to him graunted, the somme of three pounds six shillings and eight pence, which said patent the said John Taylor now hath in his owne possession, but for the joynt patent made to the said John Taylor and Thomas Taylor, sonnes of the aforesaid John Taylor, he the said John Taylor the father never received any stipend or wages upon the same patent, which said joynt patent was procured at the charge of John Taylor the father and by him intended to be a patent in reversion,[2] but by the neglecte or error of the then chapter clarke was made a joynt patent in possession to boothe the sonnes: Now forasmuch as the said office of under-cookeshipp hath beene for many yeares discontinued and of noe use within this church, wherefore wee the deane and chapter are purposed and resolved to

---

[1] The office of cook was among those laid down in the Henrician statutes. At that time the common hall (the former monastic refectory), where the choristers, lay clerks, and minor canons were expected to eat communally, was still standing, its kitchen (known then as the common kitchen) being on the site later occupied by no. 3 Millers Green.

[2] The word 'reversion' is underlined in the MS.

dissolve the said patent and to dispose of the said fee of £3 6s. 8d. upon the said patent reserved, to the betteringe and increase of the stipends (which are verry meane) of some of the quire within the church where wee shall thincke it most needefull, neverthelesse yt is concluded and agreed upon, and wee doe hereby promise and assume that if we shall hereafter be resolved and assisted by our counsell or any other learned in the lawes of this realme, that the said patent of the under-cooke's office cannot be dissolved nor the fee thereupon reserved converted to the good use formerly mentioned and by us intended, that then upon request to us made we will graunte and make to Thomas Taylor of the citty of Gloucester, clothier, a patent for terme of his life of the same office of under cooke with the same fee of £3 6s. 8d. therupon to be reserved and upon and under the same condicions that yt hath beene formerly graunted, hee the said Thomas Taylor paying the accustomed fees for the passing of yt.

William Laud, deane; Elias Wrenche; Laur[ence] Bridger; Henr[y] Aisgill; Tho[mas] Prior.

16. [*fo. 27*] ***An attestation for Dr. Loe.*** To whomsover these presents shall come, greeting in our Lord God everlastinge. Know ye that the bearer hereof William Loe, doctor of divinitie, prebendarie of the cathedrall church of Gloucester and pastor electe and allowed of the Englishe church at Hamboroughe,[1] being to reside beyond the seas, wee, the deane and chapter of the said cathedrall church, doe testifie in his behalfe that he for the terme of sixteene yeares last past lived amongst us in his said place vearie painfullie and soberly and hath performed his dutie in our said church as becommeth a man of his place withoute impeachment. Not doubtinge therefore, but that he shall there allso beyond the seas be esteemed and accoumpted of accordinge to his merit, place and paines, we being willinge to assist him with this our Christian attestation give yt under our chapter seale the tenth day of March 1618[/19].

Anth[ony] Robinson, registrarius.

17.   Wednesday 30 June 1619.   Chapter House.

Admissio elemozynarii. [*Admission of an almsman. John March, of the city of Gloucester, has affirmed before Mr. Elias Wrench, subdean, that John Grove and John Ward are dead and so the said John March is to be admitted in place of Anthony Ferris, the latest almsman of the cathedral, by virtue of letters patent of King James granted to him, addressed to the dean and chapter, whereupon the subdean admitted him, to receive the emoluments belonging to the office from the feast of the Annunciation last, provided that if Grove or Ward was alive at the time the said admission would be void.*] Johannes Marche, civitatis Gloucestriae predicte, dixit et affirmavit coram venerabili viro Magistro Elia Wrenche, subdecano ecclesie cathedralis antedicte, quosdam Johannem

---

[1] The Merchant Adventurers of England, who lived abroad and had moved around from town to town in order to sell their goods, arranged on being granted 'incorporation' to settle permanently in Hamburg. They had now elected Loe to become pastor of their church there.

Grove[1] et Johannem Ward mortuos esse, eumque prefatum Johannem Marche admittendum esse (in loco cuiusdam Anthonii Ferris ultimi elemozynarii ejusdem ecclesie cathedralis) virtute litterarum patentium serenissimi domini nostri Jacobi sibi in ea parte concessarum, decano et capitulo dicte ecclesie directarum, unde dictus venerabilis subdecanus dictum Johannem March in elemozynarium admisit habere et percipere omnia proficua et emolumenta ad officium elemozynarii spectantia, a festo Anunciacionis Beatae Mariae Virginis ultimo praeterito. Proviso tamen quod si prefati Johannes Grove vel Johannes Ward tunc temporis essent vivi quod illa prefata admissio vacua erit et nullius vigoris.

> Elias Wrenche, subdec[anus].

18.   [*fo. 27v.*] [*A*] **dispensation of absence** [*for*][2] **Dr. Anyan.** [*4 September 1619.*] James R.: Trustie and welbeloved, wee greete yow well. Whereas your founder of famous memory King Henry the Eighte hath by your locall statutes reserved to himselfe and his successors a power to dispense with any of your statutes made or to be made, and because Doctor Anyan, one of our chaplens in ordinary and prebendary of your church, by reason of his attendance upon our selfe, and necessary residency in a place of governement in one of our universities,[3] cannot reside with yow as your statutes and customs doe require, these therefore are to give yow notice, that oute of our especiall favour and regall power we doe dispense with the said Doctor Anyan for his residency with yow, requiringe yow to make him partaker of all emoluments as yf he were continually resident amonge yow, any statute or custome to the contrary notwithstandinge. Geven under our signett at our courte of Windsor the fourth day of September in the seventeenth yeare of our raigne of England, Fraunce and Ireland, and of Scotland the three and fiftithe.

> To our trustie and welbeloved the deane and chapter
> of our cathedrall church of Gloucester.

19. [*Dispensatio*] **absentiae pro** [*Willel*]**mo Loe, sacrae theologiae** [*profe*]**ssor.**[4] [*Dispensation of absence for William Loe, S.T.P. King James announces that for himself and his heirs and successors he has granted to his chaplain Dr. William Loe, vicar of Churcham and prebendary of the fifth prebend in Gloucester cathedral, that he may travel to Hamburg, to serve as minister to the English merchants there until he resigns or is recalled, dispensing him from statutory residence on his vicarage and his prebend, by letters patent dated at Westminster 30 May 1619. By privy seal letter.*] Jacobus, dei gracia Anglie, Scotie, Frauncie et Hibernie rex, fidei defensor &c., omnibus ad quos presentes

---

[1] The name is underlined. Alongside in the margin is written, in a hand which appears to be the same as that of the main entry, 'Est in plena vita ut patet postea, et ideo cassa est haec admissio. [*He is alive, as appears later, and so this admission is void.*] fol. 38': below, **51**. The word 'cassa' has been inserted over the word 'cassu', which is crossed out. March was admitted as an almsman for a second time in Nov. 1625: below, **61**.

[2] The left-hand edge of the page has been torn away.

[3] Anyan was president of Corpus Christi College, Oxford: below, p. 161.

[4] The left-hand edge of the page has been torn away.

litere pervenerint salutem. Sciatis quod multis de causis et maturis consideracionibus nos ad presens speciali moventibus de gracia nostra speciali dedimus et concessimus ac per presentes pro nobis, heredibus et successoribus nostris damus et concedimus dilecto subdito et capellano nostro Willelmo Loe, sacrae theologiae professore, vicario vicarie sive ecclesie parochiallis de Churcham in comitatu nostro Gloucestriae ac quinte prebende in ecclesie cathedrali Sancte et Individue Trinitatis Gloucestriae prebendario, ut ipse libere et licite proficiscatur in partes transmarinas, nominaliter in Hamburgum Germanie civitatem, ibique loci pro salutari, bono et commoditate mercatorum nostrorum sacre ministerii officio fungatur, ubi volumus illum tam diu remanere donec ab hoc exercitio resignaverit [*reading uncertain*] vel nobis illum revocare visum fuerit, nec teneatur quovismodo in predictis beneficiis tam vicaria quam prebenda se corporalem facere residentiam aut personaliter residere durantibus temporibus [*fo. 28*] predictis quamvis authoritate et mandata invitus impelli possit vel rogatur, et hoc absque perturbacione, vexacione, mollestacione vel contradiccione aliqua nostrum hereditorum vel successorum nostrorum aut officiariorum seu subditorum nostrorum quorumcunque, statuto de residentia clericorum de et super beneficiis et dignitatis suis, aut aliquo alio statuto, actu, ordinacione, re, causa vel materia quacunque incontrarium edictis in aliquo non obstante. In cuius rei testimonium has litteras nostras fieri fecimus patentes. Teste me ipso apud Westmonasterium tricessimo die Maii anno regni nostri Anglie, Frauncie et Hibernie decimo septimo et Scotie quinquagessimo secundo.

   Per brevem de privato sigillo &c.   Marburye.

20.   Thursday 25 October 1619.   Chapter House.
(William Laud, S.T.P., dean; Elias Wrench, subdean; Laurence Bridger; Henry Aisgill; Thomas Prior.[1])

Electio officiariorum. [*Election of officers. The dean and chapter elected Mr. Thomas Prior as subdean and Mr. Laurence Bridger as receiver and treasurer. As in* **6**, *above.*]
  Guil[ielmus] Laud, decanus; Elias Wrenche, subdec[anus];
  Henr[y] Aisgill; Laur[ence] Bridger.

Electio precentoris. [*Election of the precentor. The dean chose Thomas Tomkins. As in* **6**, *above.*] Eodem die, loco et anno [*etc.*].
  Guil[ielmus] Laud, deca[nus].

21. [*fo. 28v.*] 10 March 1619/20.
(William Laud, S.T.P., dean; Thomas Prior, subdean; Laurence Bridger; Elias Wrench.)

An acte for exchainge of lands with Wodham colledge in Oxenforde. Whereas the warden and fellowes of Wodham Colledge within the university of Oxenford hath made request unto us, the deane and chapter of this church, that they, the said warden and fellowes, or their under tenaunts, may exchaunge certayne lands parcell of their mannor of Southroppe for other lands of ours now in the possession of William Keeble, gent., our

---

[1] Thomas Prior did not put his signature at the end of the entry although he was present at the meeting.

undertenaunte, being parte and parcell of a certayne farme called by the name of Cotes,[1] and that the lands soe exchaunged may be by us or eyther of us or our undertenaunts for our greater benefitt taken in and enclosed: Yt is this day ordered and agreed on and as much as in us lyeth wee give our consents to the said exchainge and inclosure. Provided that the said warden and fellowes at their costs and charges doe or shall before any such exchainge had or made procure unto us, the said deane and chapter, the king's majestie's license of mortmaine in due forme of lawe authentically signed and sealed, and such as our learned councell in the lawe shall allowe and approve of, to enable us to make the said exchainge. And allso provided that the said enclosure extend not to the dammage or preiudice of the vicar or parson of the parish where the said lands soe to be exchaunged doe lye (or his or their consents to the said inclosure obtayned). And in case there be any parsonage impropriated in the parish where the said lands soe to be exchaunged doe lye, then the said exchaunge and enclosure to goe on withoute any respecte to be had, or consent obtayned, of the lord or farmer of any such impropriation.

William Laud, dean; Tho[mas] Prior, subd[ean]; Laur[ence] Bridger; Elias Wrenche.

Eodem die.

Smith's 2nd monition. Upon complaint made to Mr. Deane against Rowland Smyth, one of the lay singingmen of this church, for being drunk in the church in the time of devine prayers, Mr. Deane published his second monition or warning to departe the church.

William Laud, dean.

22. [*fo. 29*]   13 March 1619/20.   Deanery.

Admissio laici cantatoris. [*Admission of a lay singer. Christopher Hayes*[2] *was admitted by the dean as a lay singer in the place of Richard White, was installed in the choir by the precentor and took the oaths on the gospels touched by him. The form differs in detail from that in* **12**, *above.*] Quibus die et anno Christoferus Hayes admissus fuit per dominum decanum in locum unius laicorum cantatorum infra ecclesiam cathedralem Gloucestriae in loco Richardi White et installatus in choro per cantatorem qui quidem Christoferus subiit iuramenta respective ad sacrosancta dei evangelia per eum tacta &c.

Guil[ielmus] Laud, deca[nus].

Eodem die.

Admissio choristarum. [*Admission of choristers. Constantine Smith and Richard Dobbs were admitted by the dean as choristers in the places of Philip Bermis and William Jenninges.*] Quibus die, loco et anno Constantius[3] Smith et Richardus Dobbes admissi erant per dominum decanum in loco duorum choristarum infra hanc ecclesiam cathedralem Gloucestriae in locis Phillippi Bermis et Gulielmi Jenninges.

Guil[ielmus] Laud, decanus.

---

[1] Henry VIII had in 1541 granted to the dean and chapter of Gloucester the manor of Eastleach Martin, otherwise Coate Farm, which adjoins Southrop: *V.C.H. Glos.* vii. 56.

[2] For Hayes, below, p. 164.

[3] The reading of the name is uncertain, either 'Constantius' (with no abbreviation mark), or the English 'Constantine'.

23.   11 May 1620.   Chapter House.
(Thomas Prior, subdean; Elias Wrench.)

Lone of £20 to the Count Palatine. At which time and place Mr. Subdeane on the behalfe of the deane and chapter, having beene called upon by the reverend father in God Miles, lord bishopp of this dioces, for the lone of money to the illustrious prince Frederick, counte palatine of the Rheine, accordinge to the contents of the letters from the lord arche bishopp of Canterbury his grace to the said reverend father directed, requiring him not only to deale with the said deane and chapter but with all other the able clergye men of this dioces for the said lone of money and speedy payment thereof. And thereupon the said Mr. Subdeane having received letters from Mr. Doctor Laud, deane, and Mr. Bridger, threasurer, desiring them to treate with the said reverend father on the churche's behalfe, and specifyinge their consents to such agreements as they should make, the said Mr. Subdeane and Mr. Wrenche, after longe debate hadd and consideracion taken, agreed to the lone of twenty poundes on the behalfe of the said deane and chapter. Which said somme of twenty poundes was accepted and paid in by the threasurer accordingly.
        Tho[mas] Prior, subd[ean]; Elias Wrenche.

24.   [*fo. 29v.*]   15 May 1620.   Chapter House.
(Mr. Prior, subdean.)

Sandy his feirst monition. Upon complaint made to Mr. Subdeane of John Sandy[1] his often departinge from devine service before they are ended and allso for his overmuch noyse in talkinge and ianglinge in time of devine prayers, Mr. Subdeane gave unto him the said John Sandy his first monition to departe the church.
        Tho[mas] Prior, subd[ean].

                Eodem die.

Smith's reference to Mr. Deane. The same day likewise proofe was made against Rowland Smyth for running at one of the sarieants at mace of the citty with a knife, and likewise for diverse abuses in the time of devine prayers. Mr. Subdeane in respecte of his two former monitions allready published hath referred him and the cawse to Mr. Deane's consideracion.[2]
        Tho[mas] Prior, subd[ean].

25.   6 October 1620.   Deanery.

Smith's expultion. Whereas Rowland Smyth, a lay singingman of this church, for his sundry neglects, abuses and misdemeanors hath had two monitions or warnings given him by Mr. Deane himselfe to departe the church, and one other in the nature of a monition by Mr. Prior, subdeane, Mr. Deane for his former abuses and present necligence hath (according to the locall statutes) given unto the said Rowland Smyth his third or last monicion and decreed him expelled from the church.
        William Laud, dean.

[1] For Sandy, below, p. 168.
[2] Cf. above, **14**, **21**.

26.   16 October 1620.

Absence in residence with [. . .]. Memorandum. Mr. Dr. Loe, prebendary, this day in his residence was ready to goe to service but was dispensed with for that daye's absence by Mr. Deane and the chapter that he might stay to attende the present necessary affaires of the church.

William Laud, dean; Tho[mas] Prior, subd[ean]; Laur[ence] Bridger; Henr[y] Aisgill; Elias Wrenche.

27.   [*fo. 30*]   Thursday 19 October 1620.   Chapter House.
(William Laud, S.T.P., dean; Thomas Prior, subdean; Laurence Bridger; Henry Aisgill; Elias Wrench; William Loe, S.T.P.)

Electio officiariorum. [*Election of officers. The dean and chapter elected Laurence Bridger as subdean and Thomas Prior as receiver and treasurer. As in* **6**, *above.*]

Guil[elmus] Laud, decanus; Laur[ence] Bridger; Elias Wrenche; Will[iam] Loe.[1]

Electio precentoris. [*Election of the precentor. The dean chose Thomas Tomkins. As in* **6**, *above, omitting* 'per eum' *after* 'iuramento'.] Eodem die, loco et anno idem venerabilis decanus antedictus elegit in precentorem dicte ecclesiae pro anno futuro Thomam Tomkins, unum minorum canonicorum eiusdem ecclesiae, iuramento suscepto.

Guil[ielmus] Laud, decanus.

Eodem die.

Hayes's feirst monition. Mr. Deane this day in open chapter pronounced a solemne admonition against Christopher Hayes, a lay singingman, being the first warninge to him given for his manifoulde necligence, and especially for not applyinge himselfe to gett more knowledge in singing as was inioyned him for the better discharge of his service to the church.

William Laud, dean.

28.   [*fo. 30v.*]   19 October 1620.
[. . .] ***to commence shute*** [sc. *suit*] [***agains***]***t William Keeble.***[2] Yt is agreed upon by us, the deane and chapter of the cathedrall church of the Holy and Undevided Trinity in Gloucester, that the warden and fellowes of Wodham Colledge in Oxford shall have power to use our names in a bill in Chauncery against our tenaunte William Keeble for not giveinge way to an exchaunge to be made betweene Waadham Colledge and us for certaine lands which the said William Keeble houldeth of us belonging to his farme of Coates, which exchainge the said Keeble first desired of us by his letters, provided that it be inserted in the same bill in Chauncery, on our behalfes, that it would please my Lord Chauncellor to order that we may have power to come upon our owne lands to veiwe and see that the church be not wronged in the quantity and qualitie of the land exchaunged, in regard that the said William Keeble

---

[1] An attendance of six at a chapter meeting was unusual. Although present, Thomas Prior and Henry Aisgill did not sign their names to the entry.

[2] Cf. above, **21**.

(who formerly agreed to the exchaunge) is now fallen of and seemes to denye us leave to comme upon the churche's inheritance under pretence wee will doe him harme.

William Laud, dean; Laur[ence] Bridger; Elias Wrenche; William Loe; Tho[mas] Prior.

Eodem die in domo capitulari.

Admissio Organistae. [*Admission of the organist. Philip Hosier*[1] *was admitted by the dean as organist and instructor of the choristers in the place of Elias Smith, deceased, was installed in the choir by the precentor and took the oaths on the gospels, touched by him.*] Quibus die et anno Philippus Hosier admissus erat per decanum in locum organistae et choristarum instructoris huius ecclesiae in loco Eliae Smith, mortui, et installatus in choro per cantatorem, qui quidem Philippus subiit iuramenta respective ad sacrosancta dei evangelia per eum tacta, &c.

Guil[ielmus] Laud, decanus.

[*fo. 31*]   Acta in Domo Capitulari.
                   Eodem die.

Orders decreed in the Chapter-howse. Imprimis yt is ordered that the master of the choristers shall appoynte before the beginninge of prayers one or more of the choristers to turne the bookes reddy for such services as shalbe appoynted to be sunge, and likewise for the anthem, and lay them ready upon the singingmen's deskes to avoyd confusion and running to and fro in the time of devine service.

Allso it is ordered that if any singingman or petty cannon of this church be absent from service above twentie times in any one quarter of the yeare hee shall loose the benefitt that should come unto him oute of the perditions[2] for that quarter.

Allso it is further ordered that noe bonfiers at any time, or any fire at all, shalbe made in the farmery[3] or any parte of that greate waste roome upon any occasion whatsoever, for that yt is verry daungerous to the inhabitants on either side thereof and to the building over yt, and consequently to the whole fabricke of this church.

Allso it is ordered that if any persons be to be married within this church the chanter or any other of the quire to whom the license of mariage is directed shall before the wedding solemnised bring the same license and shew yt to Mr. Deane, or in his absence to the subdeane or senior prebendary at home, and acquaint them therewith, and proceede or desist as they directe.

And lastly yt is ordered that if any prebendary of this church shall in the absence of Mr. Deane desire eyther for himselfe or his freinds to have a peale, he shall acquainte the subdeane or senior prebendary then at home with his desire, but in case they or either of them refuse his motion yt shalbe lawful for the same prebendary of his owne authority to cawse the bells to be runge.

William Laud, dean.

[1] For Hosier, below, p. 165.
[2] Perditions were an old cathedral custom by which the money forfeited by a lay clerk or minor canon for absence from duty was shared among his colleagues.
[3] For the farmery or firmary, above, p. xxi.

Eodem die.

Mason's feirst monition. Mr. Deane this day in open chapter pronounced a solemne admonition being the first against William Mason deputy sexton, for his contemptious and evill carriage towards Mr. Prior, then subdeane, not warning a communion[1] as he was enioyned by him to doe.

William Laud, dean.

29.   [*fo. 31v.*]   26 October 1620.[2]   Deanery.

Admissio choristarum. [*Admission of choristers. Giles Dobbs and Mark Colman were admitted by the dean in the places of Thomas Goslin and Abell Randell.*] Quibus die et anno Egidius Dobbs et Marcus Colman admissi erant per dominum decanum in loca duorum choristarum infra hanc ecclesiam cathedralem Gloucestriae in locis Thomae Goslin et Abell Randell.

Guil[ielmus] Laud, decanus.

Warrant for trees. Yt is agreed upon by us, the deane and chapter of the cathedrall church of the Holy and Indevisible Trinity in Gloucester, that whereas the great dining roome in the denary house is much decayed in the flowre or boordes under foote, wee give our consents that there shalbe so many good trees felled or cutt of the coppyhould tenement of Widow Weale in Santhurst[3] as shall serve for the boording thereof, or in case yt shalbe thought fitt to boorde yt with deale boordes or oke or any other that soe many trees shalbe felled of the same tenement as shall defray the charge thereof.

Given under our hands the 26th of October 1620.

William Laud, dean; William Loe; Tho[mas] Prior; Elias Wrenche.

30.   18 December 1620.   Chapter House.
(Elias Wrenche; Thomas Prior.)

Choise of a clarke for the Convocation howse. Quibus die et loco, by vertue of a proxie from Mr. Deane dated December the fowerteenthe 1620, directed to Mr. Bridger subdeane, and Mr. Prior ioyntly and severally to give his voyce for the choise of a clarke for the convocation howse for the chapter of this church at this ensuing parliament, the said Mr. Prior gave Mr. Deane's voyce unto Dr. Anyan, a prebend of this church, for the said place, and likewise Mr. Wrench by vertue of a proxie dated octavo Decembris 1620 from the said Mr. Bridger, gave the said Mr. Bridger's voice to the said Doctor Anyan and his owne voice allso, and likewise Mr. Prior gave him the [*fo. 32*] said[4] Dr. Anyan his voice allso. By reason whereof the said Dr. Anyan was elected and chosen the clarke of the convocation howse for the body of the chapter, and yt was decreed that an instrument

---

[1] The reference is presumably to the rubric to the communion service in the *Book of Common Prayer*: 'When the Minister giveth warning for the Celebration of the holy Communion, (which he shall always do upon the Sunday . . . immediately preceding) . . .' etc. For Mason, below, p. 167.

[2] The two pieces of business entered under this date are written in different hands.

[3] The dean and chapter owned the manor of Sandhurst, 3 miles north of Gloucester.

[4] The word 'said' is also a catchword at the foot of fo. 31v.

should be made unto him under the chapter seale, which was donne accordingly, the tenor whereof followeth in these wordes. Vizt.

[*The formal instrument, dated 19 December 1620: Be it known to all that we, the dean and chapter, etc. name Thomas Anyan, S.T.P., as the chapter's representative at the convocation or synod to be held at St. Paul's, London, on 17 January next.*] Pateat universis per presentes, Quod nos, decanus et capitulum ecclesiae cathedralis Sanctae et Individue Trinitatis Gloucestriae, unanimi assensu et consensu[1] capitulariter congregati dilectum nobis in Christo Thomam Anyan, clericum, sacrae theologie professorem,[2] unum prebendariorum ecclesiae nostrae cathedralis Gloucestriae, nostrum verum, legitimum et indubitatum procuratorem, actorem, factorem, negotiorumque nostrorum gestorem et nuntium speciale ad infra scripta nominamus, ordinamus, facimus et constituimus per presentes, damusque et concedimus eidem procuratori nostro potestatem generalem et mandatum tam generale quam speciale pro nobis et nominibus nostris coram reverendissimo in Christo patre ac divino domino Georgio providencia divina Cantuariensi archiepiscopo, totius Anglie primate et metropolitano eiusve in hac parte locum tenente sive comissario quocumque in convocatione generali sive sacra synode prelatorum et cleri regni Anglie in ecclesia cathedrali Sancti Pauli Londoniensi decimo septimo die mensis Januarii proximo futurum (deo favente) celebranda cum continuacione et prorogacione dierum ex tunc sequentium et loci (si oporteat) fiendum, comparendum et interessendum nosque a personale comparicione excusandum necnon cum dicto reverendissimo patre, aut eius locum tenente sive comissario huiusmodi, aliisque prelatis et clericis regni Anglie ibidem legittime comparendis et congregandis de et super quibusdam arduis et seriis negotiis statutas, utilitatem et defensionem ecclesie Anglicane ac pacem et tranqu[i]litatem, bonum publicum et tuicionem regni predicti et subditorum eiusdem concernentibus tunc et ibidem serio communicandis et tractandis suumque consilium et auxilium sumptis impendendum et hiis [*fo. 32v.*] que ibidem, ex communi deliberacione, ad honorem dei, ecclesiae et regni predicti ac reipublicae eiusdem utilitate et commodum salubriter et concorditer ordinari et statui contigerit pro parte nostra consentiendum et assensum nostrum prebendum, juramentum etiam quodcunque licitum et honestum ac in ea parte quomodolibet requisit in animas nostras subeundum prestandum et jurandum, et generaliter omnia alia et singula faciendum, exercendum et expediendum que in premissis seu circa ea necessaria fuerint seu quomodolibet oportuna que nos, si presentes personaliter interfuissemus, faceremus aut facere potuissemus, etiam si mandatum de se magis exigant speciale quam superius est expressum. Et promittimus nos ratum, gratum et firmum perpetuo habiturum totum et quicquid dictus procurator noster fecerit in premissis aut aliquo premissorum sub hypotheca et obligacione omnium et singulorum bonorum nostrorum tam presentium quam futurorum et in ea parte caucione exponimus per presentes. In cuius rei testimonium sigillum nostrum commune presentibus apponi fecimus. Datum in domo nostra capitulari decimo nono die Decembris anno domini millesimo sexcentessimo vicessimo.

Elias Wrenche; Tho[mas] Prior.

---

[1] The words 'unanimi assensu et consensu' are underlined in the MS.
[2] The words 'sacrae theologie professorem' are underlined in the MS.

31.   4 October 1621.   Deanery.

Admissio laicorum cantatorum. [*Admission of lay singers. John Beames and Elias (MS. Ely) Smith were admitted by the dean in the places of Rowland Smith and Guy Knowles. As in* **12**, *above.*]
      Guil[ielmus] Laud, decanus.

32.   [*fo. 33*]   Friday 5 October 1621.   Chapter House.
(William Laud, S.T.P., dean; Laurence Bridger, subdean; Henry Aisgill; Elias Wrench; William Loe, S.T.P.; Thomas Prior.)

Electio officiariorum. [*Election of officers. The dean and chapter elected Thomas Prior as subdean and Laurence Bridger as receiver and treasurer. As in* **6**, *above.*]
      Guil[ielmus] Laud, decan[us]; Lawr[ence] Bridger; Elias Wrenche; Guiliel[mus] Loe.

Electio precentoris. [*Election of the precentor. The dean chose Thomas Tomkins. As in* **27**, *above.*] Eodem die, loco et anno [*etc.*].
      Guil[ielmus] Laud, decan[us].

Admissio choristae. [*Admission of a chorister. Barkeley Wrench*[1] *was admitted by the dean in the place of Ely Smith.*] Quibus die, loco et anno Barkleyus Wrench admissus fuit per venerabilem decanum chorista in loco Ely Smith.
      Guil[ielmus] Laud, decan[us].

33.   8 October 1621.   Deanery.
Admissio hypodidascali. [*Admission of the assistant schoolmaster. Thomas Daniell*[2] *was admitted by the dean. As in* **12**, *above, but abbreviated in recording the oath.*] Quibus die et anno [*etc.*].
      Guil[ielmus] Laud, decan[us].

34.   [*fo. 33v.*]   16 November 1621.   Chapter House.
(Thomas Prior, subdean; Elias Wrench.)

Tho[mas] Tully, Rich[ard] Brodgate. Quibus die et loco Thomas Tully and Richard Brodgate, two of the lay singingmen of this church, were charged by Mr. Subdeane to have refused the readinge of the feirst lesson in theyr severall courses, which they acknowledged, and promised for the time to comme that yt should be amended.
      Tho[mas] Prior, subd[ean].

---

[1] For Barkeley Wrench, below, p. 171.
[2] Thomas Daniell matriculated at St. John's College, Oxford (where William Laud was president), on 24 April 1618, aged 15, and graduated B.A. on 8 June 1621.

35.   Thursday 13 December 1621.   Chapter House.
(Thomas Prior, subdean; Elias Wrench.)

Installatio venerabilis viri Richardi Senhouse Decani Gloucestriae. 1621. [*Installation of the venerable man Richard Senhouse as dean of Gloucester. In the chapter house, before Thomas Prior, subdean, and Elias Wrench, prebendaries of the cathedral church solemnly assembled in chapter, in the presence of Mr. Edmund Randell, deputy of Anthony Robinson, gent., registrar, John Hanbury, gent.,*[1] *appeared in person and exhibited his proxy for Richard Senhouse, fellow of St. John's College, Cambridge, and chaplain to Prince Charles, prince of Wales, and made himself party for the same and presented the royal mandate, dated 21 November 1621, addressed to the chapter and residentiary prebendaries, to assign to the dean a stall in the choir and a place and voice in the chapter. And John Hanbury exhibited the dean's letters of proxy, dated 26 November 1621, appointing Mr. Elias Wrench his proxy for putting the dean in possession, etc., which* [*Mr. Wrench*][2] *accepted. Afterwards on the same day the subdean with due solemnity brought Elias Wrench to the dean's customary stall in the choir and installed him and put him in possession, and led him thence to the chapter house and assigned him his place and voice. All which the prebendaries required to be enacted, and all these things were done in the presence of John Brown, Esq., mayor of the city of Gloucester, John Jones, one of the aldermen, William Guise, Esq., John Hayward and James Powell, city sheriffs, Robert Robinson and Tobias Bullock, gents., John Workman, M.A., John Langley, M.A., Thomas Tomkins, precentor, and other servants of the said church.*] In domo capitulari ecclesiae cathedralis Gloucestriae, coram Thoma Prior, tunc subdecano, & Elia Wrench, praebendariis dictae ecclesiae cathedralis, capitulariter & solemniter congregatis, in praesentia Magistri Edmundi Randle, deputati Anthonii Robinson, generosi, dictae ecclesiae registrarii:

Quibus die et loco [*etc., as in* **1**, *above, with minor verbal variations and substituting references simply to the prebendaries for some references to the chapter and prebendaries, whose function in* **1** *in installing the dean's proxy and putting him in possession etc. is here performed by the subdean*].

[*fo. 34*] Ita testor Ed[mundus] Randell.

36. [*fo. 34v.*]   26 April 1622.   Chapter House.
(Richard Senhouse, dean; Thomas Prior, subdean; Elias Wrench.)

Decanus iurat. [*The dean takes the oath. As in* **2**, *above.*]

Richardus Senhouse, decanus; Tho[mas] Prior, subd[ecanus]; Elias Wrenche.

37.   Saturday 13 July 1622.   Chapter House.
(Thomas Prior, subdean; Elias Wrench.)

Admissio venerabilis viri Thomae Iles in sextam prebendam. [*Admission of the venerable man Thomas Iles to the sixth prebend. On Saturday 13 July 1622, before Mr. Thomas Prior, subdean, and Mr. Elias Wrench, one of the prebendaries, between the fourth and the*

---

[1] For Hanbury, below, p. 164.

[2] The MS. has 'which the said Mr. Henry Aisgill accepted'. Aisgill is not named earlier in the entry: his name was evidently copied in error from **1**, above.

fifth hour after noon, Thomas Iles, S.T.P., exhibited the king's letters patent dated 20 June granting to him the sixth canonry or prebend, vacant by the death of Henry Aisgill, and the royal mandate for his admission and installation; the subdean admitted him after he had taken the oath on the gospels to renounce the bishop of Rome, to acknowledge the royal supremacy and to observe the cathedral's statutes, and straightway led him from the chapter house into the choir of the cathedral and installed him in the stall of the said prebend, and then having returned to the chapter house assigned to him his voice and place in chapter there. All this was done in the presence of Mr. Robert Willoughby, John Langley, and Francis Lancaster, M.A., Thomas Tomkins, precentor, and other servants of the said church and of the writer, Edmund Randell, deputy of Anthony Robinson, gent., registrar.] Die Sabbathi vizt. decimotertio die mensis Julii anno domini 1622 coram venerabilibus viris Magistris Thoma Prior, subdecano ecclesiae cathedralis Gloucestriae, et Elia Wrench, uno prebendariorum dictae ecclesiae, inter horas quartam et quintam post meridiem in domo capitulari dictae ecclesiae venerabilis vir Thomas Iles, sacrae theologiae professor, exhibuit et tradidit subdecano ante dicto literas patentes illustrissimi in Christo principis domini nostri Domini Jacobi, dei gracia Angliae, Scotiae, Fraunciae et Hiberniae regis, gerentes datum vicessimo die mensis Junii, de concessione canonicatus sive prebendae sextae in ecclesia cathedrali predicta, iam per mortem naturalem Henrici Aisgill ultimi possessoris eiusdem prebendae vacantis, facta dicto Thoma Iles. Et exhibuit etiam mandatum regium pro admissione et installacione dicti Thomae Iles in prebendam praedictam iuxta consuetudinem in ea parte usitatam, unde dictus venerabilis vir subdecanus antedictus omni [cum ea] qua decuit reverentia et obedientia dictas literas patentes et mandatorias recepit[1] eisdemque perlectis ob reverentiam et obedientiam debitam prefatum Thomam Iles, prestito primitus per eum iuramento corporali ad sacro sancta dei evangelia de renuntiando Romano episcopo et de agnoscendo dictum dominum nostrum Jacobum regem &c. supremum caput &c. ac de observandis statutis dictae ecclesiae iuxta morem et ritum &c. quatenus verbo dei et legibus huius regni Angliae non repugnant &c., in canonicum et prebendarium admisit &c. Et immediate venerabilis vir subdecanus antedictus una cum antedicto Thomae Iles e domo capitulari praedicta egressus est, et ipsum Thomam Iles in chorum ecclesiae cathedralis predictae adduxit, ubi dictus subdecanus dictum Thomam Iles in stallum prebendae predictae installavit iuxta morem &c., et tunc reversus in domum capitularem predictam eidem Thomae Iles vocem et locum in capitulo ibidem assignavit &c. Et haec omnia facta fuerunt in presentia Magistri Roberti Willougby, Johannis Langley, et Francisci Lancaster, artium magistri, Thomae Tomkins, precentoris, aliorumque dictae ecclesiae ministrorum meique Edmundi Randle, deputati Anthonii Robinson, generosi, dictae ecclesiae registrarii.

Ita testor Ed[mundus] Randell.

38. [*fo. 35*]   26 November 1622.   Chapter House.
(Richard Senhouse, S.T.P., dean; Thomas Prior, subdean; Laurence Bridger; Elias Wrench.)

---

[1] The words 'reverentia et obedientia . . . recepit', much corrected, were inserted above the main text, and the words 'reverentia et obedientia dictas' are written in the margin. The words 'cum ea' were omitted. The entry contains several corrections and seems to have been carelessly written.

Admissio minoris canonici. [*Admission of a minor canon. Richard Brodgate, clerk,*[1] *was admitted and assigned a place by the dean.*] Quibus die et anno Richardus Broadgate clericus [*etc., as in* **6**, *above*].

      Richardus Senhouse, decanus.

39.   27 November 1622.

Incrementum stipendii subdecani. [*Increase of the subdean's stipend.*] Whereas the subdeanes of this church for the time being hath for many yeares past had for his fee yearly forty shillings and noe more, yt is now ordered and decreed that there shall be yearly allowed unto him for the execution of that office the somme of six pounds in regard of his paines in the execution of that office and his presence upon all occasions of the church in the deane's absence. Which said allowance of six pownds we have found to have bin formerly made unto him and therefore doe order that it shall be paid unto him by the hands of the tresurer yearly, as yt hath bin heretofore accustomed.

      Richard Senhouse, deane; Tho[mas] Prior, subd[ean]; Lawr[ence] Bridger;
      Elias Wrenche.

40.   [*fo. 35v.*]   Saturday 30 November 1622.   Chapter House.
(Thomas Prior, subdean; Laurence Bridger; Elias Wrench.)

Electio officiariorum. [*Election of officers. In the absence of the dean but with his consent, the subdean and the aforenamed prebendaries elected Laurence Bridger as subdean and Elias Wrench as receiver and treasurer. As in* **6**, *above, but replacing* Idem decanus et capitulum eligerunt *with*] Absente decano tamen consensu eiusdem venerabilis decani, idem subdecanus et prebendarii prenominati elegerunt [*etc.*].

      Tho[mas] Prior, subd[ean]; Lawr[ence] Bridger; Elias Wrenche.

Electio precentoris. [*Election of the precentor. The aforesaid men elected as precentor for the coming year Thomas Tomkins.*] Eodem die, loco et anno venerabiles viri antedicti elegerunt in precentorem dictae ecclesiae pro anno futuro Thomam Tomkins, unum minorum canonicorum eiusdem ecclesiae &c.[2]

      Tho[mas] Prior, subd[ean]; Lawr[ence] Bridger; Elias Wrenche.

41.   10 May 1623.   Chapter House.
(Laurence Bridger, subdean; Elias Wrench; Thomas Prior.)

Admissio laici cantatoris. [*Admission of a lay singer. John Freame was admitted by the subdean.*] Quibus die et anno [*etc., as in* **12**, *above, but without recording in whose place*].

      Lawr[ence] Bridger, subdeane; Elias Wrenche, treasurer; Tho[mas] Prior.

---

[1] For Brodgate and other members of his family, below, p. 162.

[2] Unlike in **6** etc., above, the election is by the prebendaries then present and there is no mention of the oath.

Eodem die.

Smith's feirst monition. Quibus die, loco et anno, Mr. Subdeane pronounced against Ely Smith, lay singingman, his feirste monition to departe this church, for his absence for one whole quarter of a yeare, and more, sence the last auditt and for sundrie other his contempts and abuses towards some of the chapter, and for his now beinge absent without any leave at all.

Lawr[ence] Bridger, subdeane; Elias Wrenche, treasurer; Tho[mas] Prior.

42.   [*fo. 36*]   16 July 1623.   Chapter House.
(Laurence Bridger, subdean; Elias Wrench; Thomas Prior.

Confirmation of a Chancellor's patent decreed. Quibus die et loco, Mr. Bridger, subdeane, exhibited a proxie under the hand and seale of the right woorshipful Dr. Senhowse, deane of this church, the contents whereof ensue in these words vizt.

'Know all men by these presentes that I, Richard Senhowse, doctor of divinitie and deane of the cathedrall church of Gloucester, doe hereby nominate, constitute, authorize and appointe my welbeloved in Christ Mr. Laurence Bridger, Mr. Elias Wrench and Mr. Thomas Prior, prebendaries of the said cathedrall church of Gloucester, iointly and severally, for me and in my name to appeare in the chapter howse of the foresaid cathedrall church and for me and in my name to give my voice and full consent to and for the confirmation of letteres patents or commission of the office, dignitie and place of chauncelor or vicar generall of, in and through the citty and dioces of Gloucester graunted by the right reverend father in God Miles, lord bishopp of Gloucester, to Mr. William Sutton, clerke, master of arts, and thereupon in the said chapter howse to seale with the chapter seale the said confirmacion annexed to the said letteres patents or commission; and to doe and performe all other things necessarie concerninge the same in as ample manner & forme as if I my selfe were personally present, ratifyinge hereby whatsoever the said Mr.[1] Laurence Bridger, Elias Wrench and Thomas Prior (iointly and severally)[2] shall for me and in my name lawfully doe in the premisses as myne owne act and deede for evermore. In wittnes whereof I have hereunto putt my hand and seale the ninth day of July anno regni domini nostri Jacobi, dei gracia Anglie, Frauncie et Hibernie regis, fidei defensoris &c. xxi⁰, Scotie vero lvi⁰, anno domini 1623. And in further confirmacion hereof I have cawsed the seale of the officialtie of the archdeacon of Gloucester to be allsoe hereunto affixed the daye and yeare above said.'

After which proxie soe read and published as aforesaid the said Mr. Subdeane ymediatly there gave Mr. Deane's voice for the confirmacion of the patent in the said proxie mencioned to Mr. William Sutton. And then and there allsoe the aforesaid Mr. Bridger, subdeane, Mr. Wrench and Mr. Prior, prebendaries, did likewise give their voices & full consents and assents to the confirmacion of the said patent. And last of all the said Mr. Subdean exhibited a proxie under the hand & seale of the right woorshipful Dr. Iles, one of the prebendaries of this church, [*fo. 36v.*] agreable in all respects, and in the same words with Mr. Deane's, bearinge date the fourteenth day of July 1623, by vertue whereof the said Mr. Subdeane gave likewise Dr. Iles his voice & full consent to the

---

[1] 'Mr.' has been inserted above the line. The reading is uncertain.
[2] The MS. omits the closing bracket.

confirmacion of the said patent. And the same day the said patent was confirmed under their chapter seale accordingly.

      Lawr[ence] Bridger, subdecanus; Elias Wrenche; Tho[mas] Prior.

Eodem die.

Smith's second monition. Quibus die, loco et anno Mr. Subdeane pronounced against Ely Smyth, lay singingman, his second monition to departe this church, for his notorious and manifest contempt of his feirst monition, and for allmost his continuall absence and neglect of his service in the church, and for his departure and absence without any leave at all.

      Lawr[ence] Bridger, subdecanus.

43.   15 September 1623.

Admissio choristae. [*Admission of a chorister. Anthony Dobbs was admitted by Mr. Laurence Bridger, subdean, in the place of John Pink.*] Quibus die et anno Anthonius Dobbs admissus fuit per Magistrum Laurentium Bridger, subdecanum, chorista in loco Johannis Pinke.

      Lawr[ence] Bridger, subdecanus.

44.   8 November 1623.

Admissio choristae. [*Admission of a chorister. Richard Price was admitted by the dean in the place of Giles Dobbs.*] Quibus die et anno Richardus Price admissus fuit per venerabilem decanum chorista in loco Egidii Dobbs.

      Richardus Senhouse, decanus.

45.   28 November 1623.   Chapter House.

Smith's expulsion. Whereas Ely Smith, a lay singingman of this church, for his sundry contempts, abuses, neglect of the churche's service and absence allmost continually for the space of this yeare last past, hath received allreddy two severall monitions to depart this [*fo. 37*] church, and since his monitions hath not reformed himselfe, but hath still absented himself from his said service, Mr. Deane, for his abuses and notorious neglect, hath (accordinge to the locall statutes)[1] given unto the said Ely Smith his third and last monition, and decreed him expelled from the said church.

      Richard Senhouse, deane.

46.   29 November 1623.   Deanery.

Admissio laici cantatoris. [*Admission of a lay singer. William Collins was admitted by the dean in the place of Elias (MS. Ely) Smith.*] Quibus die et loco [*etc., as in* **12**, *above*].

      Richard Senhouse, deane.

---

[1] The reference is evidently to Cap. XXXIII of the Henrician statutes, 'De Corrigendis Excessibus', which states that should any officer have offended 'by any great fault, if it shall be thought fit, he shall be expelled by those by whom he was admitted.'

47.   Sunday the feast of St. Andrew the Apostle, 30 November 1623.

Chapter House.

(Richard Senhouse, S.T.P., dean; Laurence Bridger, subdean; Elias Wrench; Thomas Prior.)

Electio officiariorum. [*Election of officers. The dean and chapter elected Elias Wrench as subdean and Thomas Prior as receiver and treasurer. As in* **6**, *above.*]

Richardus Senhouse, decanus; Elias Wrenche, subdecanus;
Lawr[ence] Bridger; Tho[mas] Prior.

Electio precentoris. [*Election of the precentor. The dean chose Thomas Tomkins. The form is slightly different from that in* **6**, *above.*] Eodem die, loco et anno idem venerabilis decanus antedictus elegit in precentorem dictae ecclesiae Thomam Tomkins, unum minorum canonicorum eiusdem ecclesiae cathedralis &c.

Richardus Senhouse, decanus.

48.   [*fo. 37v.*]   1 December 1623.   Chapter House.

(Elias Wrench, subdean; Laurence Bridger; Thomas Prior.)

Mr. Marwood's feirst monition. Quibus die et loco, upon complaint made by James Wood, clothier, against Mr. Marwood, one of the petticannons of this church, for the cruell and barberous whippinge and beatinge of a childe of the said Wood's, which complaint beinge manifestly proved to Mr. Subdeane and the rest that were present upon sight of the childe, and the offence for punishment of the childe being judged very small, and noe way deservinge such severe correction, Mr. Subdeane thereupon gave unto the said Mr. Marwood his feirst monition to departe the church.

Elias Wrenche, subdecanus.

49.   3 February 1623/4.   Chapter House.

(Elias Wrench, subdean; Thomas Prior.)

Choise of a clarke for the convocation howse. Quibus die et loco, by vertue of a proxie from Mr. Deane dated the 13th of January 1623[/4] for the choise of a clarke for the convocation howse for the chapter of this church at this ensuing parliament, the sayd Mr. Subdeane gave Mr. Deane's voyce unto Dr. Leo, a prebend of this church, for the sayd place, and likewise Mr. Subdeane gave his owne voice unto him the sayd Dr. Leo for the sayd place. And Mr. Prior allsoe by vertue of a proxie dated the 29th of January 1623[/4] from Mr. Bridger, gave the sayd Mr. Bridger's voice to the sayd Dr. Leo and his own voice allsoe. By reason whereof the sayd Dr. Leo was elected and chosen the clarke of the convocation howse for the body of the chapter, and yt was decreed that an instrument should be made unto him under the chapter seale which was donne accordingly, the tenor whereof followeth in these wordes, vizt. Pateat universis &c. mutatis mutandis, prout patet in pagina 32^a huius libri.[1]

Elias Wrenche, subdec[anus]; Tho[mas] Prior.

---

[1] i.e. 'Be it known to all &c., changed as necessary, as appears on page 32 of this book'; above, **30**.

50.   [*fo. 38*]   4 February 1623/4.   Chapter House.
(Elias Wrench, subdean; Thomas Prior.)

Admissio hypodidascali. [*Admission of the assistant schoolmaster. John Angell,*[1] *who had been chosen by the dean, was admitted by the subdean, after he had taken the oath on the gospels touched by him. The form of the entry is different in some respects from* **12** *and* **33**, *above.*] Quibus die, loco et anno Johannes Angell, qui in locum hypodidascali fuit electus per dominum decanum infra collegium ecclesiae cathedralis Gloucestriae, admissus fuit per Magistrum Subdecanum, sumpto prius per eum iuramento[2] respective ad sacrosancta dei evangelia per eum tacta &c.
        Elias Wrenche, subdecanus.

51.   Thursday 14 June 1624.   Chapter House.
(Elias Wrench, subdean; Thomas Prior.)

Admissio eleemosynarii. [*Admission of an almsman. John Grove appeared and sought the removal of John March from his place of almsman. March had said that Grove was dead and so the admission of March is void.*[3] *Grove asked to be admitted as an almsman by virtue of letters patent granted to him, addressed to the dean and chapter, and registered at their registry. The subdean admitted him, he having taken the almsman's oath. He is to have the emoluments of an almsman from Christmas last.*] Comparuit quidam Johannes Grove et petiit amotionem cuiusdam Johannis March a loco eleemozynarii dictae ecclesiae eo quod predictus Johannes March dixit et affirmavit ipsum Johannem Grove esse mortuum, prout in admissione dicti Johannis March plenius liquet et apparet, et ideo admissio predicti Johannis March vacua est et nullius vigoris, ut in admissione predicta similiter continetur, et unde idem Johannes Grove petiit admitti in locum eleemozynarii dictae ecclesiae, virtute literarum patentium sibi in ea parte concessarum decano et capitulo dictae ecclesiae directarum et apud registrarium eorundem decani et capituli registratarum, unde dictus venerabilis subdecanus prestito primitus per eundem Johannem Grove iuramento ab eleemozynario prestando in eleemozynarium admisit, habere et percipere omnia proficua et emolumenta ad officium eleemozynarii spectantia a festo natalis domini ultimo preterito.
        Elias Wrench, subdecanus.

52.   [*fo. 38v.*]   Wednesday 10 November 1624.   Chapter House.
(Elias Wrench, subdean; Thomas Prior, treasurer; Anthony Robinson, registrar.)

Installatio Venerabilis Viri Thomae Wynniff Decani Gloucestriae. 1624. [*Installation of the venerable man Thomas Winniffe as dean of Gloucester. In the chapter house, before Elias Wrench, subdean, and Thomas Prior, treasurer, prebendaries of the cathedral church solemnly assembled in chapter, in the presence of Anthony Robinson, registrar, John Harward, gent., appeared in person and exhibited his proxy for Thomas Winniffe, S.T.P., chaplain to Prince Charles, prince of Wales, and made himself party for the same and presented the royal mandate, dated 2 October 1624, addressed to the chapter and*

---

[1] For Angell, below, p. 161.
[2] MS. has 'sumpt' prius per eum iuramenta', an ungrammatical form which recurs in later entries.
[3] Cf. above, **17**.

prebendaries, to assign to the dean a stall in the choir and a place and voice in the chapter. And John Harward exhibited the dean's letters of proxy, dated 5 November 1624, appointing Mr. Thomas Prior his proxy for putting the dean in possession, etc., which Thomas Prior accepted. Afterwards on the same day the subdean with due solemnity brought Thomas Prior to the dean's customary stall in the choir and installed him and put him in possession, and led him thence to the chapter house and assigned him his place and voice. All which the prebendaries required to be enacted, and all these things were done in the presence of John Jones and John Brown, Esq., Thomas Harvey, William Bannester, John Huntley and Edmund Huntley, gents., John Langley, M.A., John Angell, B.A., Thomas Tomkins, precentor, and other servants of the said church.] In domo capitulari ecclesiae cathedralis Gloucestriae, coram Elia Wrench tunc subdecano, & Thoma Prior tunc thesaurario, et prebendariis dictae ecclesiae cathedralis capitulariter & solemniter congregatis. In praesentia mei Antonii Robinson, dictae ecclesiae registrarii.

Quibus die et loco comparuit personaliter quidam Johannes Harward, generosus, ac exhibuit procuratorium pro venerabili viro Thoma Wynniff (sacrae theologie professore ac sacellaro illustrissimo Principi Carolo, principi Walliae) constituto et ordinato in decanum ecclesiae cathedralis Sanctae & Individuae Trinitatis Gloucestriae, ac fecit se partem pro eodem, [*etc., as in* **1**, *above, with minor verbal variations and as modified in* **35**, *above*].

[*fo. 39*] Ita testor Anth[onius] Robinson, registrarius.

53.   26 November 1624.   Chapter House.
(Thomas Wynnyff, S.T.P., dean; Elias Wrench, subdean; William Loe, S.T.P.; Thomas Prior.)

Decanus iurat. [*The dean takes the oath. As in* **2**, *above.*]
Tho[mas] Wynnyff, deca[nus]; Elias Wrenche, subdec[anus]; Guiliel[mus] Leo; Tho[mas] Prior.

54.   [*fo. 39v.*]   Friday 26 November 1624, between eight and eleven a.m.
                                                                 Chapter House.
(Thomas Wynnyff, S.T.P., dean; Elias Wrench, subdean; William Loe, S.T.P.; Thomas Prior; Anthony Robinson, registrar.)

Electio episcopi. [*Election of the bishop. John Jones, Esq.,*[1] *registrar of Gloucester, exhibited the king's letters patent or* congé d'élire *under the Great Seal, dated 15 November 1624, for the election as bishop and pastor of the cathedral church of the episcopal see, vacant by the death of the last bishop,*[2] *of someone suitable, devout to God and useful and loyal to the king and his kingdom. He exhibited letters dated 10 November and signed by the king's hand nominating Godfrey Goodman, S.T.P., as eligible by the dean and chapter, on the strength of which the dean and chapter elected Godfrey Goodman and certified the king by a letter under the chapter seal dated 26 November. They nominated an unnamed man and Augustine Rawe, notary public of the*

---

[1] For Jones, below, p. 166.
[2] Bishop Miles Smith had died on 20 Oct. 1624, and was buried in the lady chapel.

Canterbury Court of Arches in London, jointly or severally, as their proctors to present their letter to the king and to do other things necessary. Afterwards they informed the archbishop of Canterbury, George Abbot, in a letter under the chapter seal dated 5 February 1624/5.] Quibus die et loco constitutus personaliter Johannes Jones, armiger, registrarius Gloucestriae, cum ea qua decuit reverentia et humilitate exhibuit et presentavit prefatis venerabilibus viris literas quasdam patentes sive le Congedeslire illustrissimi in Christo principis domini nostri, Domini Jacobi, dei gratia Angliae, Scotiae, Franciae et Hiberniae regis, fidei defensor &c., magno sigillo Angliae sigillatas, gerentes datas decimo quinto die Novembris anno regni sui Angliae, Franciae et Hiberniae vicesimo secundo et Scotiae quinquagesimo octavo, pro electione in episcopum et pastorem ecclesiae cathedralis Gloucestriae predictae, sede episcopali ibidem[1] iam vacante per mortem naturalem ultimi ibidem episcopi,[2] aliquem idoneum deo devotum eiusque majestati et regno suo utilem et fidelem. Ac preterea presentavit et exhibuit cum simili reverentia et humilitate eisdem venerabilibus viris literas quasdam missivas ipsius illustrissimi principis gerentes datas decimo die Novembris anno supradicto, manu sacra dicti domini regis signatas, per quas venerabilis et egregius vir Godfridus Goodman, sacrae theologie professor, prefato decano et ecclesiae cathedralis predictae capitulo nominatus et commendatus extitit et per eundem decanum et capitulum in episcopum et pastorem ecclesiae cathedralis predictae eligendus, quarum vero literarum patentium et missivarum vigore et authoritate decanus antedictus et prenominatique [*sic*] prebendarii prerecitatum venerabilem virum Godfridum Goodman, sacrae theologiae professorem, in episcopum et pastorem ecclesiae cathedralis antedictae (ut prefertur) vacantis eligerunt et eleccionem huiusmodi eorum regiae majestati certificaverunt per literas sub sigillo eorum capitulari eodem vicesimo sexto die Novembris datas. Et constituerunt et nominaverunt dilectos sibi in Christo [. . .] et Augustinum[3] Rawe, notarium publicum almae curiae Cant: de Archubus London., conjunctim et divisim, eorum procuratores &c. ad exhibendum regiae majestati dictas literas certificatorias et regalem suum assensum eleccioni predictae coram quocunque in ea parte potestatem habenti seu habituro usque ad finalem expeditionem eiusdem eorum nomine prosequendum ac confirmationem in ea parte petendum &c., et generaliter omnia et singula facienda et exercenda quae in premissis necessaria fuerint &c. Datus vero procuratorii predicti est 26 Novembris predicti. Et postea decanus antedictus prebendariique eleccionem huiusmodi eorum reverendissimo in Christo patre ac domino, Domino Georgio, providentia divina Cantuar. archiepiscopo, certificaverunt per literas sub sigillo eorum capitulari gerentes datas quinto die Februarii anno domini iuxta &c. 1624.

[*fo. 40*]   Eodem die.

A graunt to collect Tenths & Subsidyes. Quibus die et loco, a graunt was made unto Mr. John Jones, allderman of the citty of Gloucester, to be collector of the tenthes and subsedyes within the dioces of Gloucester due from the clergy within the said dioces,

---

[1] The word 'ibidem' has been written above the word 'Glouc', which has been crossed out.

[2] After 'episcopi' the words 'iam vacante' have been repeated and crossed out.

[3] The words 'et Augustinum' were written at the end of a line and crossed out, the next line being left blank except for 'et Augustinum Rawe' at the end, the space presumably being left for the insertion of the name of the other proctor.

duringe the time of the present vacancy of the bishoprick, the said Mr. Jones givinge such security for the dischardge of the said deane and chapter and their successors, as they shall approove and allow of.

> Tho[mas] Wynnyff, deca[nus]; Elias Wrenche, subd[ecanus]; Laur[ence] Bridger; W[illia]m Leo; Tho[mas] Prior.

55.   Tuesday the feast of St. Andrew the Apostle, 30 November 1624.
                                                                    Chapter House.
(Thomas Wynnyffe, S.T.P., dean; Elias Wrench, subdean; [Laurence Bridger;][1] William Loe, S.T.P.; Thomas Prior.)

Electio Officiariorum. [*Election of officers. The dean and chapter elected Thomas Prior as subdean and Laurence Bridger as receiver and treasurer. As in* **6**, *above.*]

> Tho[mas] Wynnyff, deca[nus]; El[ias] Wrenche, subd[ecanus]; Guiliel[mus] Leo; Lawr[ence] Bridger; Tho[mas] Prior.

Electio precentoris. [*Election of the precentor. The dean chose Thomas Tomkins. As in* **47**, *above.*] Eodem die, loco et anno [*etc.*].

> Tho[mas] Wynnyff, deca[nus].

                    Eodem die.
Admissio choristae. [*Admission by the dean of Thomas Lewes as a chorister in the place of Mark Colman.*] Quibus die et anno Thomas Lewes admissus fuit per venerabilem decanum chorista in loco Marci Colman.

> Tho[mas] Wynnyff, deca[nus].

56.   [*fo. 40v.*]   Monday 4 April 1625 between one and four p.m. Chapter House. (Thomas Prior, subdean; Anthony Robinson, registrar.)

Installatio episcopi. [*Installation of the bishop. Thomas Whittington, M.A., rector of Great Rissington, exhibited his letter of proxy, dated 6 March last and sealed with the episcopal seal, from Godfrey Goodman, S.T.P., recently elected as bishop of Gloucester, by which he and others (unnamed) in the bishop's name are to take possession of the see. Thomas Prior exhibited a letter, dated 23 March last, from William Kingsley, S.T.P., archdeacon of Canterbury, to whom the induction, installation and enthronement of all bishops in the province of Canterbury belonged, to Thomas Winniffe, S.T.P., dean, Thomas Prior, M.A., rector of Cowley and subdean, and Elias Wrench, M.A., rector of Lassington and prebendary, saying that on the authority of King James's letters patent George Abbot, archbishop of Canterbury, had confirmed Godfrey Goodman, dean of Rochester, to the bishopric of Gloucester, vacant by the death of Miles Smith, and that Goodman was to be put in possession; the archdeacon delegated the task to the dean, the subdean and Wrench, jointly and severally. The letters were read in public by Whittington and Prior, and leaving the chapter house and entering the cathedral Prior put the bishop, in the person of Whittington, in possession of the cathedral and enthroned him in the bishop's seat in the choir, with the bells ringing and the cathedral's servants*]

---

[1] Bridger's name, not listed at the beginning of the entry, is subscribed to the election of officers.

clothed in white. Afterwards Prior, with the proctor, entered the chapter house and assigned to the bishop the accustomed place there; then he went to the consistory place within the cathedral and delivered possession of it to the bishop; finally he went back with the proctor to the bishop's house, called the palace, within the cathedral precinct and put Whittington in possession in the bishop's name. All which was done in the presence of William Norris, B.Theol., John Jones, notary public and registrar of the bishop of Gloucester, Thomas Harvey and James Clent, notaries public, and also of the precentor, choristers and servants of the cathedral and of some others of the faithful, and of Anthony Robinson, registrar of the cathedral.] Quibus die et loco Thomas Whittington, artium magister, rector de Rysington Magna in comitatu et diocesse Gloucestriae, personaliter exhibuit quasdam literas procuratorias a reverendo patre Godfrido Goodman, sacrae theologiae professore, nuper electo in episcopum et pastorem ecclesiae cathedralis Gloucestriae predictae per quas prefatum Thomam Whittington et alios suos legitimos procuratores coniunctim et divisim nominavit et constituit pro se ac loco, vice et nomine suis in realem, actualem et corporalem possessionem ecclesiae cathedralis predictae ac dignitatis episcopalis eiusdem, cum omnibus et singulis honoribus, privilegiis, prerogativis, preheminentiis, iuribus, dignitatibus ac pertinentiis suis universis, spiritualibus et temporalibus, iuxta et secundum ipsius ecclesiae statuta, ordinationes et consuetudines laudabiles et approbatas induci, installari et inthronizari cum plenitudine iuris episcopalis in eadem ecclesia cathedramque et stallum sive sedem episcopalem in choro et locum in capitulo episcopo ibidem ab antiquo assignari consuetum sibi assignari et limitari petendi et optinendi, nec non realem et corporalem possessionem, installationem et inthronizacionem huiusmodi ingrediendi et adipiscendi, ac illas sic nactas et adeptas ad usum suum custodiendi et conservandi omniaque alia et singula faciendi et exercendi que in ea parte necessaria fuerint seu quomodolibet oportuna prout per easdem literas procuratorias gerentes datas vicesimo sexto die mensis Martii ultimo preterito sigilloque suo episcopali sigillatas plenius apparet. Quarum quidem literarum vigore idem Magister Thomas Whittington fecit se partem pro eodem reverendo patre. Ac tunc et ibidem dictus Mr. Thomas Prior subdecanus antedictus exhibuit quasdam literas mandatorias a venerabili viro Wilielmo Kingsley, sacrae theologiae professore, archidiacono Cantuariensis in ecclesia cathedrali et metropolitica Christi Cantuariense, ad quem inductio, installatio et inthronizatio omnium et singulorum episcoporum Cantuariensis provinciae de laudabili longevaque consuetudine notorie dignoscitur pertinere, gerentes datas vicesimo tertio die mensis Martii ultimo preterito ac authentice sigillatas et venerabili viro Thomae Wynnyff, sacrae theologiae professore, decano ecclesiae cathedralis predictae, prefatoque Thomae Prior, artium magistro, rectori de Cowly ac ecclesiae predictae subdecano, Eliae Wrench, artium magistro, rectori de Lassington et uni prebendariorum ecclesiae cathedralis predictae, et aliis coniunctim et divisim directas, per quas liquet et apparet reverendissimum in Christo patrem et dominum, Dominum Georgium, providentia divina Cantuariensem archiepiscopum, totius Angliae primatem et metropolitanum, auchtoritate literarum commissionalium patentium illustrissimi in Christo principis ac domini, Domini Jacobi, dei gratia Angliae, Scotiae, Franciae et Hiberniae regis &c., sibi in hac parte directarum electionem de

persona prefati venerabilis[1] viri Godfridi Goodman, ecclesiae Christi et Beatae Mariae
Virginis Roffensis decani, in episcopum et pastorem ecclesiae cathedralis Gloucestriae
predictae (sede episcopali Gloucestriae per mortem naturalem reverendi patris Domini
Milonis Smith, ultimi episcopi, ibidem vacante) alias factam et celebratam et personam
sic electam (servatis de iure et statutis huius incliti regni Angliae in ea parte servandis)
confirmari fecisse, ipsique curam, regimen et administracionem spiritualium dicti
episcopatus Gloucestriae comisisse, necnon munus consecracionis (adhibitis ritibus et
ceremoniis de usu moderno ecclesiae Anglicanae adhibendis) eidem electo et confirmato
impendisse necnon dedisse, in mandatis eidem venerabili archidiacono Cantuariensi
predicto quatenus ipse prefatum [*fo. 42*][2] venerabilem[3] virum Godfridum Goodman sic
electum, confirmatum et consecratum seu procuratorem suum legitimum eius nomine ac
pro eo in realem actualem et corporalem possessionem dicti episcopatus Gloucestriae
iuriumque, membrorum, preheminentiarum et pertinentium suorom universorum
inducerat, installaret et inthronizaret seu sic fieri faceret, per quas quoque literas apparet
similiter ante dictum venerabilem virum archidiaconum predictum vices et authoritatem
suas prememoratis decano ecclesiae cathedralis predictae et prefatis Thoma Prior et Elia
Wrench (quia ipse in presenti in quibusdam arduis et urgentibus negotiis implicitus est)
coniunctim et divisim commisisse ad inducendum, installandum et inthronizandum
prefatum reverendum patrem Dominum Godfridum Goodman in episcopum electum,
confirmatum et consecratum ut prefertur seu eius procuratorem legitimum in realem,
actualem et corporalem possessionem antedicti episcopatus Gloucestriae iuriumque,
honorum et dignitatum et pertinentium universorum &c., ceteraque omnia et singula
facienda, exercenda et expedienda quae in ea parte necessaria fuerint vel requisita &c.
prout per easdem literas mandatorias plenius appareat; quibus seperalibus instrumentis
per antedictos Thomam Whittington et Thomam Prior cum omni reverentia receptis et
publice perlectis ipsi ad executionem earundem procedere decreberunt, dictusque Mr.
Thomas Prior, cum omni reverentia et congrua festinatione exeuns e dicta domo
capitulari et accedens ad ecclesiam cathedralem predictam, antedictum reverendum
patrem Dominum Godfridum Goodman electum, confirmatum et consecratum ut
prefertur in realem, actualem et corporalem possessionem dictae ecclesiae cathedralis et
episcopatus Gloucestriae praedicti in persona prefati Magistri Thoma Whittington,
procuratoris sui predicti, induxit et eum in persona dicti procuratoris sui in episcopali
cathedra vel sede in choro dictae ecclesiae cathedralis scituata solemniter, campanis
pulsantibus et ministris ecclesiae eiusdem candidis indutis ut decantantibus installavit et
inthronizavit. Et postea dictus Mr. Thomas Prior discedens a choro predicto unacum dicto
procuratore ad domum capitularem antedictum locum in dicta domo (episcopo
Gloucestriae pro tempore existente ab antiquo solitum et consuetum) antedicto domino
episcopo in persona prememorati Thomae Whittington procuratoris antedicti assignavit,
quem idem procurator vice domini sui predicti acceptavit. Ac imediate idem Thomas
Prior abiit ad locum consistorialem infra ecclesiam cathedralem Gloucestriae predictam
cum procuratore predicto et eidem domino electo in persona dicti procuratoris sui

---

[1] The word 'venerabilis' has been written above 'reverendi', which has been crossed out.
[2] There is no folio numbered 41; fo. 40v. is numbered in a later hand as page 41.
[3] The word 'venerabilem' is also a catchword at the foot of fo. 40v.

plenam, quietam et pacificam possessionem eiusdem loci consistorialis tradidit et deliberavit, quem dictus procurator vice domini sui predicti acceptavit. Et postremo antedictus Thomas Prior recessit cum dicto procuratore ad domum mansionalem domini episcopi Gloucestriae, communiter vocatam palatium episcopale, scituatum infra precinctum ecclesiae cathedralis Gloucestriae predictae, et plenam et pacificam possessionem eiusdem domus sive pallatii prefato Thomae Whittington nomine, vice et loco domini electi antedicti tradidit etiam et deliberavit. Et haec omnia facta fuerunt in presentia venerabili viri Willielmi Norris, theologiae baccalaurii, Johannis Jones, notarii publici, registrarii episcopi Gloucestriae, Thomae Harvy et Jacobi Clent, notariorum publicorum, nec non cantatoris, choristarum et ministrorum ecclesiae cathedralis predictae et nonnullorum aliorum Christi fidelium meique Anthonii Robinson, dictae ecclesiae registrarii.

Anth[ony] Robinson, registrarius ibidem.

57.   [*fo. 42v.*]   21 April 1625.   Chapter House.
(Thomas Prior, subdean; Laurence Bridger; Elias Wrench.)

Order for church service. Quibus die, et loco, yt is ordered that upon all the solemme feast dayes, the king's holydayes and at any other times when the judges of assize or any other persons of greate qualitie shalbe present, the chaunter, or in his absence or defect the senior pettycannon, shall officiate and performe the service of the church allbeyt yt be not his course that time to officiate.

Tho[mas] Prior, subd[ean]; Laur[ence] Bridger; Elias Wrenche.

Eodem die.

Choise of a clarke for the convocation. Quibus die et loco, by vertue of a proxie from Mr. Deane dated the 2th of Aprill 1625 for the choyse of a clarke for the convocation howse for the chapter of this church, at this ensuinge parliament, the said Mr. Subdeane gave Mr. Deane's voyce unto Dr. Leo, a prebend of this church, for the said place, and likewise Mr. Subdeane gave his owne voyce unto him the said Dr. Leo for the said place. And Mr. Bridger and Mr. Wrench then present gave their voyces to the said Dr. Leo for the said place. By reason whereof [*etc., as in* **49**, *above*].

58.   15 July 1625.

Order for sermons duringe the fast. Whereas the king's most exellent majestie hath by proclamation commaunded that upon every Wednesday there shall be observed a generall publick and solemme fast duringe the continuance of this greate and heavy visitation[1] throughout the whole kingdome, and that aswell in all cathedrall as parochiall churches the duties of prayer and preachinge shall be performed, in obedience to his majestie's gratious, godly and pious commaund [*fo. 43*] yt is by Mr. Subdeane and the prebendaries present ordered and decreed that the prebendaries both present and absent shall on every the said Wednesdayes by himselfe or some other by him or them appointed performe and execute his turne and course in preachinge in the same manner and forme that they doe

---

[1] In 1625 there was a serious and widespread outbreak of bubonic plague, which fortunately did not reach the cathedral precinct. The city was not to be so lucky in 1638.

their courses and turnes on the Saboth dayes. And the next Wednesday Mr. Subdeane is to beginne, and the rest to follow in their order. And this decree to stand in force untill yt shall please allmighty God to mitigate and abate this greate contagion, and commaundement be by Mr. Deane or Mr. Subdeane given to give over and forbeare the same.

Tho[mas] Prior, subd[ean]; Lawr[ence] Bridger; Elias Wrench.

59.   1 August 1625.

Order in the time of the infection. It is ordered by Thomas Pryor, subdeane, and Elyas Wrench, one of the prebendaries of this church, that if any of the members of this church shall dureinge the time of this contagion into their howses receave any person or persons comeinge from London or any other place suspected to be infected with sicknes without the speciall lycens of the deane, or in his absence of the subdeane or senior prebend of this church, that then the partie soe offendinge shall loose the whole profitts of his place duringe pleasure.

Tho[mas] Prior, subd[ean]; Elias Wrenche.

60.   [*fo. 43v.*]   Wednesday 23 November 1625 between two and four p.m.

Chapter House.

(Thomas Prior, subdean; Elias Wrench.)

Admissio venerabilis viri Johannis Wood in tertiam prebendam. [*Admission of the venerable man John Wood to the third prebend. On Wednesday 23 November 1625, before Mr. Thomas Prior, subdean, and Elias Wrench, one of the prebendaries, between the second and the fourth hour after noon, John Wood, M.A., exhibited the king's letters patent dated 9 November granting to him the third prebend, vacant by the resignation of Laurence Bridger, and the royal mandate for his admission and installation; the subdean admitted him, as in* **37**, *above. All this was done in the presence of Christopher Capel, alderman, John Hanbury and Samuel Baynham, gents., Thomas Harvey and James Clent, notaries public, John Workman and John Langley, M.A., Richard Marwood and Richard Brodgate, minor canons, and other servants of the said church and of the writer, Anthony Robinson, registrar.*] Die Mercurii vizt. vicesimo tertio die mensis Novembris anno domini 1625 coram venerabilibus viris Magistris Thoma Prior subdecano ecclesiae cathedralis Gloucestriae et Elia Wrench uno prebendariorum dictae ecclesiae inter horas secundam et quartam post meridiem in domo capitulari dictae ecclesiae discretus vir Johannes Wood in artibus magister exhibuit et tradidit subdecano antedicto literas patentes [*etc., as in* **37**, *above, with the king's name and the date changed*].

Ita testor Anth[onius] Robinson, registrarius.

61.   Tuesday 29 November 1625.   Chapter House.
(Thomas Prior, subdean; Elias Wrench; John Wood.)

Admissio eleemozynarii. [*Admission of an almsman. John March appeared and sought admission to the place of an almsman which was vacant by the death of Roger Peirs, by virtue of letters patent granted to him, addressed to the dean and chapter, and registered* *at their registry. The subdean admitted him, he having taken the oath, to receive the emoluments belonging to the office.*] Comparuit quidam Johannes March et petiit admitti in locum eleemozynarii dictae ecclesiae, in loco cuiusdam Rogeri Peirs, nuper defuncti, virtute literarum patentium sibi in ea parte concessarum, decano et capitulo dictae ecclesiae directarum et apud registrarium eorundem decani et capituli registratarum. Unde dictus venerabilis subdecanus, prestito primitus per eundem Johannem March iuramento ab eleemozynario prestando, in eleemozynarium admisit, habere et percipere omnia proficua et emolumenta ad officium eleemozynarii spectantia.

Tho[mas] Prior, subd[ean].

[*fo. 44*]   Acta in Domo Capitulari. [*Acts in the Chapter House.*]
Eodem die.

Orders decreed in Chapter. Imprimis [*First*], In regard that the service of this church is very much neglected [by] [1] the quire, under pretence of havinge and obteyninge leave for absence [from the] subdeane for the time beinge or the senior prebendary at home, yt is therefore ordered that all licenses for absences, where the party desiringe or obteyninge yt hath bin absent above twenty times in any one quarter of the yeare before the graunt hereof, whether yt be graunted by Mr. Subdeane or any prebendary, shall be void and of none effect, and the party to whom yt is graunted shall have noe benefitt thereby.

Yt is allsoe ordered that the petty cannons, lay singingmen and choristers shall come unto such sermons as shallbe preached within this cathedrall church and there continue quietly and peaceably in their accustomed places during the sermon time. And for avoydinge of night walkinge and scandall that may arise thereby yt is ordered that noe member of the quire whose habitation is within the precincts of this church shall be abrode in the citty or else where after tenne of the clock in the night.

Whereas the moonthly communions within this church have many times bin forborne this last yeare past by reson of the great neglect of those that have bin accustomed to receave the same, for remedy whereof yt is ordered that the petty cannons and lay singingmen who shall absent themselves and not receave the communion at the times appointed shall have their absences noted by the chaunter of this church. And for every time that they shall be absent shall pay two pence, which shall be deducted out of their wages at the end of every quarter by the tresurer for the time beinge. And to be by him devided as the perditions are.

Whereas the service of God is much disturbed by such of the quire that in time of devine prayers use to talke and iangle to their fellowes or others, yt is therefore ordered that, after warning given by the chaunter to such of the said quire as shall soe offend for the feirst time, for every offence afterwards the partie offendinge shall forfeit two pence, which severall offences shall be noted by the chaunter for the time beinge, and the forfeitures shall be deducted quarterly out of the parties' wages soe offendinge by the tresurer for the time beinge. And to be by him devided as the perditions are.

Tho[mas] Prior, subd[ean]; Elias Wrenche.

---

[1] The top right-hand corner of the folio has been torn away.

62. *Admissio eleemozynarii.*[1] [*Admission of an almsman. James Webbe, of the city of Gloucester, affirmed before the subdean that John Grove was dead and that he, the said Webbe, should be admitted in Grove's place by virtue of letters patent of the late King James granted to him and addressed to the dean and chapter, whereupon the subdean admitted him, to receive the emoluments of the office from Michaelmas last past, with the proviso that if John Grove was then alive this admission would be void.*] Quibus die, loco et anno Jacobus Webbe, civitatis Gloucestriae, dixit et affirmavit coram venerabili viro Magistro Thoma Prior, subdecano ecclesiae cathedralis Gloucestriae, quendam Johannem Grove mortuum esse eumque prefatum Jacobum Webbe admittendum esse in loco eiusdem Johannis Grove ultimi eleemozynarii eiusdem ecclesiae cathedralis virtute literarum patentium serenissimi domini nostri Jacobi nuper regis sibi in ea parte concessarum, decano et capitulo dictae ecclesiae directarum, unde dictus venerabilis subdecanus dictum Jacobum Webbe in eleemozynarium admisit, habere et percipere omnia emolumenta et proficua ad officium eleemozynarii spectantia a festo Sancti Michaelis Arch-angeli ultimo preterito. Proviso tamen quod si prefatus Johannes Grove tunc temporis esset vivus, quod haec[2] prefata admissio vacua erit, et nullius vigoris.

        Tho[mas] Prior, subd[ean].

[*fo. 44v.*]   Eodem die.

[**Admissio**][3] **choristae.** [*Admission of a chorister. Anthony Smith was admitted by Mr. Thomas Prior, subdean, in the place of Henry Purlewent.*] Quibus die, loco et anno Anthonius Smith admissus fuit per Magistrum Thomam Prior, subdecanum, chorista in loco Henrici Purlewent.

        Tho[mas] Prior, subd[ean].

63.   Wednesday 30 November 1625.   Chapter House.
(Thomas Prior, subdean; Elias Wrench; John Wood.)

Electio officiariorum. [*Election of officers. The subdean and the aforenamed prebendaries elected Mr. Thomas Prior as subdean and Mr. Elias Wrench as receiver and treasurer. As in* **6**, *above, with some changes in form.*] Congregatis in domo capitulari ecclesiae Gloucestriae venerabilibus viris Magistro Thoma Prior, tunc subdecano, Elia Wrench et Johanne Wood, prebendariis, et ad eleccionem officiariorum pro anno futuro iuxta morem antiquum procedentibus, idem subdecanus et prebendarii prenominati elegerunt et continuaverunt Magistrum Thomam Prior in subdecanum et Magistrum Eliam Wrench in receptorem et thesaurarium eiusdem ecclesiae cathedralis pro hoc anno sequente usque ad finem eiusdem anni, qui quidem respective subierunt iuramenta ad sacrosancta dei evangelia per eos tacta ad eorum officia respective spectantia &c.

        Tho[mas] Prior, subd[ean]; Elias Wrenche; Johannes Woode.

---

[1] The entry, which is undated, and that which follows it may or may not belong to the meeting recorded in **61**, above.

[2] 'haec' is added above the line, to replace 'illa', crossed out.

[3] The top left-hand corner of the folio has been torn away.

Electio precentoris. [*Election of the precentor.*[1] *The aforesaid men elected as precentor for the coming year Richard Marwood,*[2] *one of the minor canons, the oath having been taken by him.*] Eodem die, loco et anno venerabiles viri antedicti elegerunt in precentorem dictae ecclesiae pro anno futuro Richardum Marwood, unum minorum canonicorum eiusdem ecclesiae, iuramento suscepto &c.

  Tho[mas] Prior, subd[ean]; Elias Wrenche; Johannes Woode.

     Eodem die.

Order for the sermons before the iudges. Whereas the judges of assize have seemed to dislike that the preachinge courses on the Saboth dayes in the morning before them have bin preached by younge men that have supplyed the course of some of the prebendaryes and not by the prebends themselves, which their dislike hath come unto the knowledge of Mr. Deane and thereupon Mr. Deane hath written to Mr. Subdeane to take care for the next supply, yt is therefore ordered that the next course before the judges on the Saboth day morninge shall be supplyed by that prebendary on whose turne yt shall fall in his owne person if he[3] will undertake the same, or otherwise Mr. Subdeane is pleased to performe yt in his owne person. And yt is ordered that if Mr. Subdeane doe performe the same for any of the prebendaryes that then the same prebendary shall by himselfe or his deputy preach a turne for Mr. Subdeane at any time when he shall require or appoint the same.

  Tho[mas] Prior, subd[ean]; Elias Wrenche; Johannes Woode.

64. [*fo. 45*] 26 January 1625/6.   Chapter House.
(Thomas Prior, subdean; Elias Wrench.)

Choise of a clarke for the convocation. Quibus die et loco, By vertue of a proxie from Mr. Deane dated the 7th of January 1625[/6] for the choyce of a clarke for the convocation howse for the chapter of this church, at this ensuinge parliament, the said Mr. Subdeane gave Mr. Deane's voice unto Dr. Leo, a prebende of this church, for the said place. And likewise Mr. Subdeane gave his owne voice unto him the said Dr. Leo for the said place. And Mr. Wrench then present gave his voice allsoe to the said Dr. Leo. And Mr. Subdeane by authority from Mr. Wood, one other of the prebendaries of this church, did give his the said Mr. Wood's voice to the said Dr. Leo for the said place. By reason whereof the said Dr. Leo was elected and chosen clarke of the convocation to serve for the body of the chapter of this church. And yt was then allsoe decreed that an instrument for the performance thereof should be made under the chapter seale unto him the said Dr. Leo, the tenor whereof followeth in these wordes. Vizt. Pateat universis &c. mutatis mutandis prout patet in pagina [3]2ᵃ huius libri.[4]

  Tho[mas] Prior; Elias Wrenche.

---

 [1] The form is as in **40**, above, with the addition of 'iuramento suscepto'.

 [2] Thomas Tomkins, however, continued to receive payment as a minor canon, precentor, and vicar of St. Mary de Lode until 1627, and Richard Marwood first received payment as precentor in the financial year 1627–8: cathedral accounts.

 [3] After 'he' the words 'be not present and' are crossed out.

 [4] Cf. **49**, above, which gives the correct cross-reference to fo. 32; the wording of the last part of the entry differs.

65.   26 April 1626.   Chapter House.
(Thomas Prior, subdean; Elias Wrench; John Wood.)

Order for frequentinge sermons. Wheras it was lately ordered in chapter that the members of the quire should come duly to sermons in this church, and since by the chanter's bill it there appeareth a generall neglect thereof:

It is now ordered that whosoever shall hencforth absent himselfe from such sermons without iust cause, as sicknes or performance of parochiall service in their cures or some other the like cause to be approvid of by the tresurer for the time beinge, shall forfit for every such neglect three pence to be deducted out of their wages.

    Tho[mas] Prior; Elias Wrenche.

Eodem die.

Order for the common orchard.[1] It is further ordered that whereas in the common orchard divers holes have beene made by the digginge and carryinge away earth there hence to privat uses to the deforminge of the said place and makinge it unfitt for the walkes and delight of the members of the church, that from henceforth it shall not be lawfull for any person to offend so again and the supervisor operum[2] is to take care that it be seene to accordingly.

    Tho[mas] Prior; Elias Wrenche.

66.   [*fo. 45v.*]   23 June 1626.   Chapter House.
(Thomas Prior, subdean; Elias Wrench.)

Hayes, Freame, and Collins to gett more skill in singinge. Whereas at the last auditt in chapter then held it was ordered[3] that Christopher Hayes, John Freame, and William Collins should endeavor to improve their skill in singing by this day, which thoughe they have done in some small measure, yet not soe as they might, they are nowe admonished to more endeavor in that kinde against the next auditt.

    Tho[mas] Prior, subd[ean]; Elias Wrenche treas[urer].

67.   12 October 1626.

Admissio choristae. [*Admission of a chorister. Luke Turner was admitted by the dean in the place of Richard Dobbs.*] Quibus die et anno Luke Turner admissus fuit per venerabilem decanum chorista in loco Richardi Dobbes.

Eodem die.

Graunt of a doore through the colled[g]e walle to Mr. Blackleech. Quibus die et anno, upon the shute [*sc.* suit] and request of Abraham Blackleeche, gent., yt is decreed and ordered that the said Mr. Blackleeche shall have liberty and power to make a doore and

---

[1] The great orchard was round the east end of the cathedral, beyond where the monks' graveyard had been. It was divided into separate parcels, which were let individually.

[2] The surveyor or clerk of works. William Mason was clerk of works at the time: below, p. 167.

[3] The order referred to seems not to have been recorded, but cf. the monition to Hayes, **27**, above.

passage (out of the grownd he houldeth of us the deane and chapter by lease[1] within the precincts of this church) through that parte of the colledge walle that is towardes St. John's church, the sayd doore not to exceede in bredth above fowre foote, and in height not above sixe foote, and to be made in and through such parte of the said walle within the compasse of the grownde soe demised unto him as shall seeme most expedient unto him. Provided neverthelesse and yt is fully agreed, that if at any time hereafter, after the makinge of the said passage and doore, there shall appeare any inconvenience, detriment or scandall to the said cathedrall church by meanes of the openinge of that passage, then upon such dislike by the said deane and chapter and notice thereof given to him the said Abraham Blackleeche he the said Abraham Blackleeche shall within one moonth next after such notice given well and sufficiently make and damme uppe the said doore soe made with sufficient stone woorke.

　　Tho[mas] Wynnyff, decan[us]; Tho[mas] Prior, subd[ecanus]; Elias Wrenche, treas[urer]; Will[elmus] Leo; Tho[mas] Iles; Johannes Woode.

I Abraham Blackleech doe for me and my assignes, affirme and promise to performe this act above-mentioned, for soe much as concerneth the stoppinge uppe of the doore, upon any inconvenience founde and warninge given as above is exspressed. Under the paine of tenne powndes.[2]

　　I, Abraham Blackleeche.

68.　　[*fo. 46*]　　24 October 1626.

Order touchinge the confirmation of the Register's patent. Quibus die et anno, whereas there hath bin tendered to us the deane and chapter of this church, by the right reverend father in God, Godfry, lord bishoppe of Glowcester, a patent of the register's office of the diocesse of Glowcester made by the said reverend father with desire from his lordshipp that the same might be by us the deane and chapter confirmed, and whereas upon communication and speech had with Mr. John Jones, the present register, the said Mr. Jones affirmeth and pretendeth to have divers confirmations of that office formerly passed to himselfe and his children by the deane and chapter of this church, by reason whereof we have thought fitt for this present to forbeare the confirmation of the said patent, neverthelesse desiringe to give all furtherance to his lordshipp's request herein, and all reall exspressions of our affections and respects to his lordshipp, we (upon any avoydance of the said patents or remooveall of the said Mr. Jones from the said office) doe agree, and by these presents conclude, that any patent of the said office graunted by the said reverend father, and tendered unto us, be fully and firmely confirmed, and that without any further meetinge, and the passinge of voices and suffrages of the deane and prebendaries, yt shall be lawfull for such as shall be then present to putt thereunto the chapter seale, and we shall

---

[1] Since 1623 Abraham Blackleech had had a lease of the house in the precinct later known as King's School House, as his father William (chancellor to the bishop of Gloucester) had done before him. After his death in 1639 his widow Gertrude stayed on in the house until the Commonwealth period. The annual rent of the house was 5s. A fine monument to Abraham and Gertrude (in the style of Nicholas Stone) is in the south transept of the cathedral: cf. *Parsons*, 420.

[2] The last six words have been squashed in above Blackleech's signature. The whole paragraph has been inserted by Blackleech at the bottom of the entry on the left-hand side.

take yt and acknowledge yt as our owne publicke act which we will be allwayes reddy to ratify and warrant. And in wittnesse whereof we have subscribed our names.

Tho[mas] Wynnyff, decan[us]; Tho[mas] Prior, subd[ecanus]; Elias Wrenche; William Leo; Tho[mas] Iles; Johannes Wood.

The patent in this act mentioned was the 25th of October 1626 by consent of Mr. Jones himselfe confirmed.

Eodem die et anno.

Order for a stable for Dr. Iles. Upon information of Dr. Iles, doctor in divinity, and one of the prebends of this church, that there hath not bin for many yeares any stable belonginge unto his prebendall house,[1] as all other the prebendaries have, and that the same hath bin negligently lost, and can by noe meanes be made appeare where the sayd stable was allbeyt yt is conceaved that at the foundation there was a stable allotted to the sayd prebendall house as well as to the rest of the prebendall houses, yt is therefore ordered that the sayd Dr. Iles shall have allotted unto him, and sett foorth soe much grownde as shall be convenient for the makinge of a stable, for the use of himselfe & his successors in the said prebendall howse, and the said grownd perpetually to be annexed to the sayd prebendall house. And yt is further ordered that the same grownde shall be allotted, set foorth and taken in, at the feirst coyne next unto the way that leadeth unto the common miskin[2] within this [*fo. 46v.*] cathedrall church, and soe to the next coyne of the said walle that encloseth the sayd miskin, to builde thereupon and in such place, and for the use of a stable only, as to the sayd Dr. Iles shall seeme most expedient.

Tho[mas] Wynnyff, decan[us]; Tho[mas] Prior, subd[ecanus]; Elias Wrenche; William Leo; Johannes Wood.

69.   Thursday the feast of St. Andrew the Apostle, 30 November 1626.

Chapter House.

(Thomas Prior, subdean; Elias Wrench.)

Electio officiariorum. [*Election of officers. In the absence of the dean but with his consent, the subdean and the aforenamed prebendary elected Elias Wrench as subdean and Thomas Prior as receiver and treasurer. As in* **6** *and* **40**, *above.*]

Tho[mas] Prior, subd[ean]; Elias Wrenche, treas[urer].

Electio precentoris. [*Election of the precentor. The aforesaid men elected Richard Marwood. As in* **63**, *above.*] Eodem die, loco et anno [*etc.*].

Tho[mas] Prior, subd[ean]; Elias Wrenche, treas[urer].

70.   3 November 1626.[3]

A confirmation of the Register's patent. Quibus die et anno, the right reverend father in God, Godfrey, lord bishop of Gloucester, sent by his servant a patent of the principall

---

[1] From 1622 Iles had lived at the house that was later no. 14 College Green.

[2] The cathedral rubbish-dump or dung-heap, located where no. 9 College Green was later built.

[3] The entry appears to have been entered in the book after the election of officers on 30 Nov.; the subdean and treasurer named are the men who held those offices before that election.

register's office of the diocese of Gloucester made by the said reverend father unto Gabriel Goodman of Ruthin, in the county of Denbighe, gent.,[1] desiringe that it might be confirmed, by and with our consents and under the seale of our church. At which time wee, hearinge that there was another patent (then in beinge) confirmed by our church unto John Jones, alderman of Gloucester,[2] who was then in the execucion of the said office, wee did desire to be excused, as havinge already confirmed one patent, and thereby concluded our selves, by our owne acte. The day followinge the said Mr. Jones came in his owne person, into the chapter howse, wee the deane and prebendaries being then mett, and signified his consent and requested that the said patent made to Gabriel Goodman might be confirmed under our chapter seale, which past by voices and was confirmed accordingly in his presence. And the same daie the said right reverend father gave unto the church a faire gilte [*fo. 47*] communion pott for the use of himself and his successors, for the use of the deane and prebendaries[3] and all others receavinge the communion there, and to remaine and be kept in the said cathedrall church perpetually from time to time and to be imployed for the time of the receavinge of the holy communion and to that and noe other use, and in the said cathedrall church only.

Tho[mas] Prior, subd[ean]; Elias Wrenche, treas[urer].

Tho[mas] Wynnyff, decan[us]; John Wood; William Leo.[4]

71.   11 January 1626/7.   Chapter House.
(Elias Wrench, subdean; Thomas Prior.)

A confirmation of 2 patents of offices belonginge to the Bishopricke. Quibus die et loco, by vertue of a proxie from Mr. Deane dated the 14th of December 1626 directed to the above named Mr. Prior and Mr. Wrench for the confirmacion of a patente of the severall offices of the collection and receavinge of the procurations, synodalls and pentecosts in the dioces of Gloucester, and of the collection and receavinge of divers pensions and portions in the countyes of Gloucester and Hereford, and allsoe the office of keepinge the pallace in Gloucester, and of the woodwardshippe of the wood called Woollridge Woods,[5] and allsoe for the confirmacion of one other patent of the severall offices of the receavorshippe of all the rents and proffitts of and in the manners of Maisemore, Droysecourt and Longford in the county of the citty of Gloucester and of the manners of Rudge and Farly[6] in the county of Gloucester, which severall patents are lately graunted by the right reverend father in God, Godfry, lord bishoppe of Gloucester, to Anthony Robinson[7] and Simon Thelwall, gent., which patents beare date the twelfe day of December 1626, the said Mr. Subdeane

---

[1] Gabriel Goodman was the bishop's cousin and brother-in-law.

[2] Cf. **68**, above.

[3] After 'prebendaries' the MS. has 'and for the use of the maior and citizens for the time beinge', crossed out.

[4] The signatures of Prior and Wrench, being those present at the meeting, are in the usual place at the end of the entry on the right-hand side of the page; the signatures of the other three, who were not present, are on the left hand side, apparently added later.

[5] Woolridge Wood, *c.* 50 acres, and a wood of 16 acres called the Perch, in the large parish of St. Mary de Lode, were part of Henry VIII's endowment of the bishopric and of the dean and chapter.

[6] The manors, which had belonged to the abbey, were also part of Henry VIII's endowment.

[7] Presumably the same man as the registrar to the dean and chapter.

gave Mr. Deane's voice for confirmacion of the said severall patents. And likewise Mr. Subdeane gave his owne voice allsoe for the confirmation of the said severall patents. And the said Mr. Prior then present by like proxie bearinge date as aforesaid from Dr. Leo, one of the prebendaries of the said cathedrall church, did give the said Dr. Leo his voice to the confirmation of the said severall patents, and allsoe gave his owne voice to the said confirmations. And by like proxie from Mr. Wood, one other of the prebendaries of the said church, Mr. Prior gave his the said Mr. Wood's voice to the said severall confirmations, thereupon the said severall patents were confirmed[1] and sealed with the seale of the said deane and chapter accordingly.

    Elias Wrenche, subd[ean]; Tho[mas] Prior.

72.   28 March 1627.   Chapter House.
(Elias Wrenche, subdean; Thomas Prior, treasurer.)

[A] **presentacion to St. Marye's.**[2] Whereas the donacion of the vicaridge of St. Mary the Virgin before the gate of the said cathedrall churche is fallen into the hands of the deane and chapter of this churche by [*fo. 47v.*] the death of the last incumbent, Thomas Tomkins deceased, the above named Mr. Wrenche and Mr. Prior, assembled and mett together in the chapter howse the day above mencioned for the passing of a presentacion to the viccaridge aforesaid, havinge received a proxie from the right worshipfull Dr. Wynnyff, deane of this churche, to that purpose bearinge date the 22th day of Marche 1626, in these words followinge, vizt. 'I Thomas Wynnyff, doctor in divinitie and deane of the cathedrall churche of Gloucester, doe hereby authorize and appoynt Mr. Elias Wrenche, subdeane of the cathedrall churche of Gloucester, to give my voice and full consent in the chapter howse of the aforesaid cathedrall churche to and for the passing of a presentacion of the viccarige of St. Maries, within the citty of Gloucester, unto Peter Brooke, clarcke, one of the singinge men of the said cathedrall churche, and thereuppon to seale with the chapter seale of the said churche the said presentation accordinglie, and to doe and performe all other things necessary concerninge the same in as ample manner and forme as if I my selfe were personallie present, rattifyinge hereby whatsoever the said Mr. Elias Wrenche shall for me and in my name lawfullie doe in the premisses as myne owne acte and deede, for evermore. In witnes whereof I have hereunto put my hande and seale the 22th day of Marche anno domini 1626.' The like proxie under the hande and seale of Mr. John Wood, one of the prebendaries of the said church, the said Mr. Prior exhibited, bearinge date as above said. Accordinge to which said severall proxies the said Mr. Wrenche and Mr. Prior gave the voyces of the said Mr. Deane and Mr. Wood accordinge as they were authorized in the proxies aforesaid, together with their owne voices allsoe, for a presentacion to be passed to Peter Brooke, clarcke, of the viccarige of St. Maries above said, who had a presentacion under seale graunted accordingly.

    Elias Wrenche, subd[ean]; Tho[mas] Prior.

---

[1] The words 'thereupon the said severall patents were confirmed' are added above the line.
[2] The rectory of the large parish of St. Mary de Lode, which before the Reformation had provided income for the abbey's lady chapel and had been granted by Henry VIII to the dean and chapter, included the right of presentation to the vicarage.

73.   [*fo. 48*]   23 April 1627.

Resignation of a lay singingman. Quibus die et anno John Freame, one of the lay singingmen of this church, did by wrytinge subscribed with his owne hande freely and voluntarily resigne and surrender upp into the hands of Mr. Elias Wrench, subdeane of this cathedrall church, all the right, title, and interest which he now hath, or ought to have, in and to a lay singingman's place within this church.

Elias Wrenche, subd[ean].

74.   10 October 1627.   Deanery.[1]

Admissio canonicorum minorum. [*Admission of minor canons. William Hulett and Edward Williams were admitted and assigned places by the dean, and they took the oaths on the gospels touched by them. The form differs in detail from that in* **6**, *above.*] Quibus die et anno Gulielmus Hulett et Edwardus Williams, clerici, admissi et assignati erant per venerabilem decanum in locos duorum minorum canonicorum, infra ecclesiam cathedralem Gloucestriae qui quidem Gulielmus et Edwardus subierunt iuramenta respective ad sacrosancta dei evangelia per eos tacta &c.

Tho[mas] Wynnyff, decan[us].

Eodem die.

Admissio laici cantatoris. [*Admission of a lay singer. Henry Purlewent*[2] *was admitted by the dean in the place of John Freame. As in* **12**, *above.*]

Tho[mas] Wynnyff, decan[us].

Eodem die.

Admissio choristae. [*Admission of a chorister. William Hosier was admitted by the dean in the place of Constantine Smith.*] Quibus die, loco et anno Gulielmus Hosier admissus fuit per venerabilem decanum chorista in loco Constantini Smith.

Tho[mas] Wynnyff, decan[us].

75.   [*fo. 48v.*] ***A dispensation of residence to Dr. Anyan.*** Charles Rex. Trusty and welbeloved we greet yow well. Whereas your founder of famous memory, Kinge Henry the Eyght, hath by your locall statuts reserved to himselfe and his successors a power to dispense with any of your statuts made or to be made, and because Doctor Anyan one of the prebendaries of your church could not the two last yeares past, vizt. 1625 & 1626, for cawses to us knowne and approved of, reside with yow as your statuts doe require, these therefore are to give yow notice that, out of our especiall favoure and regall power, we have and doe dispense with the said Doctor Anyan for his not residinge with yow those two yeares last past, (vizt.) 1625 and 1626, requiringe yow to make him partaker of all emoluments as if he had beene continuually resident amonge yow. Given under our signet at our honor of Hampton Court the eyght and twentieth day of September in the third yeare of our raigne.

To our trusty and welbeloved the deane and chapter

of our cathedrall church of Gloucester now beinge and theire successors.

Examinatur per Anthonium Robinson, registrarium.

---

[1] MS. 'In aedibus decani infra precinctum ecclesiae cathedralis Gloucestriae.'

[2] Purlewent had been a chorister from 1617 to 1625: above, **5**, **62**.

76.   Saturday 20 October 1627.   Deanery.

Admissio eleemozynarii. [*Admission of an almsman. David Parry, of the city of Worcester, affirmed before the dean, Mr. Elias Wrench, Thomas Prior and John Wood, prebendaries, that John Ward was dead and that he, the said Parry, should be admitted in Ward's place as an almsman by virtue of letters patent of the late King James granted to him and addressed to the dean and chapter, whereupon the subdean admitted him, to receive the emoluments belonging to the office from Michaelmas last past, with the proviso that if John Ward was then alive this admission would be void.*] David Parry, civitatis Wigorniae, dixit et affirmavit coram venerabilibus viris Thoma Wynnyff, sacrae theologiae professore, ecclesiae cathedralis Gloucestriae decano, Magistris Elia Wrench, Thoma Prior et Johanne Wood, dictae ecclesiae prebendariis, quemdam Johannem Warde mortuum esse eumque prefatum Davidem Parry admittendum esse in loco eiusdem Johannis Ward, ultimi eleemozynarii eiusdem ecclesiae cathedralis, virtute literarum patentium serenissimi domini Jacobi nuper regis sibi in ea parte concessarum, decano et capitulo dictae ecclesiae directarum, unde dictus venerabilis decanus dictum Davidem Parry in eleemozynarium admisit, habere et percipere omnia emolumenta et proficua ad officium eleemozynarii spectantia a festo sancti Michaelis Arch-angeli ultimo preterito. Proviso tamen quod si prefatus Johannes Ward tunc temporis esset vivus quod haec prefata admissio vacua erit et nullius vigoris.

Tho[mas] Wynnyff, dean.

77.   [*fo. 49*]   24 October 1627.   Chapter House.
(Thomas Wynniffe, S.T.P., dean; Elias Wrench, subdean; Thomas Prior; John Wood.)

An alowance to Mr. Robinson of 26s. 8d. yearely. Quibus die et loco Mr. Deane, Mr. Subdeane and the prebendaries above named, takinge into consideracion that the faithfull and diligente execution of the register's or chapter clarke's office of this church is of greate and speciall use and benefitt to the estate of this church; which sayd place or office beinge graunted by patent to Anthony Robinson, gent., hath bin by him for this fowerteene yeares past or thereabouts supplyed and executed to the good lykeinge and contente of us and our predecessors, and whereas we finde that there is noe yearely or annuall fee or annuitie from us reserved by the said patente for the execution of the sayd office other then such fees, profitts and commodities as occasionally doth acrue and become due unto him from others for the speedinge and dispatch of theire graunts, and other theire occasions that have relation unto us, we therfore, noe waye doubtinge of the future good service towards our church to be performed by the sayd Anthony Robinson, doe order and decree that the thesaurer or receiver of this church for the time beinge shall yearely at the feast of Ste. Michaell the Archangell deliver and paye to the sayd Anthony Robinson the somme of twenty six shillings and eyght pence. And we doe further order and decree that this our present acte and decree nowe made for the performance hereof shall remaine and stande in force untill by like acte or decree under our hands we shall thinke fitt to revoke or disanull the same.

78.   31 October 1627.   Chapter House.
(Elias Wrench, subdean; Thomas Prior.)

An act for confirmation of a Chancellor's patent. Quibus die et loco, whereas the right worshipfull Thomas Wynniffe, doctor in divinity and deane of this church, did on the twenty fowerth day of this instante moneth of October give his full voice and consente in open chapter for the confirmation of letters patents or commission of the office and place of a chauncelor of the citty and dioces of Gloucester graunted by the right reverend father in God, Godfrey, lord bushopp of Gloucester, to Mr. William Sutton, clerke, master of artes, and to Mr. Frauncis Baber,[1] master of artes and bachelor of lawe, and the above named Mr. Elias Wrench, subdeane of the sayd cathedrall church, and the above named Mr. Thomas Prior and Mr. John Wood, prebendaries of the sayd cathedrall church, did alsoe, the time and place [*fo. 49v.*] aforesayd, give theire full and free consents for passinge of the sayde confirmation of the sayd letters patents of the sayd office of chauncellor to the sayd Mr. William Sutton and Mr. Frauncis Baber, and alsoe, for the more full expression of the consents of the sayd Mr. Deane and Mr. Wood to the confirmation of the sayd patent soe graunted as aforesayd, they the sayd Mr. Deane and Mr. Wood left theire severall proxies under their hands and seales, which proxie under the hand and seale of the right worshipfull Dr. Wynniffe, deane of this church, was this day exhibited and shewed forth by Mr. Wrench, subdeane of this church, in open chapter, the contents wherof ensue in these words, (vizt.) 'Know all men by these presents that I Thomas Wynniffe, doctor of divinity and deane of the cathedrall church of Gloucester, doe hereby nominate, constitute, authorize and appointe my welbeloved in Christ Mr. Elias Wrench and Mr. Thomas Prior, prebendaries of the sayd cathedrall church of Gloucester, ioyntly and severally for me and in my name to appeare in the chapter howse of the foresayd cathedrall church and for me and in my name to give my voice and full consent to and for the confirmation of letters patents or commission of the office dignitie and place of chauncelor or vicar generall of, in and through the citty and diocese of Gloucester graunted by the right reverend father in God, Godfrey, lord bushopp of Gloucester, to Mr. William Sutton, clerke, master of arts, and to Mr. Frauncis Baber, bachelor of lawe, and thereuppon in the sayd chapter howse to seale with the chapter seale the sayd confirmation annexed to the sayd letters patents or commission, and to doe and performe all other thinges necessary concerninge the same in as ample manner and forme as if I my selfe were personally present, ratifyinge hereby whatsoever the sayd Mr. Elias Wrench and Mr. Thomas Prior ioyntly and severally shall for me and in my name lawfully doe in the premisses as myne owne acte and deede for evermore. In wittnes wherof I have hereunto putt my hand and seale the fower and twentieth day of October anno regni domini nostri Caroli, dei gracia Anglie, Scotie, Frauncie et Hibernie regis, fidei defensor &c., tertio annoque domini 1627, and in further confirmation hereof I have caused the seale of the officialtie of the archdeacon of Gloucester to be alsoe hereunto affixed the day and yeare above sayd.' After which proxie soe made and published as aforesayd the sayd Mr. Wrench, subdeane, imediately there[2] gave Mr. Deane's voice for the confirmation of the patent in the sayd proxie mentioned to them the sayd Mr. William Sutton and Mr. Francis Baber. And then and there alsoe the aforesayd Mr. Wrench, subdeane, and Mr. Prior, prebendary [*fo. 50*] and nowe thresurer of the sayd cathedrall church, did likewise give theire voices and full consents and assents to the confirmation

---

[1] For Baber, below, p. 161.
[2] The word 'there' has been inserted above the line.

of the sayd patent. And last of all the sayd Mr. Prior exhibited a proxie under the hand and seale of the worshipfull John Wood, one other of the prebendaries of this cathedrall church, in substance and effecte agreable with Mr. Deane's proxie, bearinge the same date, by vertue whereof the sayd Mr. Prior gave likewise Mr. Wood his voice and full consent to the confirmation of the sayd patent. And the same day the sayd patent was confirmed under their chapter seale accordingly.

79.   Friday the feast of St. Andrew the Apostle, 30 November 1627.

Chapter House.

(Elias Wrench, subdean; Thomas Prior.)[1]

Electio officiariorum. [*Election of officers. In the absence of the dean but with his consent, the subdean and the aforementioned prebendary elected Elias Wrench as subdean and Thomas Prior as receiver and treasurer. As in* **6** *and* **40**, *above.*]

Electio precentoris. [*Election of the precentor. The aforesaid men elected Richard Marwood. As in* **63**, *above.*] Eodem die, loco et anno [*etc.*].

80. [*fo. 50v.*]   8 March 1627/8.   Chapter House.
(Elias Wrench, subdean; Thomas Prior, treasurer.)

Election of a clerke for the convocation. Quibus die et loco, by vertue of a proxie from Mr. Deane dated the fifteenth day of February 1627[/8] for the choice of a clarke for the convocation howse for the chapter of this church at this ensuinge parliament, the sayd Mr. Subdeane gave Mr. Deane's voice unto Dr. Anyan, a prebend of this church, for the sayd place. And likewise Mr. Subdeane gave his owne voice unto him the sayd Dr. Anyan for the sayd place. And Mr. Prior then present gave his voice alsoe to the sayd Dr. Anyan. And the sayd Mr. Prior by severall proxies from Dr. Iles and Mr. John Wood, booth prebendaries of this church, gave theire severall voices to the sayd Dr. Anyan for the sayd place. By reason whereof the sayd Dr. Anyan was elected and chosen clarke of the convocation to serve for the body of the chapter of this church. And it was then alsoe decreed that an instrument for the performance thereof should be made under the chapter seale unto him the sayd Dr. Anyan, the tenor wherof followeth in these words, (vizt.) Pateat [*etc., as in* **64**, *above, with the correct cross-reference to fo. 32*].

81.   Thursday 17 April 1628.   Chapter House.
(Elias Wrench, subdean.)

Admissio eleemozynarii. [*Admission of an almsman. David Parry*[2] *appeared and sought to be admitted as an almsman in the place of James Webbe, deceased, by virtue of letters patent granted to him, addressed to the dean and chapter and registered at their registry,*

---

[1] Both men failed to subscribe their signatures at the end of the entry.

[2] Parry had been admitted as an almsman six months earlier: above, **76**. Presumably John Ward, whose death Parry had affirmed and whose place he had claimed, was in fact still alive.

whereupon the subdean admitted him, he having first taken the almsman's oath, to have all the emoluments belonging to the place.] Comparuit quidam David Parry et petiit admitti in locum eleemozynarii dictae ecclesiae in loco cuiusdam Jacobi Webbe, nuper defuncti, virtute literarum patentium sibi in ea parte concessarum, decano et capitulo dictae ecclesiae directarum et apud registrarium eorundem decani et capituli registratarum. Unde dictus venerabilis subdecanus prestito primitus per eundem David Parry iuramento ab eleemozynario prestando in eleemozynarium admisit, habere et percipere omnia proficua et emolumenta ad locum eleemozynarii spectantia.

Admissio eleemozynarii. [*Admission of an almsman. Francis Derricott, of the city of Worcester, affirmed before the subdean that John Ward was dead and that he, the said Derricott, should be admitted in Ward's place by virtue of letters patent granted to him by the late King James and addressed to the dean and chapter, whereupon the subdean admitted him, to receive all the emoluments belonging to the place from the Annunciation last past, with the proviso that if John Ward was then alive the admission would be void.*] Quibus die, loco et anno Franciscus Derricott, civitatis Wigorniae, dixit et affirmavit coram venerabili viro Magistro Elia Wrench, subdecano, quendam Johannem Warde mortuum esse eumque prefatum Franciscum Derricott admittendum esse in loco eiusdem Johannis Warde eleemozynarii eiusdem ecclesiae cathedralis, virtute literarum patentium serenissimi Domini Jacobi nuper regis sibi in ea parte concessarum, decano et capitulo dictae ecclesiae directarum, unde dictus [*fo.* 51] venerabilis subdecanus dictum Franciscum Derricott in eleemozynarium admisit, habere et percipere omnia emolumenta et proficua ad locum eleemozynarii spectantia a festo annuntiationis Beatae Mariae Virginis ultimo preterito. Proviso tamen quod si prefatus Johannes Warde tunc temporis esset vivus, quod haec prefata admissio vacua erit et nullius vigoris.

82.   23 June 1628.   Chapter House.
(Elias Wrench, subdean; Thomas Prior.)

Admissio hypodidascali. [*Admission of the assistant schoolmaster. Giles Workman,*[1] *B.A., who had been chosen by the dean, was admitted by the subdean, after he had taken the oath on the gospels, touched by him.*] Quibus die, loco et anno Egidius Workeman, in artibus baccalaureus,[2] [*etc., as in* **50**, *above*].

83.   11 August 1628.   Chapter House.
(Elias Wrench, subdean; Thomas Prior, treasurer.)

Readmissio ludimagistri. [*Readmission of the schoolmaster.*] Whereas Mr. John Langly, master in arts, did on the twenty fowerth day of December last past, by resignacion in writinge,[3] surrender and resigne upp into the hands of Mr. Wrench, then and yett

---

[1] For Workman, below, p. 171.

[2] The words 'in artibus baccalaureus' have been inserted above the line, apparently as an afterthought.

[3] The contents of this letter were apparently not entered in the Act Book.

subdeane of this church, his place of high scholemaster within this church, which he had dyvers yeares before that inioyed with good approbation of the deane and chapter of this church, and sithence that, the sayd Mr. Langley by perswasion and request of dyvers his freinds, is willinge to accepte of the same place againe, and to that purpose Mr. Doctor Wynniffe, deane of this church, hath exprest his desire to Mr. Subdeane that Mr. Langley should be readmitted into the same place againe, therefore accordinge to Mr. Deane's desire, Mr. Subdeane againe admitted the sayd Mr. Langly into the place of high or cheefe scholemaster within this cathedrall church, to have and to hould the sayd place with all profitts and commodities thereto belonginge, in as ample and large manner as he the sayd John Langley or any other heretofore held and enioyed the same.

[*fo. 51v.*]   Eodem die.

Ordo pro magistro choristarum. [*Order for the master of the choristers.*] Alsoe it was this day decreed and ordered that Mr. Hosier, the master of the choristers, shall from henceforth, one day in every weeke, catechise and teach the choristers in the principles of Christian religion. And the sayd Mr. Hosier was in open chapter required to see it performed.

84.   4 November 1628.   Chapter House.

(Elias Wrench, subdean; Dr. Leo; Thomas Prior, treasurer; Dr. Iles.)

Ordo. [*Order.*] It is this daye by Mr. Subdeane ordered that Mr. Chaunter shall carefully observe and dilligently take notice of all abuses and misdemeanors as shall be by any of the quire committed in the time of devine prayers, eyther in talkinge, rainglinge or quarrellinge, and thereof shall certifie the tresurer of the sayd church once every quarter, uppon which certificate the partye offendinge shall loose three pence for every such faulte, to be deducted oute of his wages by the tresurer for the time beinge. The sayd forfetures to be bestowed at the end of the yeare by Mr. Deane and the chapter uppon such of the quire as shall be found most deservinge in theire diligence and good demeanore.[1]

85.   Sunday the feast of St. Andrew the Apostle, 30 November 1628.

Chapter House.

(Elias Wrench, subdean; Thomas Prior.)

Electio officiariorum. [*Election of officers. In the absence of the dean but with his consent, the subdean and the aforenamed prebendary elected Thomas Prior as subdean and Elias Wrench as receiver and treasurer. As in* **6** *and* **40**, *above.*]

Electio precentoris. [*Election of the precentor. The aforesaid men elected Richard Marwood. As in* **63**, *above.*] Eodem die, loco et anno [*etc.*].

86.   [*fo. 52*]   17 June 1629.

Resignacio laici cantatoris. [*Resignation of a lay singer.*] Quibus die et anno John Beames, one of the lay singingemen of this church, did by writinge subscribed with his

---

[1] Cf. above, p. 19 n. 2.

owne hand freely and voluntaryly resigne and surrender upp into the hands of Mr. Thomas Pryor, subdeane of this cathedrall church, all the right, title and interest which he nowe hath or ought to have in and to a lay singingman's place within this church.

 Tho[mas] Prior, subd[ean].

87.   23 June 1629.   Chapter House.
(Thomas Prior, subdean; Elias Wrench, treasurer.)

Ordo pro Simeone Wrench.[1] [*An order for Simeon Wrench.*] Quibus die et anno Simeon Wrench, one of the sonns of Mr. Elias Wrenche, tresurer of this church, tendered in chapter a patent of one of the porters' offices made to him and to William Wrench his brother, and desired to dispose of the sayd office accordinge to his patent, whereuppon Mr. Subdeane thought meete, and accordingly ordered, that in regard the place hath long beene officiated by William Mason, a deputy appointed by Mr. Deane and approved of by the chapter, that it shall soe remayne by the sayd Mason to be executed untill the comminge of Mr. Deane and the meetinge of the chapter at the next audit.

     Eodem die.
Ordo pro Barkely Wrench. [*An order for Barkeley Wrench.*] Quibus die et anno likewise Barkely Wrench, one other of the sonns of Mr. Elias Wrench, tresurer of this church, tendered in chapter a patent of one of the sextons' offices made to him, and desired to dispose of the sayd office accordinge to his patent, wheruppon Mr. Subdeane thought meete, and accordingly ordered, that in regard the place hath longe beene officiated by William Mason, a deputy appoynted by Mr. Deane and approved of by the chapter, that it shall soe remayne by the sayd Mason to be executed untill the comminge of Mr. Deane and the meetinge of the chapter at the next audit.

     Eodem die.
Resignacio choristae. [*Resignation of a chorister.*] Eodem die anno et loco Barkely Wrench, one of the choristers of this church, freely and voluntarily surrendred his place of a chorister into the hands of Mr. Thomas Prior, subdeane of this cathedrall church.

     Eodem die.
Admissio choristarum. [*Admission of choristers. Richard White and William Dobbs were admitted by Mr. Thomas Prior, subdean, in the places of Thomas Lewes and Barkeley Wrench.*] Quibus die, loco et anno Richardus White et Gulielmus Dobbes admissi erant per Magistrum Thomam Prior, subdecanum, in loca duorum choristarum infra hanc ecclesiam cathedralem Gloucestriae, in locis Thomae Lewes et Barkeleii Wrench.

88. [*fo. 52v.*] 9 July 1629.   Chapter House.
(Thomas Prior, subdean; Elias Wrench; John Wood.)

An act for confirmation of Portham. Quibus die et loco, by vertue of a proxie from the right worshipfull Thomas Wynniffe, doctor in divinitie and deane of this church, dated

---

[1] For Simeon Wrench and his brothers Barkeley and William, below, pp. 171–2.

the second daye of July 1629 and in the fifth yeare of the raigne of our graceous soveraigne lord, Charles, by the grace of God kinge of England, Scotland, Fraunce and Ireland, defender of the fayth &c., directed to the above named Mr. Prior, subddeane of this cathedrall church, for the confirmacion of two severall leases of the one moyety or one halfe of a meadowe called Portham, otherwise called Importham, scituate, lyinge and beinge neare the citty of Gloucester in the county of the sayd citty of Gloucester and in the lordshipp of Maysemore there, for the tearme of three lives in each of the sayd severall leases, which severall leases are lately graunted by the right reverend father in God, Godfrey, lord bushopp of Gloucester, to Richard Hackett of the citty of London, dyer, and eache of the sayd leases beareth date the eight daye of July in the fifth yeare of the raigne of our soveraigne lord, King Charles that now is, and in the yeare of our Lord God 1629, the sayd Mr. Prior, subdeane, gave Mr. Deane's voice and consente for confirmacion of the sayd severall leases, and his owne voice and consent alsoe, for confirmacion of the sayd severall leases. And the sayd Mr. Wrench and Mr. Wood, prebendaries and then there both alsoe present, gave theire severall voyces and consents for the confirmacion of the sayd two severall leases, and all of them then alsoe decreed that the sayd two severall leases should be confirmed and the sayd confirmacions should be sealed with the seale of the deane and chapter of this church, which was done and performed accordingly.

89. *[fo. 53]*   6 November 1629.
An act for the Register's patent. Quibus die et anno, Upon request made by the right reverend father in God, Godfry, lord bishoppe of Gloucester, by his letter to Mr. Deane, dated the 4th of November last past, for the new confirmation of a patent of the principall register's office of the dioces of Gloucester, hertofore graunted and confirmed to Gabriell Goodman of Ruthen in the county of Denbigh, gent., yt was by Mr. Deane mooved to the prebendaries present that the said patent might be againe confirmed. And accordingly Mr. Deane gave his voice and consent for the confirmation of the sayd patent, and Mr. Prior, then subdeane, Mr. Wrench, Dr. Leo and Mr. Wood, all prebendaries of the said cathedrall church and then allsoe present, gave theyr voices and consents to the confirmation of the said patent to Mr. Gabriell Goodman of the sayd register's office.

> Tho[mas] Wynnyff, decan[us]; Tho[mas] Prior, subd[ecanus]; Elias Wrenche, thesaur[arius]; William Leo; John Wood.

> Eodem die.

Admissio choristae. [*Admission of a chorister. Richard Longe was admitted by the dean in the place of Richard Price.*] Quibus die et anno Richardus Longe admissus fuit per venerabilem decanum chorista in loco Richardi Price.

90.   9 November 1629.

Act on a concurrent lease. Whereas at the request of the right reverend father in God, Godfry, lord bishoppe of Gloucester, there was a confirmation this day passed upon a concurrent lease of the Bondhoult[1] tythes in Upton St. Leonards and Renwick tythes graunted to Mr. Gabriell Goodman, and now in the possession of Mr. Thomas Feilde[2] & Mr. James Clent,[3] yett that yt may appeare to succession how carefull the deane & chapter were on the tenants' behalfe, before the sayd confirmation passed they by this theyr act doe testify that they sent a speciall messenger and gave notice to the said Mr. Feilde & Mr. Clent that they should repaire to the sayd lord bishoppe and make theyr composition, or els to comme and shew theyr reasons to the said deane & chapter why the said lease should not be confirmed, which they refusinge to doe, havinge two dayes warninge thereof, the sayd lease was accordinge to the sayd request confirmed.

91.   [*fo. 53v.*]   Thursday the feast of St. Andrew the Apostle, 30 November 1629.

Chapter House.

(Thomas Prior, subdean; Elias Wrench.)

Electio officiariorum. [*Election of officers. In the absence of the dean but with his consent, the subdean and the aforenamed prebendary elected and continued Thomas Prior as subdean and Elias Wrench as receiver and treasurer. As in* **6** *and* **40**, *above, replacing* eligerunt *with* elegerunt et continuaverunt.]

Electio precentoris. [*Election of the precentor. The aforesaid men elected Richard Marwood. As in* **63**, *above.*] Eodem die, loco et anno [*etc.*].

92.   15 December 1629.   The Vestry.[4]

(Thomas Prior, subdean; Elias Wrench, treasurer.)

Electio laici cantatoris. [*Election, more correctly admission, of a lay singer. Richard White was admitted by Mr. Prior, subdean, in the place of John Beames, for which he took the oaths. The form differs in detail from that in* **12** *and* **22**, *above.*] Quibus die et anno Richardus White admissus fuit per Magistrum Prior, subdecanum, in locum unius laicorum cantatorum infra ecclesiam cathedralem Gloucestriae in loco Johannis Beames qui quidem Richardus subiit iuramenta respective ad sacrosancta dei evangelia per eum tacta &c.

93.   [*fo. 54*]   7 April 1630.   Chapter House.

(Thomas Prior, subdean; Elias Wrench, treasurer.)

An act for a seate in the church. Quibus die et loco it was ordered and enacted by the sayd Mr. Subdeane and Mr. Treasurer that, amonge others of the colledge and citty, it shall be lawfull from henceforth for the ministers of the sayd citty, as alsoe for Stephen

---

[1] Bondholt was presumably an area in Upton St. Leonards of woodland or former woodland.

[2] Thomas Field may be the Gloucester brewer of that name who held the office of 'aquaeductor' or water-supplier to the dean and chapter from 1603 or earlier until 1639.

[3] James Clent, a gentleman of Gloucester and notary public, died aged 70 on 5 Sept. 1645 and was buried in the lady chapel of the cathedral, where other members of his family were also buried.

[4] MS. 'In loco vocato vestria infra precinctum.'

Holford, gent.,[1] Lawrence Singleton[2] the elder, wollen draper, Nathaniell Bishopp the yonger, wollendraper, Anthony Hathway, ironmonger, and William Edwards thelder to be admitted as others already allowed are, and to sitt in the pue before the deane and chapter's seate in this colledge at sermons here; and alsoe that it shall be lawfull for the dorekeepers of the sayd seate, if there be any rome lefte there at the psalme before the sermons, to admitt as many others as may conveniently fill up the rome, which shall be named to them by the deane or in his absence by the subdeane and prebendaryes present.

Order for the quire at prayers. Eodem die the pety cannons and singinge men[3] were admonished that none of them should not talke or reade any other bookes beinge not pertinente to the service of God, nor goe out of the quire in tyme of divine service unles it be uppon urgent necessity.

94.   23 June 1630.   Chapter House.
(Thomas Prior, subdean; Elias Wrench, treasurer.)

Order for the quire. Quibus die et loco yt was ordered and decreed that the pettycannons and laye singingmen of this church should comme into the quire of this church every Sunday and holyday, in the time of devine service, before the creed be read, on payne of every of them makinge default to loose and forfeitt for every time a penny.

95. [*fo. 54v.*]   Wednesday 6 October 1630.   Deanery.
(Thomas Prior, subdean.)

Amotio eleemozynarii. [*Removal of an almsman. John Grove appeared and sought the removal of David Parry from his place of almsman because Grove's letters patent predated those of David Parry, an allegation which the subdean accepted, whereupon the subdean readmitted John Grove as an almsman, to receive the emoluments belonging to the place from Michaelmas 1629.*] Comparuit quidam Johannes Grove et petiit amotionem cuiusdam Davidis Parry a loco eleemozynarii dictae ecclesiae, quippe quod literae patentes dicti Johannis Grove antedatae fuerunt priusquam literae patentes dicti Davidis Parry, quam quidem allegationem dicti Johannis Grove dictus subdecanus allocavit [*MS.* allocat], unde dictus venerabilis subdecanus dictum Johannem Grove in eleemozynarium readmisit, habere et percipere omnia proficua et emolumenta ad locum eleemozynarii spectantia a festo sancti Michaelis Arch-angeli in anno 1629.

---

[1] He may be the Stephen Halford of the city of Gloucester, gent., who on 24 May 1660 took a lease of the college mill (later no. 2 Millers Green), at a rent of 30*s*. The next lease of the property was in 1670, to Robert Halford of Barton Street in the county of Gloucester, gent.

[2] During the Commonwealth period Alderman Lawrence Singleton was one of those who collected money for repairs to the college, i.e. the cathedral and precinct.

[3] The words 'and singinge men' have been added above the line.

96.   Wednesday 13 October 1630.   Chapter House.
(Thomas Winnyyffe, S.T.P., dean; Thomas Prior, subdean; Elias Wrench, treasurer; Dr. Loe; John Wood.)

Secrecy in Chapter affaires. Quibus die et loco Mr. Deane and the chapter present ordered and decreed that all matters and things whatsoever which shall be debated of in the chapter howse concerninge church busines or any member shall be kept secret, and noe man to divulge or publishe any thinge there handled or debated on, uppon payne that every member of the quire offendinge herein shall for every defaulte incurre the mulcte or penalty of five shillings to be by the thresurer substracted out of his wages.

                         Eodem die.

Order for takinge downe the fence-schoole.[1] Quibus die et anno, whereas a great and ruinous buildinge, at the end of the fermery, within the precincts of this church, commonly called by the name of the fencinge-schoole, is in soe greate ruine and decay that the inhabitants neare adioyninge are in greate feare and dread of themselves, theyr children and servants, in case yt should suddenly fall, as yt is very likely to doe if prevention be not therein taken, and whereas allsoe the sayd howse, for the whole time of the memory of man, hath not bin of any use or imployment but putt to the basest and wildest uses [*fo. 55*] to the[2] greate anoyance of the inhabitants neare adioyninge, and the chardge of the repaire would proove soe insupportable that the poore estate of this church is not able to beare the same, therefore yt is ordered and decreed that the thresurer of this church, accordinge to his discretion, shall take downe the same by degrees, and imploy the materialls of tile, stone and timber only upon the repaires of the church, as occasion shall require, and for the rubbish and smaller stones shall imploy them upon the repaire of the high-wayes belonginge to the church. And after the takinge downe the roof and cariage away of the materialls of buildinge, then the thresurer for the time beinge, shall give notice to the deane and chapter, at the next auditt followinge, that they the said deane and chapter may take such order for the disposinge of the vacant grounde whereon yt now standeth as for the honor of the church, and in theyr wisdomes, shall seeme most convenient.

                         Eodem die.

Alowances for Auditt to the Deane & Chapter present. Quibus die et anno, whereas the presence of the deane and prebendaryes of this church is especially required and exspected at the time of auditt, in respect of the graunt of leases, presentinge of the accounts and orderinge of all the principall matters within the church, and in regard that hertofore noe settled course by chapter act hath bin taken for competent alowance to such of the prebendaryes present as shall attende the service of the church at auditt time and accompany Mr. Deane, and be reddy to assist, for dispatch of the churche's accasions then, whereby the service hath bin neglected, and in chapter sommetimes not present to the dishonor of the church, yt is therefore for the better encouragement of those of the prebends that will be present at the auditt, and give assistance there, decreed and ordered,

---

[1] For the fencing-school, above, p. xxi.
[2] The words 'to the' are also catchwords at the foot of fo. 54v.

that the deane of the said church, whether present in person at the auditt time or sendinge his proxie shall be absent, shall have alowance by the space of one and twenty dayes after the rate of fowre shillings per diem, and every prebend of this church in person present at the auditt time, for the like space of 21 dayes, shall have alowance after the rate of two shillings per diem, for soe many dayes as he shall be present (all Sundayes within compasst of the sayd 21 dayes to be accounted as present if absent); those severall sommes to be payd to each of them, at the end of every audit by the handes of the tresurer of this church for the time beinge, and the thresurer to have alowance upon his account for payment thereof.

97.   [*fo. 55v.*]   29 October 1630.   Deanery.
Admissio choristarum. [*Admission of choristers. John Brodgate and William Collins were admitted by the dean in the places of Richard Brodgate and Anthony Dobbs.*] Quibus die, loco et anno Johannes Brodgate et Gulielmus Collins admissi erant per venerabilem decanum in loco duorum choristarum infra hanc ecclesiam cathedralem in locis Richardi Brodgate et Anthonii Dobbes.

98.   Tuesday the feast of St. Andrew the Apostle, 30 November 1630.
                                                                Chapter House.
(Thomas Prior, subdean; Elias Wrench.)

Electio officiariorum. [*Election of officers. In the absence of the dean but with his consent, the subdean and the aforenamed prebendary elected Elias Wrench as subdean and Thomas Prior as receiver and treasurer. As in* **6** *and* **40**, *above.*]

Electio precentoris. [*Election of the precentor. The aforesaid men elected Richard Marwood. As in* **63**, *above.*] Eodem die, loco et anno [*etc.*].

99.   12 February 1630/1.
Admissio choristae. [*Admission of a chorister. Thomas Hosier was admitted by Mr. Elias Wrench, subdean, in the place of William Hosier.*] Quibus die et anno Thomas Hosier admissus fuit per Magistrum Eliam Wrench, subdecanum, chorista in loco Gulielmi Hosier.

100.   [*fo. 56*]   Saturday 11 June 1631.   Chapter House.
(Elias Wrench, subdean; Thomas Prior, treasurer; Anthony Robinson, notary public, registrar of the said church.)

Installatio Venerabilis viri Georgii Warburton Decani Gloucestriae 1631. [*Installation of the venerable man George Warburton as dean of Gloucester. In the chapter house, before Elias Wrench, subdean, and Thomas Prior, treasurer, prebendaries solemnly assembled in chapter, and in the presence of the writer, Anthony Robinson, notary public, registrar, George Warburton, M.A., chaplain in ordinary to the king, appeared in person and presented the king's letters patent, dated 29 April 1631, and he exhibited the royal mandate addressed to the chapter and prebendaries to assign to the dean a stall in the* *choir and a place and a voice in the chapter. The dean asked the prebendaries to assign him the stall etc. and to put him in possession. The subdean accepted the letters patent and the mandate. After they had been read in public and the dean had taken the oaths to renounce Rome and of supremacy and to obey the statutes of the cathedral, the subdean installed the dean, gave him possession, took him back into the chapter house, assigned him a place and a voice, and gave him possession. All which the prebendaries required to be enacted, and all these things were done in the presence of William Sutton, chancellor of the diocese, Edward Forde, Esq., Philip Fleminge, Esq., Edward Cheecke, Esq., Nathaniel Mill, merchant of Southampton, Arthur Price, M.A., and John Langley, M.A., James Clent, notary public, Richard Marwood, precentor, and other servants of the said church.*] Quibus die ac loco in propria persona sua comparuit venerabilis et discretus vir Georgius Warburton, in artibus magister ac sacellanus in ordinario regiae majestati, constitutus et ordinatus in decanum ecclesiae cathedralis Sanctae et Individuae Trinitatis Gloucestriae, et ex parte sua praebendariis ecclesiae cathedralis praedictae praesentavit literas patentes illustrissimi in Christo principis domini nostri, Domini Charoli, dei gratia Angliae, Scotiae, Franciae et Hiberniae regis &c. gerentes datas vicesimo nono die Aprilis regni sui septimo,[1] et exhibuit etiam et tradidit dicto subdecano mandatum regium pro installatione dicti Georgii Warburton in decanatum Gloucestriae, capitulo et praebendariis dictae ecclesiae cathedralis Gloucestrensis directas, per quas mandatum fuit capitulo et praebendariis supra-nominatis ad assignandum sive assignari faciendum venerabili viro praedicto decano ordinato stallum in choro et locum ac vocem in capitulo in ecclesia cathedrali praedicta prout moris est. Ac insuper dictus venerabilis decanus ordinatus et constitutus virtute literarum mandatoriarum praefatarum ex parte sua et pro se petiit et requisivit a praebendariis praedictis stallum in choro et locum et vocem in capitulo in dicta ecclesia cathedrali Gloucestriae sibi assignari et limitari nec non realem, corporalem et actualem possessionem, installationem et inthronizationem sibi fieri omniaque ac singula alia perimplenda et facienda quae in hujusmodi installationis negotio necessaria fuerint seu quomodolibet opportuna. Unde dictus venerabilis subdecanus omni (qua decuit) reverentia dictas literas patentes et mandatorias acceptavit, eisdemque publice praelectis, praestito[2] primitus per praefatum Georgium Warburton decanum ordinatum iuramento corporali ad sacrosancta dei evangelia de renunciando Romano episcopo, et de agnoscendo dictum dominum nostrum Charolum regem &c. supremum caput &c. ac de observandis statutis dictae ecclesiae iuxta morem et ritum &c. quatenus verbo dei et legibus hujus regni Angliae non repugnarint, praefatus Magister Elias Wrench, subdecanus ecclesiae cathedralis Gloucestriae praedictae, omni cum solennitate qua in hac parte fieri potuerit praefatum venerabilem virum Georgium Warburton, decanum [*fo. 56v.*] ordinatum et constitutum, ad stallum in choro ecclesiae cathedralis antedictae hactenus decano ejusdem ecclesiae cathedralis Gloucestriae pro tempore existentem solitum et consuetum attulit, eumque in realem, corporalem et actualem possessionem ejusdem stalli et dignitatis decanatus ibidem cum suis membris,

---

[1] The date is enclosed in square brackets, evidently added later. The dating clause of the royal mandate, with the 18 words following it, and of the letters of proxy in **101**, below, are similarly enclosed in square brackets.

[2] The words 'praestito . . . repugnarint' are enclosed in square brackets, possibly added later.

juribus et pertinentiis universis praefato decano ordinato installavit et inthronizavit, et pacificam possessionem eorundem praemissorum ei deliberavit. Ac exinde dictum venerabilem virum Georgium Warburton decanum ordinatum et constitutum in domum capitularem dictae ecclesiae simile cum solennitate reduxit, eique locum ac vocem in capitulo eiusdem cathedralis ecclesiae prefato decano ratione decanatus huiusmodi sui debita, solita et consueta assignavit, possessionemque eorundem praefato decano ordinato et constituto dedit et tradidit. Quae omnia et singula dicti praebendarii inactitari requisiverunt. Et omnia haec antedicta facta fuerunt in praesentia venerabilis viri Guilielmi Sutton, cancellarii dioecesoes Gloucestriae, Edoardi Forde, armigeri, Philippi Fleminge, armigeri, Edoardi Cheecke, armigeri, Nathanielis Mill, mercatoris Southamptoniensis, Arthuri Price et Johannis Langley, artium magistrorum, Jacobi Clent, notarii publici, Richardi Marwood, praecentoris, aliorumque dictae ecclesiae ministrorum.

Ita testor Anth[ony] Robinson, registrarius.

101.   Tuesday 13 September 1631.   Chapter House.
(Elias Wrench, subdean; Thomas Anyan, S.T.P.; Thomas Prior, treasurer; Thomas Iles, S.T.P.; Anthony Robinson, notary public and registrar.)

Installatio Venerabilis viri Accepti Frewen Decani Gloucestriae Anno 1631.[1]
[Installation of the venerable man Accepted Frewen as dean of Gloucester in the year 1631. In the chapter house, before Elias Wrench, subdean, Thomas Anyan, S.T.P., Thomas Prior, treasurer, and Thomas Iles, S.T.P., prebendaries solemnly assembled in chapter, and in the presence of the writer, Anthony Robinson, notary public, registrar, John Harward, gent., appeared in person and exhibited his proxy for Accepted Frewen, S.T.P., and chaplain to the king, and made himself party for the same and presented the royal mandate, dated 27 August 1631, addressed to the chapter and prebendaries, to assign to the dean a stall in the choir and a place and a voice in the chapter. And John Harward exhibited the dean's letters of proxy, dated 12 September 1631, appointing Thomas Iles his proxy for putting the dean in possession, etc., which Thomas Iles accepted. Afterwards on the same day the subdean with due solemnity brought Thomas Iles to the dean's customary stall in the choir and assigned him his place and voice. All which the prebendaries required to be enacted, and all these things were done in the presence of John Newarke, clerk, John Langley, M.A., John Marks, gent., Anthony Robinson, scholar of Corpus Christi College in the university of Oxford, Christopher Prior, scholar of Balliol College in the same university, Richard Marwood, precentor, and other servants of the said church.] Quibus die ac loco comparuit personaliter quidam Johannes Harward, generosus, ac exhibuit procuratorium pro venerabili viro Accepto Frewen, sacrae theologiae professore ac sacellano regiae majestatis, [*fo. 57*] constituto et ordinato in decanum ecclesiae cathedralis Sanctae et Individuae Trinitatis Gloucestriae ac fecit se partem pro eodem [*etc. as in* **1**, *above, with minor verbal variations and as modified in* **35**, *above*].

Ita testor Anth[ony] Robinson, registrarius.

---

[1] Although installed as dean of Gloucester as recently as 11 June, George Warburton had on 3 Aug. been presented by the king to the deanery of Wells: below, p. 170.

[*fo. 57v.*]   Eodem die, loco et anno.

Act for a presentation to Rudford. Quibus die et loco, whereas the donation of the rectory of Rudford in the diocesse of Gloucester is the right of the deane and chapter of this church, and is now voyde by the late death of John Roberts, clearke, last incumbent there, whereof notice beinge given to the right worshipfull Dr. Frewen, now deane of this church, the sayd Dr. Frewen, for preservinge the right of this church in & to the sayd advowson and perpetuall patronage of the sayd church of Rudford, did by his proxie under his hand and seale bearinge date the twelfe daye of this instant September authorize & appoynte Mr. Thomas Pryor and Thomas Iles, doctor in divinity, two of the prebendaries of this church, ioyntely and severally to give his voyce and full consente to the passinge and sealinge of a presentacion of the sayd rectory of Rudford to Mr. Elias Wrench, nowe subdeane of the sayd cathedrall church, by vertue of which sayd proxie the sayd Dr. Iles gave Mr. Deane's voyce to the passinge of a presentacion of the sayd rectory of Rudford to the sayd Mr. Elias Wrench. And Thomas Anyan, doctor in divinity, and Thomas Prior, now tresurer of this church, and the sayd Dr. Iles, all prebendaryes of this church, all of them beinge then present, gave theire voyces and consents to the passinge of the sayd presentacion of the rectory of Rudford aforesayd to the sayd Mr. Wrench. And accordingly the sayd Mr. Wrench had a presentacion under the deane and chapter seale then presently graunted and delivered unto him.

102.   6 October 1631.   Chapter House.
(Accepted Frewen, S.T.P., dean; Elias Wrench, subdean; Thomas Prior, treasurer; Thomas Iles, S.T.P.; John Wood.)

Decanus iurat. [*The dean takes the oath. As in* **2**, *above, substituting the name of King Charles and adding at the end the otiose phrase*] et chartae fundacionis huius ecclesiae &c. [*i.e. and* (*according*) *to the foundation charter of this church*].

103. [*fo. 58*]   26 October 1631.   Chapter House.
(Accepted Frewen, S.T.P., dean; Elias Wrench, subdean; Doctor Loe; Thomas Prior; Thomas Iles, S.T.P.)

Mr. Hulett's feirst monition. Quibus die et loco William Hulett, clerke, one of the petty-cannons of this church, (noe occasion beinge given him) spake unto Mr. Deane in the presence of the quire there insolently and unmannerly and without such reverence as became him. Whereupon Mr. Deane in open chapter gave him the sayd Hulett his feirst monition to departe this church.
        A. Frewen, deane.

104.   27 October 1631

Admissio choristae. [*Admission of a chorister. Robert Dobbs was admitted by the dean in the place of Anthony Smith.*] Quibus die et anno Robertus Dobbs admissus fuit per venerabilem decanum chorista in loco Anthonii Smith.
        A. Frewen, deane.

105. Wednesday the feast of St. Andrew the Apostle, 30 November 1631.

Chapter House.

(Elias Wrench, subdean; Thomas Prior.)

Electio officiariorum. [*Election of officers. In the absence of the dean but with his consent, the subdean and the aforenamed prebendary elected and continued Elias Wrench as subdean and Thomas Prior as receiver and treasurer. As in* **63**, *above.*]

Electio precentoris. [*Election of the precentor. The aforesaid men elected Richard Marwood. As in* **63**, *above.*] Eodem die, loco et anno [*etc.*].

106. [*fo. 58v.*] 14 June 1632. Chapter House.

(Elias Wrench, subdean; Mr. Prior.)

Admissio hypodidascali. [*Admission of the assistant schoolmaster. Ezra Grayle,*[1] *B.A., who had been chosen by the dean, was admitted by the subdean, after he had taken the oaths.*] Quibus die, loco et anno Ezra Grayle [*etc., as in* **50**, *above*].

107. Thursday 25 October 1632, between nine and eleven a.m.

Chapter House.

(Accepted Frewen, S.T.P., dean; Elias Wrench, subdean; William Loe, S.T.P.; John Wood, S.T.B.)

Admissio venerabilis viri Georgii Palmer in primam prebendam. [*Admission of the venerable man George Palmer to the first prebend. George Palmer, S.T.B., exhibited the king's letters patent, dated 25 September last past, granting to him the prebend vacant by the death of Thomas Prior, and the royal mandate for his admission and installation; the dean admitted him, as in* **37**, *above, from which the form below differs in some ways. All this was done in the presence of Robert Willoughby, John Langley and William Loe, M.A., James Wood, gent., Richard Roberts, gent., Richard Marwood and Richard Brodgate, minor canons, and other servants of the said church and of the writer, Anthony Robinson, registrar.*] Discretus vir Georgius Palmer, sacrae theologiae baccalaureus, exhibuit et tradidit venerabili decano antedicto litteras patentes illustrissimi in Christo principis domini nostri, Domini Caroli, dei gracia Angliae, Scotiae, Fraunciae et Hiberniae regis, gerentes datas vicesimo quinto die Septembris ultimo preterito, de concessione illius prebendae sive canonicatus in ecclesia cathedrali Gloucestriae predicta quam Thomas Prior nuper habuit et iam per mortem prefati Thomae Prior ultimi possessoris eiusdem prebendae vacantis facta dicto Georgio Palmer. Et exhibuit etiam mandatum regium pro admissione et instalacione dicti Georgii Palmer in prebendam predictam iuxta consuetudinem in ea parte usitatam, unde dictus venerabilis vir decanus antedictus omni cum ea qua decuit reverentia et obedientia dictas litteras patentes et mandatorias recepit, quibus perlectis ob reverentiam et obedientiam debitam prefatum Georgium Palmer,

---

[1] For Grayle, below, p. 163. The accounts for 1630–1 show that Ezra Grayle was not the chapter's first choice, for that year they gave £1 10*s.* to a Mr. Marten 'who had a grant of the usher's place but relinquished it upon promise of his charges to London about it.'

prestito primitus per eum iuramento corporali ad sacrosancta dei evangelia de renuntiando Romano episcopo et de agnoscendo dictum dominum nostrum Dominum Carolum regem &c. supremum caput &c. ac de observandis statutis [*MS.* statuta] dictae ecclesiae iuxta morem et ritum &c. quatenus verbo dei et legibus huius regni Angliae non repugnant &c., in canonicum et prebendarium admisit &c. Et imediate venerabilis decanus antedictus unacum antedicto Georgio Palmer e domo capitulari predicta egressus est, et ipsum Georgium Palmer in chorum ecclesiae cathedralis predictae adduxit, ubi dictus decanus dictum Georgium Palmer in stallum prebendae predictae installavit iuxta morem &c., et tunc reversus in domum capitularem predictam eidem Georgio Palmer vocem et locum in capitulo ibidem assignavit &c. Et haec omnia facta fuerunt in presentia Roberti Willoughby, Johannis Langly et Gulielmi Loe,[1] artium magistri, Jacobi Wood, generosi, et Richardi Roberts, generosi, Richardi Marwood et Richardi Bradgate, duarum minorum canonicorum, aliorumque dictae ecclesiae ministrorum meique Anthonii Robinson, dictae ecclesiae registrarii &c.

    Ita testor Anth[ony] Robinson, registrarius.

108.   [*fo. 59*]   10 November 1632.
Order for Mr. Browne to shue [sc. *sue*] ***for tythes in Churcham.*** Quibus die et anno ordinatum est ut sequitur [*On which day and year it was ordered as follows*] vizt. Whereas divers parcells of tythes, parcell of the rectory of Churcham, beinge the inheritance of this church of Gloucester, have bin heretofore withheld and withdrawen from the sayd rectory, and some of the same parcells of tythes, at the costs and chardges of John Browne, esquire, our present tenant of the sayd rectory, have bin recovered and gained againe to the sayd rectory, and somme other parcells of the sayd rectory are yett still deteyned and withheld from the sayd rectory, which he the sayd John Browne (by the advise of his councell) is informed are of right belonginge to the same, yt is therefore the day and yeare above-written agreed upon and condiscended unto, by us the deane and chapter of this church, that upon any shute [sc. *suit*] or shutes to be brought and commensed for the sayd tythes soe deteyned the sayd John Browne shall have power and liberty to use the names of us the deane and chapter in the proseqution of the sayd shutes either alone, or together with himselfe, as our farmer of the sayd rectory, as by his counsell he shallbe advised. Provided allwayes that in any shute or shutes begunne commensed or prosequted for the sayd tythes the chardges and expenses soly to be borne by him the sayd John Browne.

    A. Frewen, decan[us]; E. Wrenche, subd[ecanus]; William Leo; John Wood; Geo[rgius] Palmer.

109.   13 November 1632.
Order for confirmation of the Bondhoult tithes. Quibus die et anno ordinatum est ut sequitur [*On which day and year it was ordered as follows*] vizt. upon the desire of the right reverend father in God, Godfry, lord bishopp of Gloucester, signified unto us the deane and chapter of this church, for order and authority to be given for the confirmation

---

[1] The son of Canon William Loe: below, p. 167.

of a lease for twenty one yeares, of the abbott's tythinge of the Bond-hoult in Upton St. Leonards in the county of the citty of Gloucester to be graunted to Sir John Bridgeman, knight, or George Bridgeman, esquire, we doe agree, and by these presents conclude, that upon the tender of any such lease from his lordshipp to be graunted as aforesayd to us, or any of us, at or before the feast of St. Michaell the Arch-angell next ensuinge, the same lease to be fully and firmely confirmed. And that without any further meetinge and passinge of any voices or suffrages of us the deane and prebendaries yt shall be lawfull for such of the prebendarie or prebendaries as shall be then present to such confirmation to putt the chapter seale, and we shall take yt, and acknowledge yt, as our publick act which we will be allwayes reddy to ratify and warrant.

A. Frewen, decan[us]; E. Wrenche, subd[ecanus]; W[illia]m Leo; John Wood; Geo[rgius] Palmer.

110.   [*fo. 59v.*]   Friday the feast of St. Andrew the Apostle, 30 November 1632.

Chapter House.

(Elias Wrench, subdean; William Loe, S.T.P.)

Electio officiariorum. [*Election of officers. In the absence of the dean but with his consent, the subdean and the aforenamed prebendary elected William Loe as subdean and Elias Wrench as receiver and treasurer. As in* **6** *and* **40**, *above.*]

Electio precentoris. [*Election of the precentor. The aforesaid men elected Richard Marwood. As in* **63**, *above.*]

111.   Tuesday 26 February 1632/3.   Chapter House.

(Elias Wrench, treasurer; Anthony Robinson, notary public and registrar.)

Admissio venerabilis viri Gilberti Sheldon in quartam prebendam. [*Admission of the venerable man Gilbert Sheldon to the fourth prebend. John Hayward, gent., proctor for Gilbert Sheldon, clerk, S.T.B., appeared in person and made himself proxy for the same, and exhibited the king's letters patent, dated 29 January last past, granting to Sheldon the prebend or canonry vacant by the death of Thomas Anyan, S.T.P., and he exhibited the royal mandate for his admission and installation. And Hayward exhibited letters dated 9 February 1632/3 from Sheldon nominating Jonathan Bullock, clerk, as his proxy to be installed and put in possession, which Bullock accepted. Afterwards on the same day Mr. Elias Wrench installed Bullock in Sheldon's name, etc., as in* **37**, *above. All which Mr. Wrench required to be enacted, and all these things were done in the presence of James Clent, notary public, John Langley and Ezra Grayle, M.A., Richard St. Leger, gent., Richard Marwood and Richard Brodgate, minor canons, and other servants of the said church and of the writer, Anthony Robinson, registrar.*] Quibus die ac loco comparuit personaliter quidam Johannes Hayward, generosus, ac exhibuit procuratorium pro venerabili viro Gilberto Sheldon, clerico, sacrae theologiae baccalaureo, ac fecit se partem pro eodem et ex parte eiusdem venerabilis viri exhibuit et tradidit Magistro Elia Wrench, prebendario antedicto, literas patentes illustrissimi in Christo principis ac domini nostri, Domini Caroli, dei gracia Angliae, Scotiae, Franciae et Hiberniae regis, fidei defensoris &c., gerentes datas vicesimo nono die Januarii ultimo preterito, de concessione prebendae sive canonicatus in ecclesia cathedrali Sanctae et Individuae Trinitatis Gloucestrensis per mortem Thomae Anyan, sacrae theologiae professoris, ultimi prebendarii sive canonici ibidem, iam vacantis dicto Gilberto Sheldon. Et exhibuit etiam mandatum regium pro admissione et installacione dicti Gilberti Sheldon in prebendam predictam iuxta consuetudinem in ea parte usitatam, unde dictus Mr. Elias Wrench omni cum ea qua decuit reverentia et obedientia dictas literas patentes et mandatorias recepit, et eas sic receptas publice perlegi [*MS.* perlect'] [*fo. 60*] requisivit. Ac insuper dictus Johannes Hayward ex parte dicti Gilberti Sheldon exhibuit supranominato Magistro Wrench, prebendario, literas quasdam procuratorias a praefato Gilberti Sheldon, prebendario ordinato et constituto ut supra, per quas discretum virum Jonathan Bullocke, clericum, in artibus magistrum, inter alios suum verum, certum et legitimum procuratorem nominavit, ordinavit, fecit et constituit pro se ac vice et nomine eius stallum in choro et locum et vocem in capitulo in dicta ecclesia cathedrali Gloucestriae sibi assignari et limitari petendi et obtinendi, nec non realem, corporalem et actualem possessionem et installacionem huiusmodi ingrediendi et adipiscendi, illasque sic adeptas ad usum dicti Gilberto Sheldon custodiendi et conservandi, omniaque et singula alia perimplendi et faciendi quae in huiusmodi installacionis negotio necessaria fuerint seu quomodolibet oportuna, prout per easdem literas procuratorias, gerentes datas nono die mensis Februarii anno domini 1632, plenius liquet et apparet. Quas literas procuratorias dictus Jonathan Bullocke debite recepit ac onus eorundem in se acceptavit. Postea vero eodem die prefatus Mr. Elias Wrench, prebendarius ecclesiae cathedralis Gloucestriae predictae, omni cum solennitate qua in hac parte fieri potuerit, praefatum Jonathan Bullocke ad stallum in choro ecclesiae cathedralis Gloucestriae antedictae, hactenus prebendae predictae eiusdem ecclesiae cathedralis Gloucestriae pro tempore existente solitum et consuetum, attulit, eumque in realem actualem et corporalem possessionem eiusdem stalli et dignitatis prebendae predictae ibidem cum suis membris, iuribus et pertinentiis universis, loco, vice ac nomine ac pro prefato Gilberto Sheldon prebendario ut prefertur ordinato, installavit ac pacificam possessionem eorundem premissorum ei deliberavit. Ac ex inde dictum Jonathan Bullock in domum capitularem dictae ecclesiae simili cum solennitate aduxit eique locum et vocem in capitulo eiusdem cathedralis ecclesiae prefato Gilberto Sheldon, prebendario, ratione prebendae huiusmodi sui, debita, solita et consueta assignavit, possessionemque eorundem prefato Jonathan Bullock, loco, vice ac nomine dicti Gilberti Sheldon, prebendarii, dedit et tradidit. Quae omnia et singula dictus Mr. Wrench prebendarius inactitari requisivit, et omnia haec antedicta facta fuerunt in praesentia Jacobi Clent, notarii publici, Johannis Langly et Ezra Grayle, artium magistri, Richardi St. Leger, generosi, Richardi Marwood et Richardi Brodgate, duorum minorum canonicorum, aliorumque dictae ecclesiae ministrorum meique Anthonii Robinson, dictae ecclesiae registrarii.

Ita testor Anth[ony] Robinson, registrarius.

Admissio choristae. [*Admission of a chorister. By the dean's mandate, John Hodshon was admitted by Mr. Elias Wrench in the place of Luke Turner.*] Eodem die, loco et anno per mandatum venerabilis decani Johannes Hodshon admissus fuit per prefatum Magistrum Eliam Wrench chorista in loco Lucae Turner.

112.   [*fo. 60v.*]   22 March 1632/3.   Chapter House.
(Elias Wrench, treasurer.)

A presentation to the vicaridge of Bruckthroppe. Whereas the donacion of the vicaridge
of Bruckthropp in the diocess of Gloucester is fallen into the hands of the deane &
chapter of this church by the deathe of Wytherstone Massinger, clearke, late incumbent
there, lately deceased, the above named Mr. Wrench came into the chapter howse the
daye & yeare above mencioned for the passinge of a presentacion to the vicaridge
aforesayd, havinge received a proxie from the right worshipfull Dr. Frewen, deane of this
church, under his hand & seale bearinge date the eleventh daye of February last past, to
him the sayd Mr. Wrench directed, thereby authorisinge and appointinge him, the sayd
Elias Wrench, to give his voyce and full consent to the passinge, grauntinge & sealinge of
a presentacion of the sayd vicaridge of Bruckthroppe to William Lord, bachellor in arts,
by vertue of which sayd proxie the sayd Mr. Wrench gave Mr. Deane's voyce to the
passinge of a presentacion of the sayd vicaridge of Bruckthropp to the sayd William
Lord. And likewyse by authority from Dr. Leo, now subdeane of this church, the sayd Dr.
Leo his voyce was given to the sayd presentacion of the sayd vicaridge to the sayd
William Lord. And the sayd Mr. Wrench in person gave his owne voyce allsoe to the
sayd presentacion. And by virtue of a proxie from Dr. Iles, one of the prebendaryes of this
church, to the purpose aforesayd directed, the sayd Dr. Iles his voyce was given to the
sayd William Lord to be presented to the same vicaridge of Bruckthropp aforesayd. And
lastly by virtue of two severall proxies from John Wood, bachellor in divinity, & George
Palmer, bachellor in divinity, two of the prebendaryes of this church, to the sayd Mr.
Wrench directed to the purpose aforesayd, the sayd Mr. Wrench gave theire severall
voyces of the sayd Mr. Wood & Mr. Palmer to the presentacion aforesayd to be made to
the sayd William Lord, and accordingly the sayd William Lord had a presentacion of the
sayd vicaridge of Bruckthropp aforesayd delivered unto him under the chapter seale.

113.   30 April 1633.

Admissio choristae. [*Admission of a chorister. By the dean's mandate, Thomas Longe
was admitted by Mr. Elias Wrench, treasurer, in the place of Thomas Hosier.*] Quibus die
et anno per mandatum venerabilis decani huius ecclesiae Thomas Longe admissus fuit
per Magistrum Eliam Wrench, thesaurarium, chorista in loco Thomae Hosyer.

114.   [*fo. 61*]

A dispensation for keepinge the Auditt. Charles R. Trusty and welbeloved wee greete
yow well. Whereas we are informed that amonge other your statuts for the goverment and
orderinge of that church yow have one which byndes the deane and chapter to keepe the
audit and chuse the officers of that church precisely uppon the last daye of November,
and that Dr. Frewen, your deane, by reason of his attendance both uppon our person in his
turne, and uppon the colledge whereof he is president in Oxford,[1] cannot conveniently

---

[1] Frewen was president of Magdalen College, Oxford, 1626–44.

bee there at that precise tyme, our pleasure is to alter this statute duringe the tyme he shall be deane there, and to ordayne that from henceforth that clause of your statute which bynds yow strictly to the last daye of November yearely shall cease for that tyme, and that it shall bee lawfull for yow yearely to keepe your audit and chuse your officers of the sayd church any daye which your selves shall thinke fit within the monethes of October or November. And our further pleasure is that this our letter be registred in your statute booke with the rest of your statuts which have had theire beinge from our worthie pregenitors. Given under our signett at our pallace of Westminster the seaven and twentith daye of February in the eyght yeare of our raigne.

To our trusty and welbeloved the deane and chapter of our
cathedrall churche of Gloucester.

115.   1 August 1633.   Chapter House.
(William Leo, S.T.P., subdean; Elias Wrench, treasurer; Gilbert Sheldon.)

Iuramentum venerabilis viri Gi[l]berti Sheldon. [*The oath of the venerable man Gilbert Sheldon. Gilbert Sheldon took the bodily oath on the gospels, touched and kissed by him, to renounce the bishop of Rome, to acknowledge the king as head of the church and to observe the cathedral statutes.*] Quibus die et anno venerabilis vir Gilbertus Sheldon, prebendarius antedictus, sacramentum prestitit corporale, ad sacrosancta dei evangelia per eum tacta et deosculata, de renuntiando Romano episcopo et de agnoscendo serenissimum dominum nostrum Carolum, Angliae &c. regem &c., supremum caput &c., fidei defensorem &c., ac de observando ordinaciones et statuta dictae ecclesiae cathedralis juxta morem et ritum &c. quatenus consentiunt verbo dei, ac statutis huius regni &c., et chartae fundacionis huius ecclesiae &c.

116.   [*fo. 61v*]   Wednesday 30 October 1633.   Chapter House.
(Accepted Frewen, S.T.P., dean; William Loe, S.T.P., subdean; Thomas Iles, S.T.P.)

Electio officiariorum. [*Election of officers. The dean and the aforenamed prebendaries elected Thomas Iles as subdean and William Loe as receiver and treasurer. As in* **6**, *above, replacing* capitulum *with* prebendarii prenominati.]

Electio precentoris. [*Election of the precentor. The dean chose as precentor for the coming year Richard Marwood, one of the minor canons, the oath having been taken by him.*] Eodem die, loco et anno idem venerabilis decanus antedictus elegit in precentorem dictae ecclesiae pro anno futuro Richardum Marwood, unum minorum canonicorum eiusdem ecclesiae, iuramento suscepto &c.

Admissio choristae. [*Admission of a chorister. Toby Greene was admitted by the dean in the place of Richard White.*] Quibus die et anno Toby Greene admissus fuit per venerabilem decanum chorista in loco Richardi White.

Eodem die, loco et anno.

A presentation to the Rectory of Rudford. Quibus die et loco, whereas the patronage and donation of the rectory of Ruddford in the diocese of Gloucester is the right of the deane and chapter of this church, and the same beinge now voyde by the late death of Elias

Wrench, one of the prebendaryes of this church, the last incumbent there, the above named Doctor Frewen, deane of this church, for preservinge the right of this church to the patronage of the sayd rectory of Rudford did this daye in open chapter give his voyce & free consent for a presentacion to be passed, made & sealed to William Leo, doctor in divinity & one of the prebendaryes of this church, to the sayd rectory. And the sayd William Leo himselfe & the above named Doctor Iles, one other of the prebendaryes of this church, both then allso present, gave theire severall voyces & consents to the passinge of the sayd presentacion of the rectory of Rudford aforesayd to the sayd Dr. Leo. And the sayd Dr. Frewen, deane of this church, by virtue of severall proxies under hand & seale from Mr. John Wood, Mr. George Palmer & Mr. Gilbert Sheldon, all of them prebendaryes of this church, did give theire severall voyces & full consents to the passinge of the sayd presentacion of the rectory of Ruddford aforesayd to the sayd Dr. Leo. And it was then allsoe ordered & decreed that the sayd Dr. Leo should at any tyme within the space of five moneths after the death of the sayd Mr. Wrench, the last incumbent there, shue out & take forth his presentacion under the chapter seale, or otherwyse this acte [*fo. 62*] to be voyde and the deane & chapter should then after be at liberty to dispose of the sayd presentacion to any other at theire will & pleasure.

117.   Tuesday 22 April 1634, between nine and eleven a.m.

                                                                   Chapter House.

(William Leo, S.T.P., treasurer.)

Admissio venerabilis viri Johannis English in secundam prebendam. [*Admission of the venerable man John English to the second prebend. On Tuesday 22 April 1634, before William Loe, S.T.P., prebendary, between the ninth and the eleventh hour before noon, John English, S.T.P., exhibited the king's letters patent dated 28 November last past, granting him the prebend vacant by the death of Elias Wrench and the royal mandate for his admission and installation; William Loe admitted him, as in* **37**, *above. All this was done in the presence of Anthony Ludford, Esq., James Clent and John Hayward, gents., John Langley and Ezra Grayle, M.A., Richard Marwood and Richard Brodgate, minor canons, and other servants of the said church and of the writer, Anthony Robinson, registrar.*] Die Martis vizt. vicesimo secundo die Aprilis anno domini 1634 coram venerabili viro Gulielmo Leo, sacrae theologiae professore, tunc thesaurario et prebendario ecclesiae cathedralis Gloucestriae, inter horas nonam et undecim ante meridiem, in domo capitulari dictae ecclesiae venerabilis vir Johannes English, sacrae theologiae professor, exhibuit et tradidit venerabili viro antedicto literas patentes illustrissimi in Christo domini nostri Domini Caroli, dei gracia Angliae, Scotiae, Franciae et Hiberniae regis, gerentes datas vicesimo octavo die Novembris ultimo preterito de concessione illius prebendae sive canonicatus in ecclesia cathedrali Gloucestriae predicta quam Elias Wrench nuper habuit et iam per mortem prefati Eliae Wrench, ultimi possessoris eiusdem prebendae, vacantis facta dicto Johanni English. Et exhibuit etiam mandatum regium [*etc., as in* **107**, *above*].

       Ita testor Anth[ony] Robinson, registrarius.

118.   [*fo. 62v.*]   Tuesday 8 July 1634.   Chapter House.
(John English, S.T.P., prebendary; Anthony Robinson, notary public, registrar.)

Installatio venerabilis viri Hugonis Robinson Archi-diaconi Gloucestriae. [*Installation of the venerable man Hugh Robinson as archdeacon of Gloucester. James Clent, gent., notary public, appeared and exhibited his proxy for Hugh Robinson, S.T.P., appointed as archdeacon, and made himself party for the same and presented the bishop's mandate, dated 25 June last past, for him to be assigned a stall in the choir and a place and a voice in the chapter. James Clent exhibited the archdeacon's letter, dated 30 June 1634, nominating Mr. John Allibond, M.A., as his proxy for taking possession of the archdeaconry, which letter Mr. Allibond accepted. Afterwards on the same day John English led John Allibond to the customary stall of the archdeacon and put him in possession of the stall and the archdeaconry. All this was done in the presence of James Clent, gent., John Langley, M.A., John Grayle, B.A., Richard Marwood, precentor, Richard Brodgate and William Hulett, minor canons, and other servants of the said church and of the writer, Anthony Robinson, registrar.*] Quibus die et loco comparuit quidam Jacobus Clent, generosus, notarius publicus, et exhibuit procuratorium pro venerabili viro Hugone Robinson, sacrae theologiae professore, instituto et constituto in archidiaconatum sive dignitatem archidiaconalem in ecclesia cathedrali Sanctae et Individuae Trinitatis Gloucestrensis predictae fundatum, ac fecit se partem pro eodem, et ex parte eiusdem venerabilis viri prefato prebendario ecclesiae cathedralis antedictae presentavit literas mandatorias reverendi in Christo patris et domini, Domini Godfridi, providentia divina Gloucestrensis episcopi, gerentes datas vicesimo quinto die mensis Junii ultimo preterito et eius consecrationis anno decimo, decano et capitulo ecclesiae cathedralis predictae directas, per quas mandatum fuit decano et capitulo supranominatis ad inducendum sive induci faciendum venerabili viro archidiacono ordinato predicto sive suo legitimo procuratore in realem actualem et corporalem possessionem dicti archidiaconatus et dignitatis archidiaconalis et ad assignandum sive assignari faciendum ei sive procuratori legitimo stallum in choro ac locum et vocem in capitulo prout moris est. Ac insuper dictus Jacobus Clent ex parte dicti domini archidiaconi ordinati exhibuit supranominato prebendario literas quasdam procuratorias a prefato venerabili viro Hugone Robinson, sacrae theologiae professore, archidiacono ordinato et constituto ut supra, per quas discretum virum Magistrum Johannem Allebond,[1] clericum, in artibus magistrum, suum verum certum et legitimum procuratorem nominavit, fecit et constituit, pro se ac vice et nomine suis stallum in choro ac locum et vocem in capitulo eidem archidiacono consuetam sibi assignari petendi et obtinendi nec non realem corporalem et actualem possessionem dicti archidiaconatus et dignitatis archidiaconalis vindicandi et adipiscendi omniaque et singula alia faciendi et expediendi quae dictus constitutus facere posset si personaliter interesset, prout per easdem literas procuratorias gerentes datas ultimo die Junii 1634 plenius liquet et apparet. Quas literas procuratorias dictus Magister Alleband debite recepit ac onus earundem in se acceptavit. Postea vero eodem die prefatus Johannes English, sacrae theologiae professor, prebendarius ecclesiae cathedralis Gloucestriae predictae, omni cum solemnitate qua in hac parte fieri potuerit, prefatum

---

[1] For Allibond, below, p. 161.

Johannem Allebond ad stallum in choro ecclesiae cathedralis antedictae hactenus eidem archidiacono ab antiquo solitum, consuetum et competentem attulit, eumque in realem, actualem et corporalem possessionem eiusdem stalli et dignitatis archidiaconi predicti ibidem cum suis membris, iuribus et pertinentiis universis loco, vice et nomine pro prefato Hugone Robinson, archidiacono ut prefertur ordinato, installavit ac pacificam possessionem eorundem premissorum ei deliberavit. Et haec omnia facta fuerunt in presentia Jacobi Clent, generosi, Johannis Langly, in artibus magistri, Johannis [fo. 63] Grayle, in artibus baccalaurei, Richardi Marwood, dictae ecclesiae precentoris, Richardi Brodgate et Gulielmi Hulett, duorum minorum canonicorum dictae ecclesiae, aliorumque dictae ecclesiae ministrorum meique Anthonii Robinson, dictae ecclesiae registrarii &c.

    Ita testor Anth[ony] Robinson, registrarius.

119.   [*22 June 1634.*]

His Majestie's letter to the Bishopps of Gloucester prohibitinge the lettinge of leases for yeares into lives. Charles R. Right reverend father in God, right trustie and well beloved, we greete yow well. Wee have of late taken the state of our severall bishoprickes into our princely consideracion, that wee may be the better able to preserve that livelyhood which as yet is left unto them. Upon this deliberation wee find that of later times there hath not risen a greater inconveinenc then by turneinge leases of one & twentye yeares into lives, for by that meanes the present bishop puts a greate fine into his owne purse to enriche himselfe his wife & children, and leaves all the succeedinge bishopps, of what deserts soever to us & the Church, destitute of that growinge meanes which els would come in to helpe them. By which course, should it continue, scarce any bishop would be able to live & keepe house accordinge to his place & callinge. Wee know the statute makes it alike lawfull for a bishop to lett his lease for one & twentye yeares or three lives, but time & experience have made it apparant that there is a greate deale of difference between them, especially in church leases where men are comonly in greate yeares before they come to those places. These are therefore to will & commaund yow, upon perill of our uttermost displeasure & what shall followe thereon, that notwithstandinge any statute or any other pretence whatsoever you presume not to lett any lease belonginge to your bishopricke into lives which is not in lives allreadye, and further that where any fayre opportunity is offered you, if any such be, you fayle not to reduce such as are in lives into yeares. And wee doe likewise will & require that these our royall letters may remaine upon record both with your owne register & with the register of the deane & chapter of your cathedrall church, & that by them notice be given to all your successors respectively (whome wee will that these letters shall concerne as much as yourselfe) that they presume not to breake any of these our comaunds in the least manner, as both yow & they will answere it att your & theire uttermost perills. Given under our signett at our manor of Greeneweitche the two & twentyth day of June in the tenth yeare of our raigne.

    To the right reverend father in God, our right trustie &
    wellbeloved Godfry, lord bishopp of Gloucester, & to the
    bishopp of that sea that hereafter for the time shalbe.

120.   [*fo. 63v.*]   Saturday 25 October 1634.   Chapter House.
(Accepted Frewen, S.T.P., dean; William Leo, S.T.P.; John Wood, S.T.B.; John English, S.T.P.)

Electio officiariorum. [*Election of officers. The dean and the aforenamed prebendaries elected John Wood as subdean and William Leo as receiver and treasurer. As in* **6**, *above, replacing* capitulum *with* prebendarii prenominati.]

Electio precentoris. [*Election of the precentor. The dean chose Richard Marwood. As in* **116**, *above, with* eiusdem *replaced by* dictae.] Eodem die, loco et anno [*etc.*].

Eodem die.

Admissio hypodidascali. [*Admission of the assistant schoolmaster. John Grayle, B.A.,*[1] *who had been chosen by the dean, was admitted by the dean after he had taken the oath on the gospels, touched by him.*] Quibus die, loco et anno Johannes Grayle, in artibus baccalaureus [*etc., as in* **50**, *above*].

Eodem die.

Order for the disposall of offeringes. Quibus die, loco et anno, yt was by Mr. Deane and the chapter aforesayd ordered and decreed that the mony for the offeringes, usually collected att all communions, shall be presently collected and there presently distributed to such only of the quire as shall be there present and then receave the communion.

121.   [*fo. 64*]   28 October 1634.

Order for the confirmation of a lease from the Bishoppricke. Whereas the right reverend father in God, Godfry, lord bishoppe of Gloucester, hath specified by his letter that he is minded for the benefitt of succession and profitt of his successors, bishopps of Gloucester, to make a concurrent lease to diverse persons of creditt therein trusted of diverse portions of tythes, parcell of the possessions of the sayd bishopprick, and hath made his request to us, the deane and chapter of this church, to give our consentes for the confirmation thereof accordingly, and to cause an act to be entred in this our chapter-booke for expressinge of our consents to the sayd confirmation, in case any of us should be absent at the time of the tender of any such lease unto us to be confirmed, we the sayd deane and chapter of this church, whose names are subscribed, being willinge (as much as in us lyeth) to promote the good intentions of the sayd reverend father, doe not only give our voices and free consents to the sayd confirmation, butt allsoe doe order and decree that at such time as any such lease or graunt shall be tendered to be confirmed yt shall be lawfull for the prebend or prebendaryes then att home to take the keyes of those that shall have them in keepinge and to open the chest, and take out our chapter-seale, and affix the same to such lease or demise of the sayd tythes soe tendered, and we shall allow and acknowledge the same as our act and deede. And I, Accepted Frewen, doctor in divinity and deane of the sayd church, by virtue of the severall proxies of Dr. lles, Mr.

---

[1] For Grayle, below, p. 163.

Palmer and Dr. Sheldon to me directed under theyr severall handes and seales, doe give theyr severall voices and consents to the sayd confirmation soe to be passed as aforesayd.

A. Frewen, deane; Johannes English.

122.   12 November 1634.   Chapter House.
(John English, S.T.P.)

Iuramentum Archidiaconi. [*The oath of the archdeacon. Hugh Robinson, S.T.P., recently installed in the archdeaconry of Gloucester through John Allibond, his proxy, took the bodily oath on the gospels, touched and kissed by him, to renounce the bishop of Rome and to acknowledge the king as head of the church.*] Quibus die, loco et anno venerabilis vir Hugo Robinson sacrae theologiae professor, qui in archidiaconatum sive dignitatem archidiaconalem Gloucestrensis per Johannem Allebond suum legitimum procuratorem nuper installatus fuit sacramentum prestitit corporale ad sacrosancta dei evangelia per eum tacta et deosculata de renuntiando Romano episcopo et de agnoscendo serenissimum dominum nostrum Carolum Angliae &c. regem &c. supremum caput &c. fidei defensorem &c.

123.   [*fo. 64v.*]   [*22 June 1634. The letter below, apart from being addressed to the dean and chapter rather than to the bishop, differs little in its first two-thirds from that in* **119**, *above.*]

His Majestie's letter prohibitinge the lettinge of yeares into lives. Charles R. Trusty and welbeloved, wee greete yow well. We have lately taken the state of our cathedrall & collegiate churches into our princely consideracion, that we may be the better able to preserve that livelyhood which as yet is left unto them. Upon this deliberation wee finde that of later times there hath not risen a greater inconvenience then by turninge leases of one and twenty yeares into lives, for by that meanes the present deane and chapter putt greate fynes into theire purses to inrich themselves, theire wives and children, and leave theire successors, of what desert soever to us and the Church, destitute of that growinge meanes which els would come in to helpe them. By which course, should it continue, scarce anie of them could be able to live and keepe house according to theire place and callinge. We know the statute makes it alike lawfull for a deane and chapter to lett their leases for the terme of one & twenty yeares or three lives, but time and experience have made it apparent that there is a greate deale of difference betweene them, especially in church leases, where men are comonly in yeares before they come to those places. These are therefore to will and commaund you, upon perill of our utmost displeasure and what shall follow thereon, that notwithstandinge anie statute or anie other pretence whatsoever yow presume not to let anie lease belonginge to your church in lives that is not lives allready, and further where anie faire oppertunity is offered yow, if anie such be, yow faile not to reduce such as are in lives into yeares. And wee doe likewise will and require that these our letters may remaine upon record in your owne register booke and in the registry of the lord bishopp of that diocess, that he may take notice of these our commands unto yow, and give us and our royall successors knowledge if you presume in anie sorte to disobey them. And further whereas in our late instructions we have commanded all our bishopps respectively not to lett anie lease after we have named anie of them to a better bishoprick, but did not in those instructions name the deanes whoe yet were intended by us, these are therefore to declare unto yow that noe deane shall presume to renew anie lease, either in lives or yeares, after such time as wee have nominated him either to a better deanery or a bishoprick, having observed that at such times of remove many men care not what or how they lett, to the preiudice of the Church and their successors. And this is [*fo.* 65] our[1] expresse command to yow, your chapter and your successors, which in anie case we require both yow and them strictly to observe, upon paine of our high displeasure, and as yow and they will answeare the contrary at your & their utmost perills. Given under our signet at our mannor of Greenewich the two and twentith day of June in the tenth yeare of our raigne.

> To our trusty and welbeloved the deane and
> chapter of our cathedrall church of Gloucester
> and to the deane and chapter of that
> church that hereafter for the time shalbe.

This letter above-written was shewed to the right reverend father in God, Godfry, lord bishoppe of Gloucester, and by his lordshipp read over in the presence of Dr. Frewen, now deane of this church, the 26th day of October 1634 att his lordshipp's howse called the Winyard[2] neare Glocester, and afterwardes the sayd letter was sent to Mr. Jones, register to the sayd bishoppe,[3] to register the same in the registry of the sayd lord bishoppe, who gave direction to one of his clerkes to register the same according as is hereby required.

> Ita testor Anth[ony] Robinson, decano et capitulo registrarius.

124.   3 November 1635.   Deanery.

Admissio archididascali. [*Admission of the schoolmaster. Thomas Widdowes, M.A.,*[4] *was admitted by the dean to the place of master of the free school.*[5] *In many respects the form is as in* **9**, *above, with the addition of the statement that Widdowes was admitted in the presence of the prebendaries.*] Quibus die, loco et anno Thomas Widdowes, artium magister, admissus fuit per dominum decanum in locum archididascali liberae scholae infra collegium vel ecclesiam cathedralem Gloucestriae, prius subscribens articulis tribus in ea parte requisitis ac prestito prius per eum iuramento de observandis statutis et ordinationibus dictae ecclesiae et suscepto simul iuramento allegeantiae Regi Carolo &c. In presentia praebendariorum dictae ecclesiae &c.

> A. Frewen, deane.

---

[1] The word 'our' is also a catchword at the foot of fo. 64v.

[2] The Vineyard at Over, about a mile due west of Gloucester, formerly belonging to the abbot of Gloucester, was one of the bishop's two houses, the other being the palace in the cathedral precinct. The Vineyard was ransacked by the Parliament's soldiers in 1642, and became a house 'whereof nothinge remaines but a few ruinous stone walls.'

[3] The reference to Mr. Jones as the bishop's registrar is puzzling. John Jones, who had been registrar to eight successive bishops, died in 1630 (below, p. 166), and Robinson surely knew that he was no longer alive.

[4] For Widdowes, below, p. 170.

[5] In the Act Book it is called the free school only here and in **9**, above.

125. [*fo. 65v.*]   Saturday 7 November 1635.   Chapter House.
(Accepted Frewen, S.T.P., dean; William Leo, S.T.P.; Thomas Iles, S.T.P.; John English, S.T.P.)

Electio officiariorum. [*Election of officers. The dean and the aforenamed prebendaries elected George Palmer as subdean and Thomas Iles as receiver and treasurer. As in* **6**, *above, replacing* capitulum *with* prebendarii prenominati.]

Electio precentoris. [*Election of the precentor. The dean chose Richard Marwood. As in* **116**, *above.*] Eodem die, loco et anno [*etc.*].

126.   7 November 1635.[1]   Chapter House.
(Accepted Frewen, S.T.P., dean; William Leo; Thomas Iles; John English, S.T.P.)

An act for the settlinge of the Chapter-Clerke's lodginges. Quibus die et anno, whereas the right honourable & most reverend father in God, William, lord arch-bishopp of Canterbury[2] his grace, by his grace's letter, bearinge date the sixteenth day of October last, directed to the above-named Dr. Frewen, deane of this church, and by him this day read in opne chapter, did by his grace's said letter signifye that the lodgings belonginge to the chapter-clerkes of this church had bin iniuriously detayned from Mr. Robinson, the now chapter-clerke, by Mr. Aisgill, heretofore a prebend of this church, and his successors in the said prebende, and therefore required that the said lodgings might be forthwith restored to the said Mr. Robinson, and the same roomes or lodgings for ever to remaine and be annexed to the [*fo. 66*] said office of chapter-clerke, for the safe keepinge of the colledge evidences & ledger bookes within the said church, and allsoe his grace therby appointed that the said Mr. Robinson should deliver upp to be cancelled a lease, heretofore graunted unto him by the deane and chapter of this church, of parte of the said roomes or lodgings, and his grace by his said letter further declared that a chapter act should be made, and enrolled in the chapter-booke, for the settlinge & investing the propriety of the said roomes & lodgings in the present & succeedinge chapter-clerkes of this church for ever & annexinge the same to the said office for ever, addinge moreover in his grace's said letter that if the said act should need any further or other confirmacion, or should in any sorte be impeached, his grace would be ready to give any other or further graunt or confirmacion for the strengthninge or confirminge the said act, as in the said letter is more fully declared, in obedience unto his grace's commaund soe signified, and for the full accomplishment thereof in a businesse soe behoovefull for this church, Mr. Deane & the prebendaries above-named, together with Dr. Iles (who heretofore pretended interest to the same lodgings),[3] repaired thither & tooke vew of the same, & required William Coxe, the

---

[1] Although the record of this meeting bears the same date as the previous entry, it appears to be a completely separate entry, and is in a different (very bold) hand.

[2] William Laud, formerly dean of Gloucester.

[3] Dr. Iles's prebendal house, later no. 14 College Green, was next to St. Mary's Gate, in the upper part of which were the rooms in question.

tenant in the same lodgings, to provide other where for himselfe speedyly, in regard the said lodgings were foorthwith to be restored to the said Mr. Robinson. And imediately after Mr. Deane with the prebendaryes above named (the said Dr. Iles allsoe with them) repaired to the chapter house above-named, & there being sate the said Mr. Robinson did, accordinge to his grace's comaund & in performance of what was required on his parte, deliver upp the lease of the same lodgings into the hands of Mr. Deane, who accepted thereof & cancelled the same. And then the said Mr. Deane & the prebendaries above-named in full chapter did order, declare & decree that the same lodgings, roomes & chambers over the west gate of this church, with all wayes passages and entrances with other th-appurtenancs aunciently belonginge to the chapter-clerkes of this church, should remaine (and accordinge to the primary institution & auncient course) for ever be annexed to the said office of chapter-clerk, to be used and imployed by the chapter-clerkes for the time beinge for the expeditinge and dispach of the businesse of the church and for the safe keepinge of the records evidences & ledger-bookes of the same. All which was donne, in the presence and with the allowance and consent of Dr. Iles, who willingly submitted to his said grace's order & commaund therein. And it was then likewise ordered that this present order & decree shall for the more full establishment thereof be recorded & enrolled in the chapter-booke and subscribed with the hands of the deane & prebendaries of this church, and that a true transcript of this act shall remaine with Mr. Robinson, our present [*fo. 66v.*] chapter-clerke, for the use of himselfe & his successors in the said office, as evidence for the finall settlinge of the controversy soe longe dependinge in the said matter.

  A. Frewen, deane; William Leo; John English;
  John Wood; Gilbert Sheldon; Geo. Palmer.[1]

  Eodem die.

Order for Unde[r]tenants. Quibus die et anno, yt is by Mr. Deane & the chapter present ordered & decreed, that noe petty-cannon, lay singingeman nor any other member of this foundacion, havinge any houses, roomes or lodgings belonginge to their said severall places within the precincts of this church shall nott sett or lett, take or receave into his or their houses or lodgings, in whole or in parte, any person or persons whatsoever to dwell, soiorne or inhabitt, without the especiall license allowance & consent of Mr. Deane of this church for the time beinge first had & obtayned.

  A. Frewen, deane; Geo[rgius] Palmer, subdec[anus]; W[illia]m Leo;
  Johannes English.

  Eodem die.

Order for the absence of the curates from the church service. Quibus die et anno, whereas the service of this church is very much neglected by those who have cures elswhere, under pretence of their service in the said cures, yt is therefore by especiall direction from my lord of Canterbury his grace ordered & decreed that such of the petty-cannons & lay-singingemen of this church as have cures in the citty or elswhere shall soe

---

[1] Although Thomas Iles is named at the beginning of the entry as being present at the chapter meeting he did not sign his name, while the signatures of John Wood, Gilbert Sheldon and George Palmer, who were not named as present, are written alongside the first three as though added later.

order & appoint their times & howres for divine prayers, burialls, weddings, christnings & other ministeriall dueties in their said severall cures that they nor any of them doe by reason thereof absent themselves from the prayers of this church att the times & howres appointed therefore, on payne that every of them shall forfeitt for every such default or neglect one penny to be deducted out of his wages.

A. Frewen, deane; W[illia]m Leo; Johannes English; Georgius Palmer.

127. [*fo. 67*]   12 November 1635.

Admissio choristae. [*Admission of a chorister. Thomas Barber was admitted by the dean in the place of William Dobbs.*] Quibus die et anno Thomas Barber admissus fuit per venerabilem decanum chorista in loco Willelmi Dobbes.

A. Frewen, deane.

128.   13 November 1635.   Deanery.

Admissio hypodidascali. [*Admission of the assistant schoolmaster. Christopher Prior, B.A.,[1] who had been chosen by the dean, was admitted by the dean after he had taken the oath on the gospels, touched by him.*] Quibus die et anno, Christopherus Prior in artibus baccalaureus [*etc., as in* **50**, *above, omitting the words* 'infra collegium ecclesie cathedralis Gloucestriae'].

A. Frewen, deane.

Eodem die.

A graunt of tythes. A graunt is made to Lawrence Willsheir, gent., duringe pleasure, of the tythes of corne & hey of Addams close, contayninge one acre & a halfe or thereabout, & the tythe of Mill meade, contayninge two acres or thereabouts, & the tythe of Penks, contayninge one quarter of an acre, & the tythe of two orchards, contayninge halfe an acre or thereabouts, the tythe of the Foreboords by the brooke side, all belonginge to the said Lawrence Willsheir's mill lyinge in the parish of St. Marye's,[2] payinge yearely at Michaellmas only three shillings fower pence currant mony.

A. Frewen, deane; Geo[rgius] Palmer, subdecanus; W[illia]m Leo;
Johannes English.

Eodem die.

Admissio choristae. [*Admission of a chorister. John Martin was admitted by the dean in the place of Richard Longe.*] Quibus die et anno Johannes Martin admissus fuit per venerabilem decanum chorista in loco Richardi Longe.

A. Frewen, deane.

---

[1] For Prior, below, p. 168.
[2] i.e. the parish of St. Mary de Lode in the city of Gloucester.

129.   [*fo. 67v.*]   10 February 1635/6.   Chapter House.
(John English, S.T.P.)

Admissio hypodidascali. [*Admission of the assistant schoolmaster. William Collins, B.A.,*[1]
who had been chosen by the dean, was admitted by Dr. English after he had taken the
oath on the gospels, touched by him.] Quibus die, loco et anno Gulielmus Collins in
artibus baccalaureus [*etc., as in* **50**, *above*].

130.   20 June 1636.   Chapter House.
(John Wood, S.T.B.)

Expulsion of a chorister. Quibus die et anno, uppon the receipt of certayne orders[2]
inioyned by the most reverend father in God, William, lord archbishopp of Canterbury his
grace, primate of all England & metropolitane, to be observed by the deane & chapter &
others of the cathedrall church of Gloucester, dated at Lambeth the twentith day of
February last past, yt is amongst other the ordinances thereby ordered that Thomas Longe
& Richard Longe, two of the choristers of this church, beinge presented for incorrigib[l]e
boyes, should forthwith be remooved from theire places, which said Richard Longe,
before the makinge of the said ordenances, was by Mr. Deane himselfe remooved from
his place of chorister within this church. And whereas Mr. Deane by his letter, dated the
twelfth day of this instant June, hath by his letter desired that accordinge to the said
ordinance the said Thomas Longe should be forthwith dismissed the church, in obedience
to the said ordinance & in performance of the request of Mr. Deane yt is by the
abovenamed Mr. Wood prebendary of the said church ordered & decreed that the said
Thomas Longe be from henceforth remooved & dismissed from his place of a chorister
within this church & all the proffitts & commodities thereto appertayninge.
        John Wood.

131.   28 July 1636.   Chapter House.
(Gilbert Sheldon, S.T.P.; John English, S.T.P.)

Orders from my Lo*[*rd*] *of Canterbury his Grace. Quibus die et anno, yt was ordered and
decreed that the orders and iniunctions receaved from my lord of Canterbury his grace,
and this day in opne chapter declared and published, should (according to his grace's
commaund) be registred. And it is likewise ordered that [*fo. 68*] the originall yt selfe
under his grace's hand and seale should be layd upp with other the records and evidences
of this church.
        Gilbert Sheldon; John English.

---

[1] Collins matriculated 2 Dec. 1631 at Exeter College, Oxford, aged 17, B.A. 1634.
[2] The 'certayne orders', entered as **132**, below, were the result of Laud's metropolitical visitation
in the summer of 1635. The archbishop seems to have been keeping a close eye on happenings at
the cathedral where he had been dean until fifteen years earlier.

132.   *[20 February 1635/6.]*

Orders inioyned by the most Reverend Father in God, William, Lord Archbishopp of Canterbury his Grace, Primate of all England and Metropolitane, to be observed by the Deane and Chapter and others of the Cathedrall Church of Gloucester, made uppon their answeres unto the Articles of Inquiry given them in chardge in his Grace's Metropoliticall Visitacion dependinge in the dioces of Gloucester Anno Domini 1635.

1. Inprimis. That the church evidences and muniments shall not be kept abroade in the citty or elsewhere in any particular or private man's hands, but that they shalbe kept in some private roome within the limitts of the church, and particularly in the roome which anciently was assigned unto them and was of late deteyned by Mr. Aisgill as a parte of his prebendall lodgings, and the chapter clerke by consent of the deane and chapter shall have a key to that roome and make a catalouge of all those evidences that come to his handes, together with a repertorie of the matters therein conteyned for the use of the deane and chapter aforesaid.

2. Item. That none of those who preach in your cathedrall church, eyther in their turnes or otherwise att any other time, doe in their prayers before their sermons omitt any one particular commandes in the five and fiftieth constitucion of the later canons published in anno domini 1604 mencioned in the twelveth article of inquirie ministred unto yow in our said visitacion.

3. Item. That noe place or office belonginge to your church of what sorte or on what condicion soever shall att any time hereafter be graunted in revercion.

4. Item. That those of the choristers and other ministers of your church who are disorderly, unruly or willfully negligent in performance of their severall dutyes, & doe not after wholsome admonicion or correction reforme their lives & conforme their manners, be expelled their places, that noe unseemlynes or disorder may from henceforth any way offend your church. And namely that Thomas Longe and Richard Longe, two of your choristers, who are presented for incorrigible boyes, be forthwith removed from their places or stations in your church, and others chosen in their roomes.

5. Item. That your petty-cannons and singingmen have all right done unto them concerninge their howses, whereof they make complaynt unto us in their answeres, that they have receaved butt hard measure; and therefore we require an accompt from yow touchinge the same, and that yow scearch your registrie for an act concerninge those howses made by me when I was deane of your church. And if yow find that any such was made,[1] to transcribe it & with the aforesaid accompt to signifie how it hath bin since observed, that as we shall see cause we may take further order for them.

6. Item. That yow keepe your church and churchyard from all manner of prophanacion and suffer noe encrochment to be made thereon, and if any such be, by howses there allready built or by dung miskins or any other meanes, to certifie unto us the manner of the offence & the names of the offenders, that, as is fitt, we may provide a remedy for restitucion thereof unto the former consecrated uses.

---

[1] No such act seems to have been entered in the Act Book.

7. Item. That the almsmen and officers of your church who doe not daily frequent divine service in your church, havinge noe iust impediment to hinder [*fo. 68v.*] them, be taken notice of, and presented eyther to us or your ordinary, that they may receave condigne punishment for such their neglect, or att the least that his majesty may be informed in whose guift they are, to the end they may be better regulated hereafter.

8. Item. In regard it is his majestie's expresse pleasure that the bodyes of cathedrall churches should not be pestered with standinge seates, contrary to the course of cathedralls & the dignity of those goodly piles of building, we must & doe require yow that all standinge & fixt seates, aswell those where the mayors' & aldermen's wives use to sitt as others betweene the pillars, be taken downe & other moveable ones fitted into their roomes, according to such direcions as we gave to the deane by our late letters written to him. Butt the seate where the mayor & his bretheren used to sitt, as alsoe that where the deane & prebends used to sitt in sermon time, because to our owne knowledge they are without all blemish to the church & more convenient then they can any where else be placed, we doe hereby require that they be left standinge to the use aforesaid.

9. Item. We require that these our iniuncions be carefully registred & observed.

In wittnes hereof we have hereunto putt our archiepiscopall seale. Yeaven att our mannor of Lambeth the twentith day of February in the yeare of our Lord God (accordinge to the computation of the Church of England) one thousand six hundred thirty & five, and of our translation the third.

W. Cant[uariensis]; Willelmus Sherman, registrarius.

133.   28 September 1636.

Admissio choristae. [*Admission of a chorister. By the dean's mandate, Richard Elliotts was admitted by Dr. English in the place of Thomas Longe.*] Quibus die et anno per mandatum venerabilis decani huius ecclesiae Richardus Elliotts admissus fuit per dominum Doctorem English, prebendarium, chorista in loco Thoma Longe.

134.   10 November 1636.

A catalogue of the Evidences of the church. Quibus die et anno, Anthony Robinson, gent., chapter-clerke of this church, did present unto us the deane & chapter whose names are subscribed a cattalouge in parchment or repertorie of our evidences remayninge in the chapter-clerkes lodgings, according to the first order made by my lord arch-bishopp of Canterbury his grace above inrolled. And it is ordered that the said catalogue or repertorie shalbe layd upp in the greate chest in the vestry for the use of the church, which was presently donne accordingly.

A. Frewen, deane; William Leo; Tho[mas] Iles; Jo[hn] Wood;
Gilb[ert] Sheldon; John English.

135. [*fo. 69*]   Thursday 10 November 1636.   Chapter House.
(Accepted Frewen, S.T.P., dean; William Leo, S.T.P.; Thomas Iles, S.T.P.; John Wood, S.T.B.; Gilbert Sheldon, S.T.P.; John English, S.T.P.)

Electio officiariorum. [*The dean and the aforenamed prebendaries elected Gilbert Sheldon as subdean and John Wood as receiver and treasurer. As in* **6**, *above, replacing* capitulum *with* prebendarii prenominati.]

Electio precentoris. [*Election of the precentor. The dean chose Richard Marwood. As in* **116**, *above.*] Eodem die, loco et anno [*etc.*].

                              Eodem die.

Ordinance of the schole-master's increase of stipend.[1] Quibus die, loco et anno,[2] whereas Mr. Thomas Widdowes, master in artes & schoolemaster of the grammer schoole within this church, hath seince his admission to that place bin very diligent in his instrucion of the youthes under his chardge, aswell in their manners as learninge, to the greate good likinge of us the deane and chapter & the credditt of the said schoole, we doe therefore order and decree that the same wages & stipend formerly paid to Mr. Langly, his imediate predecessor in that place, shalbe continued and payd to him, and his first quarter to beginne and to be payd unto him att the feast of the birth of our Lord God next ensuinge.

136.   12 November 1636.
Abolition of the Cook's, Butler's & other places.[3] Quibus die et anno, wee the deane & chapter upon a petition exhibited by the quire to Sir Nathaniel Brent, his grace's vikar general, at the metropolitical visitation, and according to his grace's directions given therein, doe order & decree that the stipends of al such officers now not useful to that church, as cookes, butlers and others, when theire places shal become voyd, shal not be granted agayne to any other persons as formerlye but be imployed onlye to increase the[4] wages of the said quire-men, as the deane & chapter shal thinke fit to distribute it.

          A. Frewen, deane; Tho[mas] Iles; Gilb[ert] Sheldon.

137. [*fo. 69v.*]   27 January 1636/7.   Chapter House.
(John English, S.T.P.)

Confirmation of a lease of Camme Rectory. Quibus die et loco, by vertue of a proxie from the right worshipfull Accepted Frewen, doctor in divinity and deane of this church, under his hand and seale dated the eyghteenth day of this instant January 1636 and in the twelfth yeare of the raigne of our gratious soveraigne lord, Charles, by the grace of God kinge of England, Scotland, Fraunce and Ireland, defender of the fayth &c., directed to the above-named Dr. English, prebendary of this church, for the confirmacion of a lease

---

[1] The account book shows that while the headmaster and assistant master were regularly together paid £24 13*s*. 4*d*. a year, in some years the head master was given an increment of 13*s*. 4*d*.
[2] After the word 'anno' the rest of the entry and the whole of the next are in a different hand.
[3] The heading is written in a modern hand.
[4] MS. 'that', overwriting and correcting, wrongly, another word.

of the parsonage of Camme in the county of Gloucester, with the appurtenances thereto belonginge, graunted by the right reverend father in God, Godfry, lord bishopp of Gloucester, to Walter Woodward, Christopher Woodward and Richard Woodward and their assignes, bearinge date the twenty seventh day of December last past, the said Dr. English gave Mr. Deane's voice and consent for confirmacion of the said lease of the said parsonage of Camme, and alsoe by vertue of two severall proxyes, the one from Thomas Iles, doctor in divinity, the other from Gilbert Sheldon, doctor in divinity, both prebendaryes of this church, under their severall hands and seales, dated the said eyghteenth day of this instant January 1636 and likewise directed to the said Dr. English for the confirmacion of the said lease of the said parsonage of Camme, the said Dr. English gave the severall voices and consents of the said Dr. Iles and Dr. Sheldon to the confirmacion aforesaid to be made to them, the said Walter Woodward, Christopher Woodward and Richard Woodward. And the said Dr. English in person then alsoe gave his owne voyce and consent to the said confirmacion, & then alsoe decreed that the said confirmacion should be sealed with the seale of the deane and chapter of this church, which was then donne and performed accordingly.

138.   20 March 1636/7.   Chapter House.
(Accepted Frewen, S.T.P., dean.)

A presentacion to Greate Marlow vicaridge. Quibus die et loco, whereas the patronage & donacion of the vicaridge of Greate Marlow in the county of Buckingham and in the diocese of Lincolne is & of right belongeth to the deane & chapter of this church, and the same vicaridge is now becomme voyd by the late death of Anthony Wattson, clerke, last incumbent there, the above named Dr. Frewen, deane of this church, for preservinge the right of this church to the patronage of the said vicaridge of Greate Marlow did this day in open chapter give his voyce & full consent for a presentacion to be passed, made & sealed to John Lee, clerke, master in arts, to the said vicaridge. And the said Dr. Frewen, deane of this church, then exhibited and openly caused to be read severall proxyes under the severall hands and seales of Gilbert Sheldon, doctor in divinity, subdeane of this church, Thomas Iles, doctor in divinity, & John Wood, batchelor in divinity, all of them prebendaryes of this church, authorizinge him, the said Dr. Frewen, to the choice & nominacion of a vicar there to succeed the said Anthony Wattson, clerke, lately deceased, and all & every other thinge to doe & performe touchinge the said nominacion and eleccion, by vertue of [*fo. 70*] which said severall proxyes the said Dr. Frewen, deane of this church, did give the severall voices & full consents of them the said Dr. Sheldon, Dr. Iles & Mr. Wood to the passinge, makinge & sealinge of the said presentacion of the said vicaridge of Greate Marlow to the said John Lee, clerke, and did alsoe then order & decree that the said presentacion should be sealed with the seale of the deane & chapter of this church, which was then donne & performed accordingly.

139.   5 October 1637.
Admissio choristae. [*Admission of a chorister. By the dean's mandate, Peter Chambers was admitted by Dr. English in the place of Toby Greene.*] Quibus die et anno per mandatum venerabilis decani huius ecclesiae Petrus Chambers admissus fuit per dominum Doctorem English chorista in loco Tobiae Greene.

140.   Monday 13 November 1637.   Chapter House.
(Accepted Frewen, S.T.P., dean; William Leo, S.T.P.; John Wood, S.T.B.; Gilbert Sheldon, S.T.P.; John English, S.T.P.)

Electio officiariorum. [*Election of officers. The dean and the aforesaid prebendaries elected John English as subdean and Gilbert Sheldon as receiver and treasurer. As in* **6**, *above, replacing* capitulum *with* prebendarii prenominati.]

Electio precentoris. [*Election of the precentor. The dean chose Richard Marwood. As in* **116**, *above.*] Eodem die, loco et anno [*etc.*].

[*fo. 70v.*] ***Gulielmus Mason, supervisor operum, jurat.*** [*William Mason, surveyor of the works,*[1] *takes the oath. Mason, in the presence of the dean and the aforesaid prebendaries, took the oath, touching the gospels, that he would perform his said office devoutly and faithfully.*] Eodem die, loco et anno Gulielmus Mason, supervisor operum huius ecclesiae, in presentia decani et prebendariorum predictorum suscepit iuramentum, tactis sacrosanctis dei evangeliis, se sanctissime et fidelissime officium suum predictum esse observaturum &c.

141.   7 March 1637/8.   Chapter House.
(John English, S.T.P., subdean.)

Admissio hypodidascali. [*Admission of the assistant schoolmaster. Richard Lovell, BA.,*[2] *who had been chosen by the dean, was admitted by Dr. English, subdean, after he had taken the oath on the gospels, touched by him. The form differs from* **50**, *above, in the order of the words.*] Quibus die, loco et anno Richardus Lovell, in artibus baccalaureus, qui in locum hypodidascali infra collegium ecclesiae cathedralis Gloucestriae fuit electus per dominum decanum, admissus fuit per dominum Doctorem English, subdecanum, sumpto prius per eum iuramento[3] respective ad sacrosancta dei evangelia per eum tacta &c.

142.   7 April 1638.   Chapter House.
(John English, S.T.P., subdean.)

Confirmation of Portham lease. Quibus die et loco, by vertue of a proxie under the hand and seale of the right worshipfull Accepted Frewen, doctor in divinity and deane of this church, dated the 26th day of March 1638 and in the thirteenth yeare of the raigne of our gratious soveraigne lord, Charles, by the grace of God kinge of England, Scottland, Fraunce and Ireland, defender of the faith &c., directed to the above-named Dr. English, subdeane of this cathedrall church, for the confirmacion of two severall leases of the moyety of one halfe of a meadow called Portham, otherwise called Importham, scituate lyinge and beinge neare the citty of Gloucester in the county of the said citty of

---

[1] The office was later called clerk of works.
[2] For Lovell, below, p. 167.
[3] MS. 'iuramenta'; cf. above, p. 29 n. 2.

Gloucester and in the lordshipp of Maysemore there, for the tearme of three lives in each of the said severall leases, which severall leases are lately graunted by the right reverend father in God, Godfry, lord bishoppe of Gloucester, to James Wood of the cittie of Gloucester, clothier, and each of the said severall leases beareth date the thirtith day of March in the fowreteenth yeare of the raigne of our soveraigne lord Kinge Charles that now is and in the year of our Lord God 1638, the said Dr. English, subdeane, gave Mr. Deane's voice and consent for the confirmation of the said two severall leases, and his own voice and consent alsoe for the confirmation of the said two severall leases, and allsoe by vertue of severall proxies under the severall hands and seales of William Leo and Thomas Iles, doctors in divinity, John Wood and George Palmer, batchelors in divinity, and Gilbert Sheldon, doctor in divinity, all of them prebendaryes of the cathedrall church of Gloucester, [*fo. 71*] to the said Dr. English directed to the purpose aforesayd, the said Dr. English gave theire severall and respective voices and consents for the confirmacion of the said two severall leases, and then alsoe decreed that the two severall leases should be confirmed and the said confirmacions should be sealed with the seale of the deane and chapter of this church, which was donne and performed accordingly.

Eodem die, loco et anno.

Admissio laici cantatoris. [*Admission of a lay singer. John Cuttler, having been chosen by the dean, was admitted by Dr. English, subdean, and he took the oaths on the gospels, touched by him. The form differs in detail from* **12**, *above.*] Quibus die, loco et anno Johannes Cuttler, electus per dominum decanum,[1] admissus fuit per dominum Doctorem English, subdecanum, in locum unius laicorum cantatorum infra ecclesiam cathedralem Gloucestriae, qui quidem Johannes subiit iuramenta respective ad sacrosancta dei evangelia per eum tacta &c.

143.   17 November 1638.   Chapter House.
(John English. S.T.P., subdean.)

An act to demaund the rents of the mannors of Barnewood, Wootton & Crenham.[2] Quibus die et loco, by vertue of a proxie under the hand and seale of the right worshipfull Accepted Frewen, doctor in divinity and deane of this church, dated the sixth day of this instant November, directed to the above named Dr. English, subdeane of this cathedrall church, for the makinge & grauntinge of a letter or warrant of atturny to Anthony Robinson, gent., to aske, demaund and take all such rent and rents as are due and payable to the deane and chapter of Gloucester in and out of the mannors of Barnewood, Croneham and Wootton, in the county of Gloucester or in the county of the citty of Gloucester, upon any demise or lease thereof formerly made, and payable upon the feast day of St. Michaell the arch angell last past, according to the reservations in the said lease expressed, and upon failer [*sc.* failure] of payment of the said rent or rents beinge lawfully demaunded to reenter, and the same and every parte and parcell thereof to

---

[1] The words 'electus per dominum decanum' have been inserted above the line.
[2] The annual rent due from the manors of Barnwood, Wotton and Cranham was £79 19*s.* 2½*d.*

claime, reteine and keepe to the use and behoofe of us, the deane and chapter, and with the chapter seale the said warrant or letter of attorny to seale, and to doe and performe all other things concerninge the same, ratifyinge whatsoever the said John English shall doe in the premisses, by vertue whereof the said Dr. English, subdeane, gave Mr. Deane's voice and consent to the makinge grauntinge and sealinge of the said letter or warrant of attorny to the said Anthony Robinson, and likewise gave his owne voice and consent allsoe to the grauntinge and sealing of the said letter or warrant [*fo. 71v.*] of attorny. And allsoe by vertue of two severall proxies bearing date as aforesaid under the severall hands and seales of Thomas Iles, doctor in divinity, and Gilbert Sheldon, doctor in divinity, both of them prebendaries of this cathedrall church of Gloucester, to the said Dr. English directed, to the purpose aforesaid, the said Dr. English gave theire severall and respective voices and consents to the makinge grauntinge and sealinge of the said letter or warrant of attorny to the said Anthony Robinson. And then allsoe decreed that the said letter or warrant of attorny should be sealed with the seale of the deane and chapter of this church, which was soe donne and performed accordingly.

Eodem die, loco et anno.

Admissio choristarum. [*Admission of choristers. By the dean's mandate, John Painter and John Tyler were admitted by Dr. English, subdean, in the places of William Collins and John Brodgate.*] Quibus die, loco et anno per mandatum venerabilis decani huius ecclesiae Johannes Painter et Johannes Tyler admissi erant per dominum Doctorem English, subdecanum, in locis duarum choristarum huius ecclesiae cathedralis Gloucestriae in locis Willelmi Collins et Johannis Brodgate.

144.   29 November 1638.   Chapter House.
(Accepted Frewen, S.T.P., dean; John English, subdean; William Leo, S.T.P.; George Palmer, S.T.B.; Gilbert Sheldon, S.T.P.)

For takinge in straingers into howses. Quibus die, loco et anno, whereas by a former act made in chapter[1] yt was decreed and ordered that noe petty-cannon, lay singingman nor any other member of this foundacion should take into theyr howses any person to dwell, soiurne or inhabitt without the consent of Mr. Deane feirst had and obteyned, in respect of divers inconveniences hapyninge by the breach of the sayd order yt is now decreed and further ordered that the thresurer for the time beinge, upon breach of the sayd order, shall forbeare to pay such person or persons his or theyr wages or stipend untill they bringe good testimony that they have putt away such tenant or inmate out of theyr howses.

[*fo. 72*]   Eodem die.

Electio officiariorum. [*Election of officers. The dean and the aforenamed prebendaries elected William Loe as subdean and George Palmer as receiver and treasurer. The form differs slightly from that in* **6**, *above.*] Congregatis venerabilibus viris preantea nominatis et ad eleccionem officiariorum pro anno futuro iuxta morem antiquum solempniter procedentibus [*MS.* procedentes], idem decanus et prebendarii prenominati elegerunt hos officiarios, vizt. Dominum Gulielmum Leo, sacrae theologiae professorem,

---

[1] Cf. **126** (p. 73), above.

in sub-decanum et Magistrum Georgium Palmer, sacrae theologiae baccalaureum, in receptorem et thesaurarium [*etc. as in* **6**, *above*].

Electio precentoris. [*Election of the precentor. The dean chose Richard Marwood. As in* **116**, *above.*] Eodem die, loco et anno [*etc.*].

Eodem die.

Electio minoris canonici. [*Election, more correctly admission, of a minor canon. John Cuttler*,[1] *clerk, was admitted and assigned* (*a place*) *by the dean, and he took the oaths on the gospels, touched by him. The form is as in* **74**, *above.*] Quibus die, loco et anno Johannes Cuttler, clericus, admissus et assignatus erat per venerabilem decanum in locum unius minorum canonicorum infra ecclesiam cathedralem Gloucestriae, qui quidem Johannes subiit iuramenta respective ad sacrosancta dei evangelia per eum tacta &c.

Eodem die.

Admissio organistae. [*Admission of the organist. Barkeley Wrench*[2] *was admitted by the dean as organist and instructor of the choristers in place of Philip Hosier, deceased, and was installed in the choir by the precentor and took the oaths on the gospels, touched by him. The form is as in* **28**, *above.*] Quibus die, loco et anno Barkeleius Wrench admissus erat per venerabilem decanum in locum organistae et choristarum instructoris huius ecclesiae, in loco Philippi Hosyer, nuper defuncti, et installatus in choro per cantatorem qui quidem Barkeleius subiit iuramenta respective ad sacrosancta dei evangelia per eum tacta &c.

145.   [*fo. 72v.*]   Tuesday 2 April 1639.   Chapter House.
(George Palmer; Dr. English.)

Admissio eleemozynarii. [*Admission of an almsman. John Sandy*[3] *appeared and sought to be admitted as an almsman in place of John March lately deceased, by virtue of letters patent granted to him and addressed to the dean and chapter, and registered at their registry, whereupon George Palmer, on the strength of the dean's mandate, admitted John Sandy, he having first taken the almsman's oath, to receive the emoluments of the office. The form is as in* **81**, *above, with the addition of the phrase in parentheses.*] Comparuit quidam Johannes Sandy et petiit admitti in locum eleemozynarii dictae ecclesiae in loco cuiusdam Johannis March, nuper defuncti, virtute literarum patentium sibi in ea parte concessarum, decano et capitulo dictae ecclesiae directarum et apud registrarium eorundem decani et capituli registratarum, unde dictus venerabilis vir Georgius Palmer (vigore mandati venerabilis decani huius ecclesiae), prestito primitus per eundem Johannem Sandy iuramento ab eleemozynario prestando in eleemozynarium admisit, habere et percipere omnia proficua et emolumenta ad officium eleemozynarii spectantia.

---

[1] Evidently the John Cuttler who had been admitted as a lay singer on 7 April 1638: above, **142**. The accounts show that he was paid as a lay singer for the one year only.

[2] For Wrench, below, p. 171.

[3] Evidently not the John Sandy who was a minor canon 1610–41: cf. below, p. 168.

146. 21 May 1639. Chapter House.
(John Wood, S.T.B.)

Admissio hypodidascali. [*Admission of the assistant schoolmaster. William Elbridge, B.A.,*[1] *who had been chosen by the dean, was admitted by Mr. Wood, after he had taken the oath on the gospels, touched by him.*] Quibus die, loco et anno Gulielmus Elbridge, in artibus baccalaureus, [*etc., as in* **50**, *above*].

Eodem die.

Admissio laici cantatoris. [*Admission of a lay singer. Richard Brodgate,*[2] *having been chosen by the dean, was admitted by Mr. Wood in the place of John Merroe, deceased,*[3] *for which he took the oaths. The form is as in* **142**, *above, but records in whose place the new singer was admitted.*] Quibus die, loco et anno Richardus Brodgate electus per dominum decanum admissus fuit per Magistrum Wood in locum unius laicorum cantatorum infra ecclesiam cathedralem Gloucestriae in loco Johannis Mero defuncti, qui quidem Richardus subiit iuramenta respective ad sacrosancta dei evangelia per eum tacta &c.

Eodem die.

Admissio choristae. [*Admission of a chorister. By the dean's mandate, Thomas Merrett was admitted by Mr. Wood in the place of John Hodshon.*] Quibus die, loco et anno per mandatum venerabilis decani huius ecclesiae Thomas Merrett admissus erat per Magistrum Wood chorista in loco Johannis Hodshon.

147. [*fo. 73*] 11 June 1639. Chapter House.
(John English, S.T.P.)

Admissio minoris canonici. [*Admission of a minor canon. William Hosier, clerk, B.A.,*[4] *who had been chosen by the dean, was admitted by Dr. English, having first taken the oath on the gospels, touched by him.*] Quibus die, loco et anno Gulielmus Hosyer, clericus, in artibus baccalaureus, qui in locum unius minorum canonicorum infra ecclesiam cathedralem Gloucestriae fuit electus per dominum decanum, admissus fuit per dominum Doctorem English, sumpto prius per eum iuramento[5] respective ad sacrosancta dei evangelia per eum tacta &c.

148. 6 September 1639. Chapter House.
(John English, S.T.P.)

Confirmation of the lease of Bruckthruppe. Quibus die, loco et anno, by vertue of a proxie under the hand and seale of the right worshipfull Accepted Frewen, doctor in divinity and deane of this church, dated the twenty seaventh day of August last past,

---

[1] For Elbridge, below, p. 163.
[2] For Brodgate, below, p. 162.
[3] Merroe died on 23 March 1636 and was buried in the lady chapel beside his wife Elizabeth, his epitaph including the couplet, 'I once did sing in this, Now in the choir of bliss.'
[4] For Hosier, below, p. 165.
[5] MS. 'iuramenta'; cf. above, p. 29 n. 2.

directed to the above named Dr. English, prebendary of this church, for the confirmacion of a lease of the scite and demesne of the mannor of Brookthropp, in the county of the citty of Gloucester, with the appurtenances thereto belonging, graunted by the right reverend father in God, Godfry, lord bishopp of Gloucester, to Silvanus Wood of Brookthropp aforesaid, esquire, and his assignes, bearing date the twentyth day of August last, the said Dr. English gave Mr. Deane's voice and consent for the confirmacion of the said lease. And alsoe by vertue of severall proxies under the severall handes and seales of Thomas Iles and Gilbert Sheldon, doctors in divinity and prebendes of the cathedrall church of Gloucester, directed[1] to the said Dr. English, gave their severall and respective voices and consents for the confirmacion of the said lease. And the said Dr. English in person then alsoe gave his owne voice and consent to the said confirmacion, and then alsoe decreed that the said confirmacion should bee sealed with the seale of the deane and chapter of this church, which was then donne and performed accordingly.

149. [*fo. 73v.*]   Thursday 14 November 1639.   Chapter House.
(Accepted Frewen, S.T.P., dean; William Leo, S.T.P., subdean; Thomas Iles, S.T.P.; George Palmer, S.T.B.; Gilbert Sheldon, S.T.P.; John English, S.T.P.)

Electio officiariorum. [*Election of officers. The dean and the aforenamed prebendaries elected Dr. Iles as subdean and Dr. John English as receiver and treasurer. As in* **6**, *above,* replacing capitulum *with* prebendarii prenominati.]

Electio precentoris. [*Election of the precentor. The dean chose Richard Marwood. As in* **116**, *above, with* eiusdem *at first replaced by* dictae, *which has been crossed out, with* eiusdem *restored.*] Eodem die, loco et anno [*etc.*].

                    Eodem die.

An increase of the organists stipend [*of*][2] ***£6 13s. 4d.*** Quibus die, loco et anno, yt was decreed and ordered by the deane and the prebendaryes above-named that upon the admittinge of an able and very sufficient organist, the place beinge now voyd, there shall be for his better maintenance an addition of six poundes thirteene shillinges and fowre pence yearely[3] to his former stipend of tenne poundes, to be payd him quarterly by the handes of the thresurers of this church for the tyme beinge, as the residue of former stipend hath bin accustomed to be payd.

150. [*fo. 74*]   19 February 1639/40.   Chapter House.
(John English, S.T.P.)

Admissio choristae. [*Admission of a chorister. By the dean's mandate, John Burruppe was admitted by Dr. English in the place of Robert Dobbs.*] Quibus die, loco et anno per mandatum venerabilis decani huius ecclesiae Johannes Burruppe admissus erat per dominum Doctorem English chorista in loco Roberti Dobbs.

---

[1] The words 'directed to the church aforesaid to the said Dr. English' have been inserted between the lines, the last five words repeating what was already in the MS.

[2] The word 'to' has been crossed out but not replaced, as necessary, by 'of' or 'by'.

[3] This word has been inserted above the line.

151.   Tuesday 10 March 1639/40, between nine and eleven a.m.

Chapter House.

(John English, S.T.P., treasurer.)

Admissio venerabilis viri Gilberti Osborne in tertiam prebendam. [*Admission of the venerable man Gilbert Osborne to the third prebend. On Tuesday 10 March 1639, before John English, S.T.P., treasurer and prebendary, between the ninth and the eleventh hour before noon in the chapter house, Gilbert Osborne, clerk, S.T.B., exhibited the king's letters patent, dated 15 February last past, granting him the prebend vacant by the death of John Wood, and the royal mandate for his admission and installation; Dr. English admitted him, as in* **37**, *above. All this was done in the presence of James Clent, Stephen Brice, notaries public, John Baylis, gent., Thomas Widdowes, M.A., Richard Marwood, precentor, William Hulett, minor canon, and other servants of the said church and of the writer, Anthony Robinson, registrar.*] Die Martis vizt. decimo die Martii anno domini 1639, coram venerabili viro Johanne English, sacrae theologiae professore, tunc thesaurario et prebendario ecclesiae cathedralis Gloucestriae, inter horas nonam et undecimam antemeridiem eiusdem diei, in domo capitulari dictae ecclesiae cathedralis venerabilis vir Gilbertus Osborne, clericus, sacrae theologiae bacchalaureus, exhibuit [*etc., as in* **107**, *above*].

[*fo. 74v.*]   Ita testor Anth[ony] Robinson, registrarius.

152.   2 April 1640.   Chapter House.

(Dr. English, S.T.P., treasurer.)

Choise of a clerke for the convocation. Quibus die et loco, by vertue of a proxie from Mr. Deane dated the 29th day of March last for the choice of a clerke for the convocation howse for the chapter of this church at this ensuinge parliament, the sayd Dr. English gave Mr. Deane's voice unto Dr. Gilbert Sheldon, a prebend of this church, for the sayd place. And likewise by vertue of a like proxie from Dr. Iles, subdeane of this church, dated the same day the sayd Dr. English gave his the sayd Dr. Iles his voice unto him the sayd Dr. Sheldon for the sayd place. And likewise the sayd Dr. English then present gave his owne voice unto him the sayd Dr. Sheldon for the sayd place. And the sayd Dr. English by vertue allsoe of a proxie from Mr. Gilbert Osborne, prebendarie of this church, bearinge date the last day of March last past, gave his the sayd Mr. Osborne's voice to the sayd Dr. Sheldon for the said place. By reason whereof the sayd Dr. Sheldon was elected and chosen clerke of the convocation to serve for the body of the chapter of this church. And yt was then alsoe decreed that an instrument for the performance thereof should be made under the chapter seale unto him the sayd Dr. Sheldon, the tenor whereof followeth in these wordes (vizt.), Pateat [*etc., as in* **64**, *above, with the correct cross-reference to fo. 32*].

153. [*fo. 75*]   Feast of St. Mark 25 April 1640.   Chapter House.

(John English, S.T.P.)

Admissio organistae. [*Admission of the organist. John Okeover,*[1] *who had been chosen by the dean as organist and instructor of the choristers, was admitted by Dr. English and*

---

[1] For Okeover, below, p. 168.

installed in the choir by the precentor, and took the oaths on the gospels, touched by him.] Quibus die, loco et anno Johannes Okeover, qui in locum organistae et choristarum instructoris huius ecclesiae fuit electus per dominum decanum, admissus fuit per dominum Doctorem English et installatus fuit in choro per cantatorem qui quidem Johannes Okeover subiit iuramenta respective ad sacrosancta dei evangelia per eum tacta &c.

154.   31 October 1640.   Chapter House.
(Thomas Iles, S.T.P., subdean; John English, S.T.P., treasurer.)

Choice of a clerke for the convocation. Quibus die et loco, by vertue of a proxie from Mr. Deane and Dr. Sheldon, a prebend of this church, dated the 26th day of this instant October, for the choice of a clerke for the convocation howse for the chapter of this church att this ensuinge parliament, the sayd Dr. Iles, subdeane, gave Mr. Deane's voice unto Mr. George Palmer, a prebend of this church, for the sayd place, and his owne voice allsoe. And likewise by vertue of the sayd proxie the sayd Dr. Iles gave his the sayd Dr. Sheldon's voice unto him the sayd Mr. Palmer for the sayd place. And likewise the sayd Dr. English, then allsoe present, gave his owne voice unto him the sayd Mr. Palmer for the sayd place. By reason whereof the sayd Mr. Palmer was elected and chosen clerke of the convocation to serve for the body of the chapter of this church. And yt was then allsoe decreed that an instrument for the performance thereof should be made under the chapter-seale unto him the sayd Mr. Palmer, the tenor whereof followeth in these wordes (vizt.) Pateat [*etc., as in* **64**, *above, with the correct cross-reference to fo. 32*].

155. [*fo. 75v.*]   Thursday 12 November 1640.   Chapter House.
(Accepted Frewen, S.T.P., dean; Thomas Iles, S.T.P., subdean; Gilbert Sheldon, S.T.P.; John English, S.T.P.; Gilbert Osborne, S.T.B.)

Electio officiariorum. [*Election of officers. The dean and the aforenamed prebendaries elected Dr. Sheldon as subdean and Gilbert Osborne as receiver and treasurer. As in* **6**, *above, replacing* capitulum *with* prebendarii prenominati.]

Electio precentoris. [*Election of the precentor. The dean chose Richard Marwood. As in* **116**, *above.*] Eodem die, loco et anno [*etc.*].

156.   18 November 1640.   Deanery.
(Thomas Iles, S.T.P.)

Admissio minoris Canonici. [*Admission of a minor canon. Peter Brooke, clerk, who had been chosen by the dean, was admitted by Dr. Iles, having first taken the oath on the gospels, touched by him.*] Quibus die, loco et anno Petrus Brooke, clericus, qui in locum minoris canonici huius ecclesiae fuit electus per dominum decanum, admissus fuit per dominum Doctorem Iles, sumpto prius per eum iuramento ad sacrosancta dei evangelia per eum tacta.

Eodem die.

Admissio laici Cantatoris. [*Admission of a lay singer. Robert Muddin, who had been chosen by the dean in the place of Peter Brooke, was admitted by Dr. Iles, after he had taken the oath on the gospels, touched by him.*] Quibus die, loco et anno Robertus Muddin, qui in locum unius laicorum [cantatorum][1] huius ecclesiae fuit electus per dominum decanum in loco Petri Brooke, admissus fuit per dominum Doctorem Iles, sumpto prius per eum iuramento ad sacrosancta dei evangelia per eum tacta &c.

157. [*fo. 76*]   Thursday 17 June 1641.   Chapter House.
(John English, S.T.P.; Gilbert Osborne.)

[*Admission of almsmen.*[2] *William Coxe and William Collins appeared and sought to be admitted in the places of John Grove and John Ward, lately deceased, by virtue of several letters patent granted to them and addressed to the dean and chapter, and registered at their registry, whereupon John English and Gilbert Osborne, with the dean's consent, admitted the same William Coxe and William Collins, they having first taken the almsman's oath, to have the emoluments belonging to the office.*] Comparuerunt Gulielmus Coxe et Gulielmus Collins et petierunt admitti in loca duorum eleemozynariorum dictae ecclesiae, in locis cuiusdam Johannis Grove et Johannis Ward nuper defuncti,[3] virtute seperatium literarum patentium ipsis in ea parte concessarum decano et capitulo dictae ecclesiae directarum et apud registrarium eorundem decani et capituli registratarum. Unde dicti venerabiles viri Johannes English et Gilbertus Osberne (cum consensu venerabilis decani huius ecclesiae), prestito primitus per eosdem Gulielmum Coxe et Gulielmum Collins iuramento ab eleemozynariis prestando, in eleemozynarios admiserunt, habere et percipere omnia proficua et emolumenta ad officia eleemozynariorum spectantia.

Eodem die.

Confirmation of Diocesan Registrar.[4] Quibus die, loco et anno, whereas the right reverend father in God, Godfry, lord bishoppe of Gloucester, specified his request to Mr. Deane & the chapter for the confirmation of the principall register's office of the diocese of Gloucester graunted by his lordshipp to Edward Goodman of Ruthin in the county of Denbigh, notary publick,[5] which patent beareth date the 29th day of May last past, unto which request of the said reverend father Dr. Frewen, deane of this church, gave his consent under his hand, and likewise Dr. Sheldon, now subdeane, & Dr. Iles, prebends of this churche, under their hands gave their severall consents to the confirmation of the said patent of the office of principall register as aforesaid to the said Mr. Goodman. And Dr. English and Mr. Osberne, then present, gave their voices & consents alsoe, & by virtue of the authority given to Mr. Osberne hee, the said Mr. Osberne, gave the severall voices

---

[1] The word 'cantatorum' is omitted.
[2] The MS. omits a heading.
[3] Correct grammar requires 'quorumdam . . . nuper defunctorum'; the MS. has 'cuiusdam . . . nuper defunct' '.
[4] The heading is written in a modern hand.
[5] Edward Goodman was presumably a relation of the bishop, who was born at Ruthin.

and consents of the said Dr. Frewen, deane, Dr. Sheldon, subdeane, & Dr. Iles, prebendaryes, in open chapter. And then alsoe the said Dr. Englishe and Mr. Osberne decreed that the said patent should be confirmed and the said confirmacion to bee sealed with the seale of the deane and chapter of this churche, which was donne and performed accordingly.

158. *[fo. 76v. blank except for]* **Electio officiariorum.**[1] *[Election of officers.]*

159. *[fo. 77]* **The King's Letters Patents to Dr. William Brough to be Deane of Gloucester.**[2] *[The king has granted to William Brough, S.T.P. and one of his chaplains in ordinary, the deanery of Gloucester, vacant by the promotion of Accepted Frewen, S.T.P., to the bishopric of Coventry and Lichfield, to hold for life with all its rights etc., commanding the bishop, chapter and prebendaries to admit him and to do whatever else is necessary. Dated at Oxford, 4 May 1644, by privy seal.]* Carolus, dei gracia Anglie, Scotie, Frauncie & Hibernie rex, fidei defensor &c., omnibus ad quos presentes litere pervenerint, salutem. Sciatis quod nos, de gracia nostra speciali ac ex certa scientia & mero motu nostris, dedimus & concessimus & ac per presentes pro nobis, heredibus & successoribus nostris damus & concedimus dilecto nobis in Christo Gulielmo Brough, sacre theologie professori & uni capellanorum nostrorum ordinariorum, decanatum ecclesie nostre cathedralis Gloucestriae, iam per promocionem Accepti Frewen, sacre theologie professoris, ultimi decani ibidem, ad episcopatum Coventrie et Lichenfeldie vacantem & ad nostram donacionem pleno iure spectantem, ac ipsum Gulielmum Brough decanum ecclesiae cathedralis predictae facimus, ordinamus & constituimus per presentes, habendum, gaudendum & tenendum decanatum predictum Gulielmo Brough durante vita sua naturali, cum omnibus et singulis juribus, jurisdiccionibus, libertatibus, privilegiis, titulis, quotidiem distribucionibus, dividentiis, excrescentiis, refeccionibus, mancionibus, domibus, edificiis, terris, tenementis, pratis, pastis, pasturis, hortis, pomariis, gardinis, clausuris, boscis, subboscis, redditibus, revencionibus, serviciis, communiis, aquis, stagnis, piscariis, piscacionibus ac omnibus & omnimodis aliis proficiis, allocacionibus, comoditatibus, advantagiis, emolumentis & hereditamentis quibuscunque ad dictum decanatum pertinentibus sive spectantibus vel qualitercunque annexis vel imposterum annexandis, in tam amplis modo & forma prout ultimus decanus ibidem vel aliquis alius decanus ecclesie cathedralis predicte eundem decanatum habens tenuit, habuit vel quovis fuit aut habere, tenere vel gaudere debuit. Mandamus ac per presentes pro nobis, heredibus [et] successoribus nostris firmiter iniungendo [et] percipiendo episcopo, capitulo, prebendariis & aliis quibuscunque potestatem in hac parte licentibus sufficiendis ad dictum decanatum ecclesie cathedralis predicte prefatum Gulielmum Brough admittat & admittant, ipsumque decanum ibidem rite & legitime instituat & instituant & investiri faciat & faciant, ceteraque omnia & singula que in hac

---

[1] The marginal heading is the only reference in the Act Book to an election of officers between 1640 and 1661. The rest of the page is blank.

[2] The handwriting of this entry and the one that follows clearly indicates that they were added after the Restoration.

parte quomodolibet fuerint opportuna & necessaria faciant, paragant & perimpleant & quilibet eorum faciat peragat & perimpleat, eo quod expressa inductio de vero valore annuo vel de certitudine premissorum vel eorum alicuius aut de aliis donis sive concessionibus per nos seu per aliquem progenitorum sive predecessorum nostrorum prefato Gulielmo Brough ante haec tempora factis in presentibus minime factis existit aut aliquo statuto, actu, ordinacione, provisione, proclamacione sive restriccione in contrarium inde ante hac habito, facto, edito, ordinato sive proviso aut aliqua alia re, causa vel materia quacunque in aliquo non obstante. In cuius rei testimonium has literas nostras fieri fecimus patentes. Teste me ipso apud Oxoniam quarto die Maii anno regni nostri vicesimo. Per breve de privato sigillo.   Hastings.[1]

[*fo. 77v. blank*]

160.   [*fo. 78*] ***Dr. Brough, Dean of Gloucester, his Mandamus.*** [*The king's mandate to the bishop, chapter and prebendaries informing them of his grant of the deanery to William Brough, as in* **159**, *above, and commanding them to assign to him a stall in the choir and a voice and a place in the chapter. Dated at Oxford, 4 May 1644.*] Carolus, dei gracia Anglie, Scotie, Francie & Hibernie rex, fidei defensor &c., dilectis nobis in Christo episcopo Gloucestrensis, capitulo & prebendariis ecclesie nostre cathedralis Gloucestrensis predicte aut aliis quibuscunque in hac parte authoritatem habentibus, salutem. Cum nos per literas nostras patentes sub magno sigillo nostro Anglie sigillatas, gerentes datas apud Oxon. die dato presentium, dedimus & concessimus dilecto nobis in Christo Gulielmo Brough, sacre theologie professori, decanatum ecclesie nostre cathedralis Gloucestrensis predicte per promocionem Accepti Frewen, sacre theologie professoris, ultimi decani ibidem, ad episcopatum Coventrie & Lichenfeldie vacantem & ad nostram donacionem pleno iure spectantem, habendum, gaudendum & tenendum decanatum predictum prefato Gulielmo Brough durante vita sua naturali [*etc. as in* **159**, *above, but with* 'quotidianis' *for* 'quotidiem', '& omnibus' *for* 'ac omnibus', 'aliqualiter' *for* 'qualitercunque', *as far as* 'gaudere debuit'], prout per easdem literas patentes plenius liquet & apparet. Vobis igitur mandamus quod eidem Gulielmo Brough stallum in choro & vocem & locum in capitulo assignetis assignarive faciatis in omnibus diligenter prout moris est. Teste me ipso apud Oxoniam quarto die Maii anno regni nostri vicesimo.

Hastings.

161.   [*fo. 78v.*] ***Dispensation for Dean Brough to keep the Audit any time in November or October.*** Charles R. II[us]. Trusty and welbeloved we greete yow well. Whereas wee are informed that among other your statutes for the governinge & orderinge of that church yow have one which binds the deane and chapter to keepe the audit and chuse the officers of that church precisely upon the last day of the moneth of November, and that Dr. William Brough your deane, by reason of his attendance both upon our person in his turne and his residence at his cannon's place in our royall chappell at Windsor coincident at the same time, cannot conveniently be there at that precise time,

---

[1] The royal official Hastings has not been identified.

our pleasure is to alter this statute duringe the time he shall be deane there and to ordeine that from henceforth that clause of your statute which binds yow strictly to the last day of November yearely shall cease for that time, and that it shalbe lawfull for yow yearely to keepe your audit & chuse your officers of the said church any day which yow your selves shall thinke fitt within the monethes of October or November. And our further pleasure is that our letter be registred in your statute booke with the rest of your statutes which have had their being from our worthy progenitors. Given under our signett at our court at Whitehall the 14th day of September 1661 in the thirteenth yeare of our reigne.

By his majestye's command.   Edw[ard] Nicholas.[1]

162.   *Assignment of Rectories for repaire of Gloucester Ch[urch].*[2] Charles R. Whereas we are informed that the cathedrall church of Gloucester is become very ruinous in the late ill tymes, and being desirous to contribute what may lye in us towards a worke of soe great piety as the reparacion & preservacion of that ancient structure, we are gratiously pleased to assigne the improved rents of all impropriacions belonginge to the said church which were made payable to us the 29th of September last past towards the repayring of that fabrick, and doe hereby require and authorise yow to receive & collect the same and to imploy it to the end aforesaid and none other, willinge & requiringe all those in whose hands the said rents remaine to pay them to yow accordingly. For which this shalbe to yow & them a suffcent warrant & discharge. Given at our court at Whitehall the 24th day of October in the twelfe yeare of our reigne [1660].

By his majestie's command.   Edw[ard] Nicholas.

To our trusty & well beloved the deane &
chapter of our cathedrall church of Gloucester.

163.   [*fo. 79*] *Dispensacion for Dr. Blandford his Residences.* Charles R. Trusty and welbeloved wee greete yow well. Whereas your founder of famous memory, Kinge Henry the Eight, hath by your locall statutes recerved [*sc.* reserved] to himselfe and his successors a power to dispence with any of your statutes made or to be made, and because Dr. Blandford, one of the prebendaryes of your church, by reason of his necessary residence in a place of goverment in our university of Oxon. as vice-chancellor, cannot reside with yow as your statutes and customs doe require, these are therefore to signifie to yow that out of our speciall favour and royall power wee have dispensed and by these presents doe dispence with the said Dr. Blandford for his residence with yow, requiringe yow to make him partaker of all the profitts and emoluments of his prebend there, as if he were continually and actually resident among yow, any statute or custome

---

[1] Sir Edward Nicholas (1593–1669) was Secretary of State to Charles I and Charles II.

[2] The original letter, once sealed at top left, is pasted into the book between fos. 82 and 83. On it the title is written very small at the foot. The text as given above is from that original letter. The copy on fo. 78v., with the same title in the usual marginal form, has a few changes in spelling: 'lat ill times', 'beinge', 'so great piety', 'repairinge', 'sufficient', 'twelfth'.

to the contrary notwithstandinge. For which this shall be your warrant. Given at our court at Whitehall the 21th day of August 1663 in the 15th yeare of our reigne.

By his majestie's command.   Henry Bennet.[1]

To our trusty & welbeloved the deane &
chapter of our cathedral church of Gloucester.

[fo. 79v. blank]

164. *[fo. 80]* ***Dispensacion for Dr. Blandford.*** Charles R. Trusty and welbeloved wee greet you well. Whereas your founder of famous memory, King Henry the Eight, hath by your locall statutes reserved to himself and his successors a power to dispense with any of your statutes made or to be made, and to order as he or they shall see cause, and because Doctor Walter Blandford, one of our chaplaines in ordinary and prebendary of your church, by reason of his indisposition of health the last yeare and his preperation of late for the bishopricke of Oxon. (unto which wee have nominated him), hath not resided with you as your statutes and customes doe require, wee have therefore thought fitt to signifie our pleasure unto you on his behalf that out of our especiall favour and regall power wee doe dispense with the said Doctor Blandford for his residency with you, requiring you to make him partaker of all emoluments as if he were continually resident amonge you, and to allowe him the benefitt of all fines that have bene or shall be treated of while he is prebendary, particulerly of that of Sherston, any statute or custome to the contrary notwithstandinge. Given under our signe manuall at our court at Oxford the 10th day of November 1665 in the seaventeenth yeare of our reigne.

By his majestie's command.   Will[iam] Morice.[2]

To our trusty and welbeloved the deane and chapter
of our cathedrall church of Gloucester.

165. *[fo. 80v.]* Memorandum, that the fines treated of before Dr. Blandford was consecrated were, ultimo [*sc.* recently],

Sir Thomas Stephens for Barnwood &c. Aprill 1665. March 1664.[3]
Sherston, ultimo, Mr. Hodges lately & long before.
Churcham at the audit &c.

166.   *[fo. 81]*   Tuesday 26 November 1661.   Chapter House.
(Thomas Warmstry, S.T.P.; Walter Blandford, S.T.P.; Hugh Naish, A.M.)

Electio officiariorum. [*Election of officers. The said prebendaries being assembled in the chapter house and solemnly proceeding to the election of officers for the coming year, in the absence of the dean but with his consent, elected and continued Thomas Washbourne as subdean and Hugh Naish as receiver and treasurer.*] Congregatis in domo capitulari

---

[1] Sir Henry Bennet (*c.* 1620–1685), created earl of Arlington in 1672, had become Secretary of State following the enforced retirement of Sir Edward Nicholas on 15 Oct. 1662.
[2] Sir William Morice (1602–76), Secretary of State 1660–8.
[3] The date 'March 1664', inserted above the line, appears to have been added as an afterthought.

ecclesiae cathedralis Gloucestriae venerabilibus viris Thoma Warmstry, S.T.P., Gualtero Blandford, S.T.P., et Hugone Naish, A.M., praebendariis dictae ecclesiae, et ad electionem officiariorum pro anno futuro solenniter procedentibus (absente decano, tamen cum consensu eiusdem venerabilis decani), iidem praebendarii praenominati elegerunt et continuarunt hos venerabiles viros in officiarios, viz. Thomam Washbourne, S.T.P., in subdecanum et Magistrum Hugonem Naish in receptorem et thesaurarium eiusdem ecclesiae pro hoc anno sequente usque ad finem eiusdem anni, qui quidem [*unfinished*].

[*The aforesaid men, with the dean's consent, elected as precentor for the coming year Mr. Hanslape,*[1] *one of the minor canons, who took the oath.*] Eodem die, loco et anno venerabiles viri antedicti, cum consensu decani, elegerunt in praecentorem dictae ecclesiae pro anno futuro Magistrum Hanslape, unum minorum canonicorum eiusdem ecclesiae, qui iuramentum suscepit &c.

167.   Wednesday 26 November 1662.   Chapter House.
(Thomas Washbourne, S.T.P.; Hugh Naish, A.M.; Richard Harwood, S.T.P.)

Electio Officiariorum. [*Election of officers. In the absence of the dean but with his consent, the prebendaries elected and continued Thomas Washbourne as subdean and Richard Harwood as receiver and treasurer.*[2] *As in* **166**, *above, ending with the statement that they took the oaths for their offices on the gospels, touched by them.*] Qui quidem respective subierunt juramenta ad sacrosancta dei evangelia per eos tacta ad eorum officia repective spectantia &c.

168.   [*fo. 81v.*]   Saturday[3] 25 November 1663.   Chapter House.
(Dr. Washbourne; Mr. Naish; Richard Harwood.)

Electio officiariorum 1663. [*Election of officers. In the absence of the dean but with his consent, the prebendaries elected and continued Thomas Washbourne as subdean and Richard Harwood as treasurer and receiver. As in* **166–7**, *above.*]

169.   26 November 1664.

Electio officiariorum 1664. [*Election of officers. Richard Harwood was elected by the same venerable men*[4] *as treasurer for the following year.*] Idem Ricardus Harwood electus fuit per eosdem venerabiles viros 26 Novembris 1664 in officium thesaurarii pro anno sequente &c.

---

[1] The MS. omits a heading. For Hanslape, below, p. 164.

[2] The record implies that Richard Harwood was 'continued' as treasurer, but Hugh Naish had been elected as treasurer the year before (**166**).

[3] MS. 'Die Saturni'. Since 25 Nov. 1663 was a Wednesday, the date, though clearly written as 25, was perhaps 21 or 28 Nov.

[4] The same venerable men were presumably prebendaries Washbourne, Naish and Harwood, the clerk looking back to the preceding entry. Although the Act Book does not record the election of a subdean for the year 1664–5 or of a precentor for the years 1662–4, the cathedral accounts show that Dr. Washbourne received £6 as subdean for the year 1664–5 and that Francis Hanslape was paid as precentor for the years 1662–4.

170.   Thursday 30 November 1665.   Chapter House.
(Dr. Deane; Dr. Wasburne [*sic*]; Dr. Harwood; Mr. Viner; Mr. Andrewes.)

Electio officiariorum 1665. [*Election of officers. The dean and the aforenamed prebendaries elected Thomas Washbourne as subdean and Thomas Vyner as treasurer and receiver. Beginning as in* **166**, *above, and continuing*] Venerabilis decanus et iidem prebendarii prenominati elegerunt venerabiles viros in officiarios [in officiarios *repeated*], viz. Thomam Washburne, S. theologiae professorem, in subdecanum & Thomam Viner, in theologia baccalaureum, in thesaurarium et receptorem eiusdem ecclesiae pro hoc anno sequente usque ad finem eiusdem anni. Qui quidem respective subierunt juramenta ad sacrosancta dei evangelia per eos tacta ad eorum officia respective spectantia &c.

Mr. Viner, Martii 30 1666. Subdecanus.[1]

[*The dean and the aforesaid men, the dean being present, elected as precentor*[2] *for the coming year Mr. Hanslape, who took the oath.*] Eodem die, loco & anno, decanus & venerabiles viri antedicti, decano presente, pro anno futuro Magistrum Hanslape in precentorem dictae ecclesiae elegerunt, qui juramentum suscepit &c.

Mr. Lambe chosen Chapter clark Nov. 30 1665. [*William Lamb was chosen by the dean, with the chapter's consent, as chapter clerk in succession to Mr. John Theyer.*[3]] Eodem die, loco & anno, Guilielmus Lamb eligitur a decano cum consensu capituli in successionem Magistri Johannis Theyer, in officio clerici capitularis, nemine contradicente.

Mr. Lamb is to give good security in the colledge before he execute the office of chapter clarke.

> Guil[ielmus] Brough, decanus; Tho[mas] Washbourne; Ri[cardus] Harwood;
> Tho[mas] Vyner; Antonius Andrewes.

171. [*fo. 82*][4] ***Installatio Venerabilis Viri Willelmi Brough Decani Gloucestriae.***
[*Installation of the venerable man William Brough as dean of Gloucester. Be it known that, by virtue of a commission or letter of proxy of William Brough, clerk, S.T.P. and dean of Gloucester, and of a royal mandate for him to be inducted, addressed to Gilbert Osborne, S.T.B., prebendary, Samuel Temple of Shipton Oliffe, clerk, and Samuel Broad, rector of Rendcomb, jointly or severally, dated 12 October 1644, authorising Osborne, Temple and Broad jointly or severally to ensure that Brough be instituted, admitted and inducted to the stall in the choir and the place in the chapter belonging to the deanery and usually held with it, the aforesaid Samuel Broad, on 20 November 1644, because the mandate could not at the time be executed before the prebendaries, as best he could, while the force of rebellion raged and the frenzy of arms prevailed over law through*

---

[1] The line seems to have been inserted at a later date than the entries above and below it. Its significance is obscure: Viner was treasurer as stated above; Washbourne appears to have remained subdean throughout 1666.

[2] The MS. omits a heading.

[3] For Lamb and Theyer, below, pp. 166, 169.

[4] The leaf was formerly pasted in after fo. 77 and also numbered 77 in a modern hand; there was then no fo. 82. At the rebinding of 1998 the leaf, which is 1 cm. shorter than the others, was placed as fo. 82. Cf. above, p. xxix.

almost all of England and especially at Gloucester (then fortified against the king), took care to be admitted etc. in the dean's name, as Broad's certificate can show. Its tenor is to be inserted on the page or pages of the book following the rest of this matter as told above. The dean required William Lamb, gent., notary public, to put the above act in this book in writing.[1]] Pateat universis praesens scriptum visuris quod, virtute cuiusdam comissionis, instrumenti sive mandati procuratorii sub nomine et sigillo venerabilis viri Gulielmi Brough, clerici, sacrae theologiae professoris ac decani ecclesiae cathedralis Sanctae et Individuae Trinitatis Gloucestriae rite et legitime constituti, atque mandati regii authoritate ad se inducendum sive induci faciendum venerabili Gilberto Osborne, sacrae theologiae baccalaureo, eiusdem ecclesiae prebendario, Samueli Temple de Shipton Oliffe in comitatu Gloucestrensi, clerico, et Samueli Broade, rectori de Rencombe in comitatu predicto, coniunctim et divisim directi,[2] gerentis datas duodecimo die Octobris anno domini 1644 annoque regni Caroli &c. vicesimo, in quo mandato procuratio idem Gulielmus Brough inter cetera in eodem contenta predictis Gilberto Osborne, Samueli Temple et Samueli Broade coniunctim et divisim tanquam suis procuratoribus veris et legitimis dedit et concessit potestatem generalem et mandatum speciale ut suo nomine et jure coram venerabilibus viris eiusdem ecclesiae prebendariis vel aliis quibuscunque in hac parte authoritatem sive potestatem habentibus coniunctim et divisim curarent, sive quilibet eorum curaret, ut idem prefatus venerabilis vir Gulielmus Brough in decanum eiusdem ecclesiae cathedralis canonice institueretur, admitteretur nec non in actualem et corporalem possessionem eiusdem induceretur inque stallum in choro et locum in capitulo eidem decanatui competentem et cum eodem teneri solitum imponeretur sive ius haberet, prout ex tenore eiusdem instrumenti sive mandati procuratorii vel ex intentione et scopo eiusdem plenius liquet et apparet, predictus Samuell Broade vicesimo die Novembris anno regni domini nostri Caroli, dei gratia Angliae, Scotiae, Franciae et Hiberniae regis, fidei defensoris &c., vicesimo, quia idem mandatum tunc temporis exequi non potuit coram venerabilibus &c. vel aliis ius sive potestatem in hac parte habentibus, eundem Gulielmum Brough omnibus melioribus viis, mediis et modis quibus ille idem facere et illud idem fieri potuit, dum per totam fere Angliam et precipue Gloucestriae (quae civitas presidio contra regem tunc munita fuit) rebellionis impetus saeuiebat et furor armorum plusquam ius prevaluit, in decanatum eiusdem ecclesiae cathedralis admitti et pariter canonice institui curavit nec non nomine et vice eiusdem in realem et actualem possessionem eiusdem decanatus inductus et installatus fuit, stallumque in choro ecclesiae predictae atque locum in capitulo eidem decanatui competentem nomine et vice ejusdem decani occupavit et recepit, prout ex certificatorio sive certificatoriis eiusdem Samuelis Broade plenius et clarius apparere et constare poterit. Instrumenti vero sive mandati procuratorii predicti itemque certificatorii sive certificatoriorum predictorum tenor vel tenores sequetur sive sequentur, inseretur sive inserentur, in pagina sive paginis libri sequentibus caeterum super tota huius rei gestae

---

[1] The 'rest . . . as told above' evidently refers to nos. 159–60. The certificate was not so inserted (unless the brief declaration that follows on fo. 82v. was a sufficient certificate), but the intention may have been to write it on fo. 77v. and, if necessary, fo. 79v., which remain blank.

[2] MS. 'directo'.

materia prout supra ponitur et narratur. [*fo. 82v.*] Idem[1] venerabilis vir Gulielmus Brough requirivit a me Gulielmo Lambe, generoso, notario publico, ut actum desuper conficerem et in hoc libro in scriptis redigerem.

Ita testor Willelmus Lambe, notarius publicus.

[*I Samuel Broad, asked specially, declare all the words above to be true as recited, and witness it by subscription in my own hand.*] Ego vero praenominatus Samuell Broade specialiter ad hoc rogatus omnia supra dicta vera esset (prout recitantur) pronuncio et declaro propriaeque manus subscriptione attestor.

Sam[uel] Broade, rect[or] de Rendcombe.

[*The dean aforesaid took the oath on the gospels, touched and kissed by him, to renounce the Roman pontiff, and to acknowledge King Charles II as head of the church and to observe the cathedral statutes.*] Venerabilis vir decanus antedictus sacramentum prestitit corporale ad sacrosancta dei evangelia, per eum tacta & deosculata, de renunciando Romano pontifico & de agnoscendo serenissimum dominum nostrum Carolum secundum regem &c. supremum &c. fidei defensorem &c. ac de observandum ordinaciones & statuta dictae ecclesiae cathedralis quatenus consentiunt verbo dei & statutis hujus regni.

[*fo. 83 and v. blank*; *pasted in between fos. 82 and 83 is the original letter entered above as no.* **162**.]

172.   [*fo. 84*]   8 August 1665.

Broadgate & Painter their first Monition. Quibus die, loco & anno, Mr. Deane pronounced against Richard Broadgate & John Painter, two of the singing men of this church, their first monition to depart this church for their often absence & contempt of the dean & chapter's authority, in not asking their leave, when many tymes commaunded the contrary by the said deane, and particularly for neglecting the morning prayers on Sundaies at 7 of the clock, for which they had no leave nor asked any.

William Brough; Tho[mas] Washbourne; Tho[mas] Warmstry;
Ri[chard] Harw[a]rd; Tho[mas] Vyner.

Thomas Loe chosen Organist. Eodem die, Thomas Loe[2] was admitted to be organist of this church, & took the oath appointed for the same.

173.   9 August 1665.

Thomas Viner, prebendary, his instalment: Entrie by Mr. Deane. [*Having taken the oath to renounce the bishop of Rome, to acknowledge the king as head of the church and to observe the cathedral statutes, according to the king's mandate he was admitted by Dr. Washbourne, subdean.*] Quo die, loco & anno, prestito primitus per eum juramento corporali ad sacrosancta dei evangelia de renunciando Romano episcopo & de

---

[1] The word 'idem', without an initial capital, is also a catchword at the foot of the recto.

[2] Both this entry and **173** seem to be in the handwriting of Dean Brough. For Thomas Loe, below, p. 166.

agnoscendo dominum nostrum Carolum 2dum regem & supremum caput &c., ac de observandum statutis dictae ecclesiae juxta morem & ritum &c. quatenus verbo dei & legibus hujus regni Angliae non repugnant &c., juxta literas domini regis mandatorias admissus est in canonicatum & prebendarium hujus ecclesiae venerabili viro Dr. Washburn, subdecano.

Guil[ielmus] Brough.

174. 24 November 1665.

Quo die anno & loco, A pettent [*sc.* patent] for the porter's place[1] void by the death of Mr. John Angell was granted & sealed to Richard Morrall, & Mr. Thomas[2] appointed to be his deputie in that office.

175. 14 April 1666.[3]

[*Richard Morrall was admitted by the dean to the place of one of the porters, having first taken the oath on the gospels, touched by him.*] Quo die et anno Ricardus Morrall admissus fuit per venerabilem dominum decanum in locum unius janitorum infra ecclesiam cathedralem, prestito prius juramento iuxta statutis ad sacro sancta dei evangelia per eum tacta &c.

Guliel[mus] Lambe, notarius publicus.

176. 13 December 1665.

Quo die, loco & anno, Mr. Deane pronounced agaynst Mr. Wrench,[4] one of the porters of this church, his first monition to depart this church, for his unpeaceable demeanour towards others, but especially for his contempt of the deane & chapter's authority.

Tho[mas] Washbourne, subd[ean]; Ric[hard] Harwood; Tho[mas] Vyner.

[*fo. 84v. blank*]

177. [*fo. 85*] 14 December 1665.

An Order to save harmless Dr. Harwood about the sale of Wood. Quo die, loco et anno, whereas the deane and chapter of the church of Gloucester have not bene able by the contribucion of theire friends and other helpes to raise moneys sufficient to discharge the great summes to be paid for theire new organ,[5] and were therefore forced to make sale of some of theire woods at Woolridge towards the making up of those summes, and did for

---

[1] Cf. above, p. xvii.

[2] Griffith Thomas, for whom see below, p. 169.

[3] This entry, squashed tightly and chronologically out of place so that it appears as an afterthought, is in William Lamb's hand, most of the others on the page being in the dean's.

[4] William Wrench, for whom see below, p. 172.

[5] The organ was built by Thomas Harris, who was paid *c.* £400. The account book names those who gave money towards the cost: little was given by the citizens of Gloucester. The chief carpenter seems to have been Thomas Elbridge. The pipes were gilded and painted by John Campion with the coats of arms of the king, the duke of York, the earl of Clarendon, the dean and chapter and the see of Gloucester along with the personal coats of arms of the dean and prebendaries.

that end give power in theire names to Dr. Harwood, then treasurer and receivor[1] of theire church, to contract & covenunte for the sale of woods, soe farr as by law and statute they may and will be forced for the benefitt and proffitt of the church, wee doe hereby iustifie that our act of givinge him such power and all acts by him done in pursuance of the said churche's right. And therefore against all suits which are or shall be commenced against him for any such acts by him done wee doe hereby promise and engage our selves to defend and assist him, as occasion shall be, accordinge to the intent and order of the deane and chapter in that perticuler to be provided and observed.

Guil[ielms] Brough, decanus; Tho[mas] Washbourne, subd[ecanus];
Tho[mas] Vyner; Hugh Naish.

178.   12 April 1666.

The Sub-Deane to receive £10 per Annum. Quo die et anno, whereas the sub-deanes of this church for the time beinge have for many yeares last past received onely the yearely fee of six pounds, it is hereby ordered and decreed that for the future there shall be allowed unto the sub-deane for the time beinge the yearely sume of tenne pounds for the execucion of the said office and for and in respect of the paines and trouble therein upon all occasions in the absence of Mr. Deane. Which said sume of tenn pounds is to be paid yearely by the hands of the treasurer for the time beinge.

Ita testor Guil[ielmus] Lambe, notarius publicus.

179. [*fo. 85v.*]   Friday 30 November 1666.   Chapter House.
(The Dean; Dr. Harwood; Mr. Viner; Mr. Andrewes.)

Electio Officiariorum 1666. [*Election of officers. The dean and the aforenamed prebendaries elected Thomas Washbourne as subdean and Thomas Vyner as treasurer and receiver. As in* **170**, *above. Alongside in the margin is written*] Juramentum subiit thesaurarii Thomas Vyner die 6to Decembris 1666. Guil[ielmus] Brough.[2]

[*The dean and the aforesaid men, the dean being present, elected as precentor*[3] *Mr. Hanslape, who took the oath. As in* **170**, *above.*] Eodem die, loco et anno [*etc.*].

Guil[ielmus] Brough, decan[us]; Ri[cardus] Harwood; Hugo Naish per
procuratorem suum, Tho[mam] Vyner; Antonius Andrewes.

180.   6 December 1666.
[*The dean and the aforesaid men,*[4] *the dean being present, elected as sacrist for the coming year Mr. Jackson,*[5] *for which he took the oath.*] Quo die et anno decanus et

---

[1] Harwood was treasurer for the year 1664–5; in Nov. 1665 Thomas Vyner had been elected as treasurer: above, **169–70**.

[2] The addition, presumably in Dean Brough's hand, suggests that, notwithstanding the record, Vyner did not take the oath at the meeting where he was elected.

[3] The MS. omits a heading.

[4] The 'aforesaid men' were presumably those present at the meeting a week earlier (**179**).

[5] Edward Jackson, who was a minor canon 1664–77. The election of the sacrist is recorded here for the first time in the book.

venerabiles viri ante dicti (decano presente) pro anno futuro Magistrum Jackson in sacristam dictae ecclesiae elegerunt qui juramentum suscepit &c.

Guil[ielmus] Lambe, notarius publicus.[1]

181.[2] [*The dean and the aforesaid men, the dean being present, admitted Daniel Henstridge*[3] *as master of the choristers or organist, and Daniel took the oath according to the statute. And they admitted Edward Fidkin*[4] *as a minor canon, and he took the oath on the gospels, touched by him, on 27 December 1666.*] Quo die et loco decanus et venerabiles viri antedicti (decano presente) Danielem Henstridge in locum magistri coristarum sive organistae admiserunt, et dictus Daniel iuramentum subiit secundum statutum.

Quo die et loco decanus et venerabiles viri antedicti (decano presente) Edoardum [*sic*] Fidkin elegerunt unum minorum canonicorum.

Qui quidem Edvardus Fidkin subiit juramentum ad sacrosancta dei evangelia per eum tacta &c. Dec. 27 1666.

Tho[mas] Vyner.

182.   [*fo. 86*]   6 December 1666.[5]

Noe repaires to be without Orders. p. 22.[6] Quo die et anno, whereas by an order dated the twentith day of October 1617 it was agreed that the treasurer for the time beinge should not appointe any worke of reparacions in or about this church exept he should have it first obtayned under the deane's hand, and alsoe that the sayd lycence soe obtayned should be shewed at the audit, and that if the treasurer should doe otherwise it should be required againe at his hands, and that neither Mr. Deane nor any prebend of this church should cause any reperacions of leade-worke to be done in or about his or theire house or houses without the consent of the deane and chapter first had and obtayned, it is hereby ordered that the said former order be and is hereby ratified and confirmed, and all persons concerned are to take notice thereof and to observe the same accordingly.

Guil[ielmus] Brough, decan[us].

Pattents to be Durante bene placito [sc. *during pleasure*] ***without distress.*** Quo die et anno, whereas severall inconveniencyes have befallen to the deane and chapter by granting of pattents at large with power of distresse, which hath and may be the occasion of further suits in law, to prevent the like for the future it is hereby ordered concluded and agreed that all pattents hereafter to be made or granted to any officer belonginge to this

---

[1] The signature is compressed, and was presumably added later.

[2] The whole entry is in a hand (Thomas Vyner's, to judge from the signature at the end) different from that of the entries immediately before and after, and although those two entries are both dated 6 Dec. it is possible that **181** was inserted as an afterthought and so may not belong to the same meeting.

[3] For Henstridge, below, p. 165.

[4] For Fidkin, below, p. 163.

[5] After the date is a space matching that in which in other entries the names of those attending the meeting are written. At this meeting of 6 Dec. 1666 it seems that only the dean was present.

[6] The reference to page (*recte* folio) 22 is in a different hand and was probably added later. Cf. above, **7**.

church shall have this clause inserted 'Durante bene placito decani et capituli' and the other clause of distresse to be omitted.

Guil[ielmus] Brough, decan[us].

183.   22 October 1666.

Upon request made to Mr. John Robins[1] (late council to the deane & chapter) by order of Mr. Deane that he would surender up the office of council to the deane & chapter, in regard the distance of his abode from this church rendered him unserviceable to it in the aforesayd office,[2] he the said Mr. Robins did freely & ingeniously surrender up the said office & fee thereto belonging to the deane & chapter to dispose the same to theyr better advantage.

Whereupon, in the absence of the deane, Mr. Subdeane offered the said office & fee to the acceptance of Thomas Williams, esquire, which being by him accepted the said Mr. Williams was chosen & admitted council to the deane & chapter.

Tho[mas] Washbourne.

[*fo. 86v. blank*]

184.   [*fo. 87*]   *A concurrent Lease of the Bishop's. Sealed in Chapter June 1667.*[3]

[*fos. 87v.–88v. blank*; *between fos. 87 and 88 is an original letter, given below as Appendix II, p. 160.*]

185.   [*fo. 89*]   8 April 1661, 13 Charles II.   Chapter House.

Foure pounds to Mris. Allibond. Quibus die, loco & anno, by vertue of a proxie from the Reverend William Brough, doctor in divinity, deane of the said cathedrall church, dated the twenty seaventh day of March anno domini 1661 directed to Thomas Washbourne, doctor in divinity, subdeane, it was agreede and ordered by the said subdeane and by Hugh Naish, master of arts, treasurer, and Richard Horwood, doctor in divinity, prebendaryes of the said cathedrall church, that the somme of ffower pounds shalbe given unto Margaret Allibond widow, relict of John Allibond, doctor in divinity, deceased, in regard of the good service performed by the said Dr. Allibond to the church and also of the great necessity and want of her the said Margaret.

186.   10 April 1661, 13 Charles II.   Chapter House.

Order for Cutting of Timber. Quibus die anno & loco, by vertue of a proxie from Mr. Deane directed to Mr. Subdeane, dated the twenty seaventh day of March 1661, it is agreed & ordered by the said subdeane, Mr. Treasurer and Dr. Harwood that Mr. John

---

[1] For Robins, below, p. 168.
[2] A gap after the word 'office' suggest that a word was to be added.
[3] The chapter's confirmation of the lease was never entered in the book.

Theyer, chapter clerk of the said deane and chapter, shall with the assistance of a carpenter to be assigned by the said treasurer make choice of such tymber trees growinge upon any of our mannors of Barnewood, Cranham, Wotton, Churcham, Tyberton, Taynton, Bulley & Sandhurst which in the judgement of such carpenter shall seeme necessary or convenient for the use of, or to be imployed by, the said deane & chapter for the repayringe of the said cathedrall church or reedifyinge or repayeringe of any the howses within the precincts of the said church inhabited by any of those who as members or officers doe apperteyne to the said church, and also to seize and imploy to our use all such tymber as is already illegally cutt downe within any of the mannors aforesaid.

[*fos. 89v–90v. blank*]

187.   [*fo. 91*]   25 October 1663.

The Font consecrated.[1]

188.   19 October 1664.
[*In the chapter house Edward Jackson, clerk, was admitted by the dean as a minor canon, and he took the oath.*] Quibus die et anno in domo capitulari Edvardus Jackson, clericus, admissus et assignatus erat per venerabilem decanum in locum unius minorum canonicorum infra ecclesiam cathedralem Gloucestriae, qui quidem Edvardus Jackson [*unfinished; sc.* subiit juramentum *etc.*].

[*fos. 91v.–95v. blank*]

189.   [*fo. 96*]   7 August 1660, between nine and eleven a.m.   Chapter House.
(William Brough, S.T.P., dean.)

Admissio venerabilis viri Thomas Washbourne. [*Admission of the venerable man Thomas Washbourne. Before William Brough, S.T.P., dean, between the ninth and the eleventh hour before noon in the chapter house, Thomas Washbourne exhibited the king's letters patent, dated 23 June last past, granting to him the prebend vacant by the death of Gilbert Osborne, and the royal mandate for his admission and installation; the dean admitted him, as in* **37,** *above. All this was done in the presence of John Theyer, gent., John Vaulx and Gilbert Jones, notaries public, Richard Witherston, gent., and other servants of the said church.*] Vizt.[2] septimo die Augusti anno domini 1660 coram venerabili viro Willemo Brough, sacrae theologiae professore, decano ecclesiae cathedralis

---

[1] The heading is followed by a space that remained unused. The font, consecrated by Bishop Nicholson, was made by a Mr. Baldwyn for £5 and painted and gilded by John Campion in Oct. 1663; in Dec. 'Skillum the Taylor' was paid 6*s.* for making a leather cover for it, and in March 1664 a Mr. Beale was paid 11*s.* 11*d.* for the red leather so used. The font, whose making had upset the puritan citizens of Gloucester, was given away in 1865. In 1928, through the efforts of Dean Gee, it was discovered in the Travellers' Rest chapel at Swimbridge, Devon, and later passed into the hands of an antique dealer: letters in *Country Life*, 24 Feb., 24 April 1983.

[2] A gap at the beginning of the line may have been intended for an addition, perhaps of the day of the week, Tuesday.

Gloucestriae inter horas nonam et undecimam ante meridiem in domo capitulari dictae ecclesiae venerabilis vir Thomas Washbourne exhibuit [*etc.*, *as in* **107**, *above*].

[*fo. 96v. blank*]

190.   [fo. *97*]   [Sunday 19 August 1660.]¹

Dr. Warmestry.² [*Before* (*the dean*), *between the ninth and the eleventh hour before noon in the chapter house, Thomas Warmestry, S.T.P., exhibited the king's letters patent granting to him a vacant prebend, and he exhibited the royal mandate for his admission and installation;* (*the dean*) *admitted him.*] Coram venerabili viro [. . .] cathedralis Gloucestriae, inter horas nonam et undecimam ante meridiem in domo capitulari dictae ecclesiae, venerabilis vir Thomas Warmstry, sacrae theologiae professor, exhibuit et tradidit [. . .] antedicto literas patentes illustrissimi in Christo principis domini nostri, Domini Caroli Secundi, dei gratia Angliae, Scotiae, Franciae et Hiberniae regis, fidei defensoris, &c., gerentes datas [. . .] ultimo preterito, de concessione illius prebendae sive canonicatus in ecclesia cathedrali Gloucestriae predicta iam [. . .] vacantis facta dicto Thoma Warmstry. Et exhibuit etiam mandatum regium pro admissione et installacione dicti Thomae Warmstry in prebendam praedictam iuxta consuetudinem in ea parte usitatam. Unde dictus venerabilis vir [. . .] antedictus omni cum ea qua decuit reverentia et obedientia dictas literas patentes et mandatorias recepit. Quibus perlectis ob reverentiam et obedientiam debitam prefatum Thomam Warmstry, prestito primitus per eum iuramento corporali ad sacrosancta dei evangelia de renunciando Romano episcopo et de agnoscendo dictum dominum nostrum Dominum Carolum regem &c. supremum caput &c. ac de observandis statuta dictae ecclesiae iuxta morem et ritum &c. quatenus verbo dei et legibus huius regni Angliae non repugnant &c., in canonicum et prebendarium admisit &c.

[*fo. 97v. blank*]

191.   [*fo. 98*]   22 August 1660, between nine and eleven a.m.   Chapter House.
(William Brough, S.T.P., dean.)

Admissio venerabilis viri Walteri Blandford. [*Admission of the venerable man Walter Blandford. Before William Brough, S.T.P., dean, between the ninth and the eleventh hour before noon in the chapter house, Walter Blandford, S.T.P., exhibited the king's letters patent, dated 6 August last past, granting to him a vacant prebend, and the royal mandate for his admission and installation; the dean admitted him, as in **37**, above. All this was done in the presence of Thomas Washbourne, S.T.P., John Vaulx, notary public,*

---

¹ The entry is undated and incomplete, with gaps left blank, as is indicated here by ellipses in square brackets, for the name of the dean, the date of the letters patent and the name of the previous holder of the prebend. It breaks off with the statement of Warmestry's admission. The date and the fact that the dean performed the ceremony, in the presence of John Vaulx and William Pierson, notaries public, and Thomas Washbourne, S.T.P., are supplied by G.D.R. 142a, p. 61.

² The name is written in the margin in an almost illegible hand, possibly that of Dean Brough.

Henry Brett,[1] gent., Walter Church and Edward Williams, one of the minor canons, and other servants of the said church.] Vicesimo secundo die Augusti anno domini 1660, coram venerabili viro Willelmo Brough, sacrae theologiae professore, decano ecclesiae cathedralis Gloucestriae, inter horas nonam et undecimam ante meridiem in domo capitulari dictae ecclesiae, venerabilis vir Walterus Blandford, sacrae theologiae professor, exhibuit et tradidit venerabili decano antedicto literas patentes illustrissimi in Christo principis domini nostri, Domini Caroli Secundi, dei gratia Angliae, Scotiae, Franciae et Hiberniae regis, fidei defensoris &c., gerentes datas sexto die Augusti ultimo preterito, de concessione illius prebendae sive canonicatus in ecclesia cathedrali Gloucestriae predicta iam legitime et de iure vacantis facta dicto Waltero Blandford. Et exhibuit [*etc., as in* **107**, *above*].

[*fo. 98v. blank*]

192.   [*fo. 99*] **Mr. Naish.**[2]

193.   [*fo. 99v.*] **Mr. Harris.**[3]

194.   [*fo. 100*]   11 November 1660, between nine and eleven a.m.   Chapter House. (William Brough, S.T.P., dean.)

Admissio venerabilis viri Ricardi Harwood. [*Admission of the venerable man Richard Harwood. Before William Brough, S.T.P., dean, between the ninth and the eleventh hour before noon in the chapter house, Richard Harwood, S.T.P., exhibited the king's letters patent, dated 3 November last past, granting to him the prebend vacant by the preferment of Gilbert Sheldon to the bishopric of London, and the royal mandate for his admission and installation; the dean admitted him, as in* **37**, *above. All this was done in the presence of Thomas Washbourne, subdean, Anthony Harwood, Robert Muddin,[4] Richard Brodgate[5] and other servants of the said church.*] Undecimo die Novembris anno domini 1660, coram venerabili viro Willelmo Brough, sacrae theologiae professore, decano ecclesiae cathedralis Gloucestriae, inter horas nonam et undecimam ante meridiem in domo capitulari dictae ecclesiae, venerabilis vir Ricardus Harwood, sacrae theologiae professor, exhibuit [*etc., as in* **107**, *above*].

195.   [*fo. 100v.*] **Mr. Jacob.**[6]

---

[1] For Brett, below, p. 162.

[2] It was presumably intended to enter after the heading the record of the admission of Hugh Naish, M.A, to a prebendal stall on 10 Sept. 1660.

[3] It was, similarly, presumably intended to enter after the heading the record of the admission of Robert Harris, M.A, to a prebendal stall on 24 Sept. 1660.

[4] Robert Muddin was a lay singer 1660–71 (cf. above, **156**), clerk of works 1661–70 and almsman 1669–71.

[5] For Brodgate (MS. Bradgate), below, p. 162.

[6] As in **192** and **193**, it was presumably intended to enter after the heading the record of the admission of Francis Jacob to the prebend vacant by the death of Robert Harris, to which the king had presented him on 12 Nov. 1662.

196.   [*fo. 101*]   Monday 20 November 1665, between nine and eleven a.m.

Chapter House.

(William Brough, S.T.P., dean.)

Admissio venerabilis viri Thomae Viner. [*Admission of the venerable man Thomas Vyner. Before William Brough, S.T.B., dean, between the ninth and the eleventh hour before noon in the chapter house, Thomas Vyner, S.T.B., exhibited the king's letters patent, dated 10 November last past, granting to him the prebend vacant by the death of Thomas Warmestry, and the royal mandate for his admission and installation; the dean admitted him, as in* **37**, *above. All this was done in the presence of John Langley, gent., William Pierson, gent., William Lamb, gent., Francis Hanslape (MS. Anslip), minor canon, and other servants of the said church.*] Die Lunae, vizt. vicessimo die Novembris 1665, coram venerabili viro Willelmo Brough, sacrae theologiae professore, decano ecclesiae cathedralis Gloucestriae, inter horas nonam et undecimam ante meridiem in domo capitulari dictae ecclesiae, venerabilis vir Thomas Viner, sacrae theologiae baccalaureus, exhibuit [*etc., as in* **107**, *above*].

[*fo. 101v. blank*]

197.   [*fo. 102*]   Monday 20 November 1665, between nine and eleven a.m.

Chapter House.

(William Brough, S.T.P., dean.)

Admissio venerabilis viri Anthonii Andrews. [*Admission of the venerable man Anthony Andrews. Before William Brough, S.T.B., dean, between the ninth and the eleventh hour before noon in the chapter house, Anthony Andrews, M.A., exhibited the king's letters patent, dated 13 November last past, granting to him the prebend vacant by the resignation of Thomas Vyner, and the royal mandate for his admission and installation; the dean admitted him, as in* **37**, *above. All this was done in the presence of John Langley, gent., William Pierson, gent., William Lamb, gent., Francis Hanslape (MS. Anslip), minor canon, and other servants of the said church.*] Die Lunae (vizt.) vicessimo die Novembris 1665, coram venerabili viro Willelmo Brough, sacrae theologiae professore, decano ecclesiae cathedralis Gloucestriae, inter horas nonam et undecimam ante meridiem in domo capitulari dictae ecclesiae, venerabilis vir Anthonius Andrews, in artibus magister, exhibuit [*etc., as in* **107**, *above*].

198.   [*fo. 102v.*]   Friday 12 January 1665/6, between nine and eleven a.m.

Chapter House.

(Thomas Washbourne, S.T.P., subdean; Thomas Vyner, S.T.B.)

Admissio Venerabilis viri Henrici Savage. [*Admission of the venerable man Henry Savage. Before Thomas Washbourne, S.T.B., subdean, and Thomas Vyner, prebendary, between the ninth and the eleventh hour before noon in the chapter house, Henry Savage, S.T.P., exhibited the king's letters patent, dated 14 December last past, granting to him* *the prebend vacant by the preferment of Walter Blandford to the bishopric of Oxford, and the royal mandate for his admission and installation; the subdean*[1] *admitted him, as in* **37**, *above. All this was done in the presence of the said Thomas Vyner, John Powell, alderman, Francis Hanslape* (MS. *Anslip*), *precentor, Edward Jackson, minor canon, and other servants of the said church.*] Die Veneris vizt. duodecimo die Januarii 1665, coram venerabilibus viris Thoma Washbourne, sacrae theologiae professore, subdecano ecclesiae cathedralis Gloucestriae, et Thoma Viner, S.T.B., uno prebendariorum dictae ecclesiae, inter horas nonam et undecimam ante meridiem in domo capitulari dictae ecclesiae, venerabilis vir Henricus Savage, sacrae theologiae professor, exhibuit [*etc., as in* **107**, *above*].

199.   [*fo. 103*]   Saturday 8 May 1669, between nine and eleven a.m.   Chapter House. (Thomas Washbourne, S.T.P., treasurer.)

Admissio Venerabilis viri Willelmi Washbourne. [*Admission of the venerable man William Washbourne. Before Thomas Washbourne, S.T.P., treasurer and prebendary, between the ninth and the eleventh hour before noon in the chapter house, William Washbourne, M.A., exhibited the king's letters patent dated 23 April last past, granting to him the prebend vacant by the death of Richard Harwood, and the royal mandate for his admission and installation; the said prebendary admitted him, as in* **37**, *above. In the presence of Charles Pierson, notary public.*] Die Sabati vizt. octavo die Maii anno 1669, coram venerabili viro Thoma Washbourne, S.T.P., tunc thesaurario et prebendario ecclesiae cathedralis Gloucestriae, inter horas nonam et undecimam ante meridiem in domo capitulari dictae ecclesiae, venerabilis vir Willelmus Washbourne, clericus, in artibus magister, exhibuit [*etc., as in* **107**, *above, except that the statement about witnesses is reduced to*] In presentia Caroli Pierson, notarii publici.

[*fo. 103v. blank*]

200.   [*fo. 104*]   7 August 1666.

Quo die & loco,[2] it was agreed & ordered that ten pounds be allowed by this church towards the better maintenance of a minister for Chippin-Norton, provided that my Ladie Covet[3] allow so much, who is our tenant for the parsonage of Chippin-Norton. And that the toune allow ten pounds lyke wise per annum. And the bishop of Oxford[4] is to be writt to & desired to nominate & appoint a man for discharge of the cure such as he shall think fitt to discharge the cure.

William Brough, dean; Tho[mas] Washbourne, subd[ean]; Tho[mas] Vyner.

---

[1] Where the subdean is recorded as receiving the king's letters, but not elsewhere, the clerk, evidently copying from an earlier entry, has mistakenly referred to him as the dean.

[2] The location of the meeting is not stated.

[3] For Lady Covert, below, p. 162.

[4] The bishop was Walter Blandford, a former prebendary of Gloucester cathedral.

201.   26 October 1667.   Deanery.

For repaire of the Chancell of Matson.[1] Quo die et loco, it was aggreed & ordered that at time convenient in the next spring the treasurer for the time being shal see that the chancel of Matisden shal be putt in al necessarie and convenient reparacion & that due care shal be used at present for prevencion of further ruine unto it.

> William Brough, dean; Tho[mas] Washbourne; Ri[chard] Harward;
> Tho[mas] Vyner; Anthony Andrewes.

202.   26 October 1667.   Deanery.

Exchange of Tithes &c.[2] Quo die et loco, whereas there hath beene formerlie a controversie touching certayne roomes with appurtenances &c.[3] adjoyneing to the prebendal house formerlie Dr. Inglish his house,[4] which said roomes were lately leased out to Mrs. Bridget Vaulx, daughter of the said Doctor Inglish, and whereas by a graunt of the deane & chapter to Mrs. Bridget Vaulxe of the tithes of Insworth the controversie about the sayd roomes is now ceased, it's now ordered for prevencion of further controversie about the sayd roomes that for the time to come the sayd roomes shal be taken & deemed to be a part of the said prebendal house, & that noe other person clayme any right therein but he that shal have right in the sayd prebendal house.

> William Brough, dean; Tho[mas] Washbourne, subd[ean]; Anthony Andrewes;
> Henry Savage, D.Th.

[*fo. l04v. blank*]

203.   [*fo. 105*]   24 June 1667.   Chapter House.

Admissio choristarum E. Tyler, T. Wilcox, J. Painter. [*Admission of the choristers E. Tyler, T. Wilcox, J. Painter. Edward Tyler was admitted by the dean in the place of Godfrey Founes, who has left, Thomas Wilcox in the place of Edward Thomas,*[5] *lately deceased, and Jesse Painter in the place of John Lug, who has left, his voice for a long time not in tune.*] Quo die & anno, Edward Tyler admissus fuit a domino decano in choristam, in loco Godfrei Founes, qui ab ecclesia nuper discessit.

Eodem die, loco & anno, Thomas Wilcox admissus fuit a domino decano in choristam, in loco Edwardi Thomas, nuper mortui.

Eodem die & anno, Jesse Painter admissus fuit a domino decano in choristam, in loco Johannis Lug, qui ab ecclesia discessit, voce diuturnus non favente.

---

[1] The rectory of Matson, which had belonged to the abbey, as also the manor of Matson, had been granted by King Henry VIII on 4 Sept. 1541 as part of the endowment of the newly established dean and chapter of Gloucester. The heading is in a different hand from that of the rest of the entry.

[2] The heading is in a different hand from that of the rest of the entry.

[3] The words 'with appurtenances &c.' have been added above the line.

[4] Cf. below, p. 163.

[5] Son of Griffith Thomas, for whom see below, p. 169.

Wells admitted a clarke. [*John Wells,*[1] *once one of the choristers, was admitted as a lay singer in the place of Richard Brodgate, lately deceased, by the dean, and he took the oath on the gospels, touched by him.*] Eodem die & anno & loco Johannes Wells, unus olim de choristis, admissus fuit in laicum cantorem, in loco Richardi Broadgate, nuper defuncti, a domino decano. Qui quidem Johannes subiit juramenta respective ad sacrosancta dei evangelia per eum tacta.[2]

    Guil[ielmus] Brough, decanus.

204.   29 June 1667.   Chapter House.

John De[i]ghton, a Peticanon. [*John Deighton was admitted and assigned* (*a place*) *by the dean as a minor canon, after he had taken the oaths on the gospels, touched* (*by him*).] Eodem die, loco & anno Johannes Deighton admissus & assignatus fuit a Domino decano in minorem canonicum hujus ecclesiae, praestitis prius juramentis requisitis sacrosanctis dei evangeliis tactis &c.

    Guil[ielmus] Brough, decanus.

205.   23 October 1670.   Deanery.

Electio Minoris Canonici. Mr. Evans. [*Election of a minor canon, Mr. Evans. George Evans was admitted and assigned* (*a place*) *by the dean as a minor canon, after he had taken the oaths on the gospels, touched* (*by him*).] Quibus die et anno Georgius Evans admissus et assignatus fuit a domino decano in minorem canonicum huius ecclesiae, praestitis prius juramentis requisitis, sacrosanctis dei evangeliis tactis &c.

    Guil[ielmus] Brough, decanus.

206.   [*fo. 105v.*] 26 October 1667.[3]   Chapter House.
(The Dean; Dr. Washbourne, subdean; Dr. Harwood; Mr. Viner, and by the same as proxy Mr. Naish;[4] Mr. Andrewes, and by the same as proxy Dr. Savage.)

Electio Officiariorum 1667. [*Election of officers. The dean and the aforenamed prebendaries elected Thomas Washbourne as subdean and Thomas Vyner as treasurer and receiver. As in* **170**, *above, stopping at* eiusdem anni.]

[*The aforesaid Thomas Washbourne and Thomas Vyner each took the oaths belonging to their respective offices on the gospels, touched by them, on 4 December 1667.*] Qui quidem antedicti Thomas Washburne & Thomas Vyner juramenta subierunt ad officia suarum respective spectantia ad sacra dei evangelia per eos tacta Decembris 4to 1667.

---

[1] John Wells the elder, a chorister 1660–5 and a lay singer 1667–1703.

[2] The sentence appears to have been inserted after the dean had signed his name.

[3] The entries for the meeting are in three different hands, the sentences recording the oaths taken by the subdean, the treasurer and the precentor being in much darker ink and presumably added later. Cf. above, p. xxx.

[4] Naish's name has been added as a correction, after Savage's name, which should evidently have been deleted there since it recurs in the next line.

[*The dean chose as precentor Edward Jackson, one of the minor canons. Jackson took the oath belonging to his office, touching and kissing the gospels.*] Eodem die, loco & anno idem venerabilis decanus antedictus elegit in praecentorem dictae ecclesiae Edwardum Jacksen, unum minorum canonicorum eiusdem ecclesiae cathedralis &c.

Qui quidem Edwardus Jackson prestitit juramentum corporale ad officium suum spectans tactis et deosculatis sacrosanctis deo evangeliis.

Ita testor Guil[ielmus] Lambe, notarius publicus.

Twenty Tunn of Timber allowed for Erectinge a Tenement upon a Piece of ground called the Old Parliament house.[1] Quo die, loco et anno, whereas Mr. Deane hath occasion of timber for the buildinge and erectinge of one tenement upon a certaine plott or parcell of grounde knowne by the name of the old Parliament Howse, it is concluded and agreed that Mr. Deane be allowed twenty tunn of timber, the same to be taken out of the woods called Birdewood or Woolridge, and not elsewhere, for the uses aforesaid.

Tho[mas] Washbourn, subd[ean]; Tho[mas] Vyner; Anthony Andrewes; Henry Savage per procuratorem suum [*by his proxy*].

207. [*fo. 106*]   15 February 1667/8.   Chapter House.

Presentacion Dr. Washbourne. St. Mary de Loade. Quo die, loco et anno &c., whereas the patronage and donation of the vicaridge of St. Mary de Loade within the citty of Gloucester is the right of the deane & chapter of Gloucester, and the same being now void by the surrender of Mr. Francis Hanslape, the last incumbent there, Dr. William Brough, deane of Gloucester, for preservinge the right of this church to the patronage of the said vicaridge of St. Mary's did this day in open chapter give his voyce and free consent for a presentacion to be pass'd, made and sealed to Thomas Washbourne, doctor in divinity and sub-deane of this church, of the said vicaridge. And Mr. Thomas Vyner and Mr. Anthony Andrewes, both prebendaryes of this church, gave theire severall voyces and consents to the passing of the said presentacion. And the said Mr. Vyner by proxie under the hand and seale of Mr. Hugh Naish and the said Mr. Andrewes by proxie under the hand and seale of Dr. Henry Savage, both prebendaries of this church, did likewise give theire severall voyces and full consents to the passinge the said presentacion to the said Dr. Washbourne, which was then ordered to be sealed with the chapter seale and was performed accordingly.

Guil[ielmus] Brough, decanus; Tho[mas] Vyner; Anth[ony] Andrewes.

208. [*fo. 106v.*]   12 October 1667.   Chapter House.

[*The dean, Mr. Vyner, Mr. Andrews, canons, Mr. Naish by his proxy Mr. Vyner and Dr. Savage by his proxy Mr. Andrews being then and there present.*[2]] Quo die et loco &c. presentibus tunc et ibidem domino decano, Magistro Vyner, Magistro Andrews, canonicis, Magistro Naish per procuratorem Magistrum Vyner et Doctore Savage per Magistrum Andrewes procuratorem suum.

---

[1] The site became that of no. 7 Millers Green, built between 1667 and 1670 by William Lamb, for which the timber was allowed. It had been part of the site of a huge building called the old workhouse and old schoolhouse, let *c.* 1649 to Thomas Pury, who repaired it and shortened it, leaving empty the site of no. 7. The building preserved by Pury is now known as the Parliament Room.

[2] The statement of those present has been added in the margin, apparently at a later date.

Mr. Hanslape petticanon and precentor of the church of Glouc. was by Mr. Deane convented, and the power of the deane to punish errors and enormityes reade before him the said Mr. Hanslape out of the statute, De Corrigendis Excessibus, in haec verba [*Of Correcting Excesses, in these words*] as followeth,[1]

'Statuimus et volumus, si quis minorum canonicorum, clericorum, aut aliorum ministrorum, in levi culpa deliquerit, arbitrio decani aut eo absente, vicedecani, corrigatur. Sin gravius fuerit delictum ab eisdem expellatur, a quibus fuit admissus'.

Mr. Hanslape's Suspension. By vertue of this he was suspended from all offices & services of the church of Gloucester with all theire benefitts and perquisites any wayes to be had or gott, or which he may claime as due by reason of the said offices or otherwise in the church aforesaid. For beinge very scandalous in the church and in the citty by his comon gaminge, lyinge and being out of the colledge at un-statutable howres, sometimes all night, drinkinge with younge gentlemen. And perticulerly and lately after he had preached at the cathedrall on Sunday October the sixth, and dined at the maior's feast on Monday after, October the seaventh, went to the Boothall (a comon inn) neare mid-night, and then and there inordinately behaved himself in drinkinge, quarrellinge and swearinge. And going away in the morninge, as is very probably suggested, one cominge by, who helped him up when he was falne in the streete, made a noise in the towne that he lay drunke in the kennell, and at the best with other passages within doores of the inn caused a greate scandall and offence.

For all which crimes and scandalls, of which many he confessed or not gainsaid, some could not be denyed, he was by the deane suspended onely, though he might have expell'd him. The scandalls being by him given in unlawfull marriages in an ale-howse and after dinner and in prohibited degrees being left to the censure of the chancellor and bishop, as proper to theire cognizance.

    William Brough, dean.

    Ita testor Guil[ielmus] Lambe, notarius publicus.

209. [*fo. 107*]   21 August[2] 1668.   Chapter House.

Presentacion. Mr. John English. Llantrissen.[3] Quo die, loco & anno &c., whereas the patronage & donacion of the vicaridge of Llantrissen in the county of Glamorgan is the right of the deane and chapter of Gloucester, and the same being now void by the death of Mr. David Lloyd, the last incumbent there, Dr. William Brough, deane of Gloucester, for preservinge the right of this church to the patronage of the said vicaridge of Llantrissen, did this day in open chapter give his voice and free consent for a presentacion to be pass'd, made and sealed to John English, clerke, of the said vicaridge. And Mr. Anthony Andrewes and Dr. Henry Savage, both prebendaryes of this church, gave theire severall

---

[1] Cap. XXXIV of the statutes, 'we ordain and will that if any one of the minor canons, clerks or other officers shall be guilty of any lesser fault he shall be punished according to the discretion of the dean, or in his absence of the subdean, but if he hath offended by any great fault he shall be expelled by those by whom he was admitted.' In quoting the statute the MS. omits 'ut' before 'si quis'.

[2] The word 'Augusti' has been substituted for 'Octobris', which has here been crossed out.

[3] The rectory of Llantrisant (Glam.) had belonged to Tewkesbury abbey and was granted by King Henry VIII on 4 Sept. 1541 as part of the endowment of the dean and chapter of Gloucester.

voyces and consents to the passinge of the said presentacion. And the said Dr. Henry Savage by proxie under the hand and seale of Dr. Thomas Washbourne, subdeane of this church, did likewise give his full consent to the passinge the said presentacion to the said John English, which was then ordered to be sealed with the chapter seale and was performed accordingly.

  William Brough, dean.

  Ita testor Guil[ielmus] Lambe, notarius publicus.

210.   17 September 1668.   Chapter House.

Whereas Griffith Thomas hath delivered a note of severall moneys by him claymed and for other services by him done for the use of the church, it is thought fitt at present that Mr. Lambe doe pay him the summe of five pounds in parte of the said note, and the remainder to be left to consideracion till the next audit, what he shall have for the time past and what shall be thought fitt to be ordered for the time to come.

  William Brough, dean; Tho[mas] Washbourne; Anthony Andrewes &

  Henry Savage per procuratores suos [*by their proxies*].

211. [*fo. 107v.*] 30 November 1668.   Deanery.[1]

(William Brough, S.T.P., dean; Dr. Washbourne; Mr. Viner; Mr. Andrewes; Dr. Savage.)

Electio Officiariorum 1668.[2] [*Election of officers. The dean and the aforenamed prebendaries elected Richard Harwood as subdean and Thomas Washbourne as treasurer and receiver, as in* **166**, *above, stopping at* ejusdem anni, *with a separate note, presumably added later, that on 14 December 1668 they took the oaths belonging to their respective offices.*] Idem decanus et iidem prebendarii prenominati elegerunt venerabiles viros in officiarios, vizt. Richardum Harwood, sacrae theologiae professorem, in sub-decanum et Thomam Washbourne, S.T.P., in thesaurarium et receptorem ejusdem ecclesiae pro hoc anno sequente usque ad finem ejusdem anni.

  Qui quidem antedicti Ricardus Harward et Thomas Washbourne juramenta subierunt ad officia sua respective spectantia ad sacra dei evangelia per eos tacta decimo quarto die Decembris 1668.

[*The dean chose as precentor Edward Jackson. As in* **206**, *above, omitting the word* antedictus *and with the spelling* Jackson.] Eodem die, loco et anno [*etc.*].

  Ita testor Guil[ielmus] Lambe, notarius publicus.

212. [*fo. 108*] 29 April 1669.   Chapter House.

(Thomas Washbourne; Thomas Vyner.)

Presentacion. Mr. Edw[ard] Jackson. Rudford. Quibus die et loco, whereas the patronage & donacion of the rectory of Rudford in the diocesse of Gloucester is the right of the deane and chapter of this church, and the same beinge now void by the death of Dr. Richard Harwood, one of the prebendaryes of this church, the last incumbent there, the above named

---

[1] MS. 'In aedibus domini decani infra precinctum ecclesiae cathedralis Gloucestriae.'

[2] The main heading (here calendared) and the first two words 'Idem decanus' appear to be in the hand of Dean Brough; the marginal heading and the rest of the entry are in that of William Lamb.

Dr. Washbourne and Mr. Vyner, being all that were resident at that time, assembled and mett together in the chapter howse the day abovemencioned for the passinge of a presentacion to the rectory of Rudford aforesaid. The said Dr. Washbourne exhibited a proxie under the hand and seale of the right worshipfull Dr. William Brough, deane of Gloucester, bearinge date the twenty first day of Aprill instant,[1] authorisinge and appointinge the said Dr. Washbourne to give his voice and full consent to the passinge and sealinge a presentacion of the said rectory of Rudford to Edward Jackson, batchelor of arts and one of the minor canons of this church. And the said Dr. Washbourne and Mr. Vyner then likewise gave theire severall voyces and consents to the passinge of the said presentacion of the rectory of Rudford aforesaid to the said Edward Jackson. And the said Mr. Thomas Vyner by vertue of severall proxies under hand and seale from Mr. Hugh Naish and Dr. Henry Savage, both prebendaryes of this church, did give theire severall voyces and full consents to the passinge of the said presentacion of the rectory of Rudford aforesaid to the said Edward Jackson. And accordingly the said Mr. Edward Jackson had a presentacion under the deane & chapter seale then presently granted and delivered unto him.

Presentacion. Mr. Edw[ard] Fidkyn. Matsdon. Quibus die, loco et anno, the like consents were given and pass'd for the presentacion of the rectory or vicaridge of Matsdon unto Edward Fidkyn, clerke, one of the minor canons of this church.

> Tho[mas] Washbourne; Tho[mas] Vyner.
> Ita testor Willelmus Lambe, notarius publicus.

213.   [*fo. 108v.*]   31 July 1669.

Quo die et anno &c. By vertue of the statute 'De Visitacione ecclesiae cathedralis Gloucestriae'[2] cap: 37, the lord bishop of Gloucester was desired to hold a visitacion for the regulatinge of some disorders and abuses in this church and to appoint a certaine time and place for the doinge thereof.

> Tho[mas] Washbourne; Anthony Andrewes; Will[iam] Washbourne.
> Willelmus Lambe, notarius publicus.

214.   19 August 1669.

Mr. William Wrench his second Monition. Quo die et anno &c., at a visitacion holden by the lord bishop of Gloucester the day and yeare abovesaid his lordship pronounced against Mr. Wrench, one of the porters of this church, his second monition to depart this church for his uncivill demeanour to the deane and chapter but especially for his contempt of his lordship's authority.

> Willelmus Lambe, notarius publicus.
>
> This is to be entred in the lord bishop's register.[3]

---

[1] Here a word which might be 'last' has been crossed out, and the word 'instant' inserted above.

[2] Cap. XXXVII, 'Of the Visitation of the Church', appointed the bishop as visitor of the cathedral: if asked by the dean or by two canons, or in any case every three years, the bishop was bound to make an official visitation.

[3] The sentence is in a hand, probably that of Dean Brough, different from that of the main entry.

215. [*fo. 109*]   20 August 1669.   Chapter House.
(William Brough, S.T.P., dean; Thomas Washbourne, S.T.P., treasurer; Anthony Andrewes; William Washbourne.)

Confirmacion of the Chancellor's Patent. Dr. Nicholson.[1] Quo die, loco et anno, the said right worshipful Dr. William Brough, deane of this church, together with the sayd Dr. Washbourne, Mr. Anthony Andrewes and Mr. William Washbourne, prebendaryes, did give theire severall voices and full consents for the continuacion of letters pattents or comission of the office and place of chancellor of the citty and dioces of Gloucester, granted by the right reverend father in God, William, lord bishop of Gloucester, unto John Nicholson, doctor of lawes, and the same day the said patent was continued under theire chapter seale accordingly.
        Ita testor Willelmus Lambe, notarius publicus.

216.   7 September 1669.

Tithes. St. Mary. Quo die et anno, whereas the deane and chapter of Gloucester have by lease granted unto Elianor Boyle, widdow, a certaine parcell of tithes formerly granted unto Walter Harris of the citty of Gloucester, gent., in trust for Mr. Charles Jones, deceased, brother of the said Elianor, which said parcell of tithes was amongst others given unto the viccar of St. Mary de Loade, it is therefore concluded and agreed upon that the said viccar, in liewe of the tithes soe granted as aforesaid, shall receive of the said deane and chapter the yearely summe of six poundes to be duly paid him untill some more convenient way of tithe or other meanes shall be founde out to recompence the said viccar. The foure pounds formerly promised to be paid yearely to the said Elianor henceforth to cease & determine.
        William Brough, deane; Tho[mas] Washbourne; Hugh Naish per
        procuratorem Will[iam] Washbourne; Will[iam] Washbourne.

217. [*fo. 109v.*]   7 September 1669.[2]

The Treasurer to sue for Arrears.[3] Quibus die et loco &c., whereas it appeares that there are upon the audit booke many arrearages of rents due to this church from the yeare 1660 to this present yeare, and also that for time to come we may expect the increase of such arreares by the negligence of tennants to pay theire rents hereafter, and forasmuch as by this meanes the treasurer of the church for the time beinge may be disappointed soe much in receivinge the rents of the church that he shall not be able to pay salaries and other payments in behalfe of the church, wee doe therefore hereby, by our consents in chapter, authorise the said treasurer (soe farr as by law he may) to aske, demand and sue for the said arrearages that for present are, and from time to time duringe his continuacion in the said office shall be, due to the church.
        Willelmus Lambe, notarius publicus.

---

[1] For Nicholson, below, p. 167.

[2] Although the entry bears the same date as the previous one, it is not clear that the decision which it records was taken at the same meeting.

[3] The account books record many lawsuits against tenants who, having acquired chapter property under the Commonwealth, refused to pay their rents. A major offender was Sir Thomas Stephens, lessee of Wotton, Barnwood and Cranham manors, who eventually paid £81 2*s.* 6*d.* as an entry fine.

218.   Wednesday 17 December 1669.   Chapter House.
(Thomas Vyner, subdean.)

James Evans. Eleemozinarius.[1] [*James Evans, almsman. James Evans appeared and sought admission to the place of an almsman by virtue of letters patent granted to him and addressed to the dean and chapter, and registered at their registry, whereupon the subdean admitted him, he having first taken the almsman's oath, to receive the emoluments belonging to the place.*] Comparuit quidam Jacobus Evans [*etc., as in* **81**, *above*].
      Ita testor Willelmus Lambe, notarius publicus.

219.   [*fo. 110*]   Tuesday the feast of St. Andrew the Apostle, 30 November 1669.
                                                          Chapter House.
(William Brough, S.T.P., dean; Thomas Washbourne, S.T.P.; Thomas Vyner; Anthony Andrewes; William Washbourne.)

Electio Officiariorum 1669. [*Election of officers. The dean and the aforenamed prebendaries elected Thomas Vyner, S.T.B., as subdean and Thomas Washbourne, S.T.P., as receiver and treasurer. As in* **170**, *above, adding* hos *after* elegerunt.]
      Ita testor Willelmus Lambe, notarius publicus.

Electio Precentoris. [*Election of the precentor. The dean chose as precentor Edward Jackson, one of the minor canons, who took the oath. The form differs from that in earlier entries of the kind.*] Eodem die, loco et anno idem venerabilis decanus elegit in precentorem dictae ecclesiae Edvardum Jackson, unum minorum canonicorum ejusdem ecclesiae cathedralis &c., qui juramentum suscepit &c.
      Ita testor Willelmus Lambe, notarius publicus.

220.   Wednesday the feast of St. Andrew the Apostle, 30 November 1670.
                                                          Chapter House.
(Thomas Vyner, subdean; Thomas Washbourne, S.T.P.; Anthony Andrewes; Henry Savage, S.T.P.)

Electio Officiariorum 1670. [*Election of officers. In the absence of the dean but with his consent, the subdean and the aforenamed prebendaries elected Thomas Vyner as subdean and Anthony Andrews as receiver and treasurer. As in* **166–7**, *above, omitting* et continuarunt *and adding* iuxta morem antiquum.]

Electio Precentoris. [*Election of the precentor. The aforesaid men elected as precentor Edward Jackson, one of the minor canons, who took the oath.*] Eodem die, loco et anno venerabiles viri antedicti elegerunt in praecentorem dictae ecclesiae Edvardum Jackson, unum minorum canonicorum ejusdem ecclesiae, [qui] juramentum suscepit &c.
      Ita testor Willelmus Lambe, notarius publicus.

---

[1] MS. 'Eleesimozinarius'.

221. [*fo. 110v.*] ***Orders enioyned by the Reverend Father in God, William, by God's permission Lord Bishop of Gloucester, to be observed by the Deane and Chapter of the Cathedrall Church of Gloucester, given them in charge in his Lordship's Trienniall Visitacion of the Diocesse of Gloucester Anno Domini 1668/9.***

1. Imprimis that the order enioyn'd by Archbishop Laud when he was deane of the aforesaid church, which are registred [on] page 31, and alsoe those orders which he enioyn'd afterward in his archiepiscopall visitacion 1635, which are registred [on] page (68), be duly observed.[1]

2. Ordered that besides what is ordered about mariages by Deane Laude, page (31), there be a register booke kept in the church by the chantor, wherein he is to register the names, day, moneth, yeare and the parish of all those who are married, as alsoe the names of all those who are christned in the cathedrall or buried in church or churchyard, and that the chantor in the cathedrall only marry, except the deane or any of the prebendaryes please to doe that office or appoint some other. And then the precentor to be acquainted therewith that the marriages be entred accordingly.

3. Ordered that the petty canons read the letany on the dayes appointed[2] at the deske in the midst of the quire.

4. Ordered that the master of the choristers be very diligent in teaching the choristers to sing, and give his approbacion of the voice and aptnes of the boy who is to be chosen chorister, and one day in every weeke catechize the choristers in the principles of Christian religion as is sett downe in the church chatechisme the better to prepare them for confirmacion.

[*fo. 111*]

5. Ordered that a place or two of the choristers be kept void till a boy be found who hath a good voice and aptnes for musique. And that for the first yeare choristers be admitted as probationers onely, that soe, if they fitt not themselves to doe the quire service by the end of the yeare, they may be removed; yet be it provided, that they receive the usuall stipend for that yeare of probacion quarterly, as if they were actually admitted.

6. Ordered that the eucharist or holy communion be better and oftner frequented by all that have places in the church capable to receive, and for their neglect be punishable per arbitrio decani [*at the dean's discretion*] or in his absence vice decani [*the subdean's*] or senior prebendarie. And that the moneys given at the offertory be at the dispose of the deane (if present) or subdeane or any other prebend that is present in their absence.

7. Ordered that the money received for burialls in the cathedrall be bestowed upon the reparacion of the church, which is to be accompted for by the treasurer at the audit, and that the treasurer permitt not the grounds to be broken up till the fees be paid.

8. Ordered that the janitors for the future according to the statute be Virgae-Bajuli.[3]

---

[1] Cf. above, **28**, **132**. The references to pages are in fact to folios.

[2] Presumably as was directed in the *Book of Common Prayer*.

[3] i.e. wand-bearers. Cap. XXVII of the statutes provided for 'two door-keepers, who shall also do the office of virgers . . . who shall also faithfully keep the keys of the gates; and shall also keep the gates and outward doors of the precincts of our church'.

9. Ordered that the offices of butler, cooke and the like that may be spared be never more by patent granted to any;[1] and in those inferior offices which shall be granted by patent (which I wish none were, and I am sure the statutes are silent in it) that there be noe lycence given to distraine upon any of your mannors or tenements, in case their stipends be not payd, noe, nor yet any liberty given them to appoint a deputy for their life, nay, nor any at all without the consent of the deane and chapter.

[*fo. 111v.*]

10. Ordered that the almesmen be vested as they ought, weare on their right [*sic, recte* left] shoulder a redd rose of silke, attend and helpe to cleane the church, and to their power helpe the sexton to toll the bells, and doe their dutyes which are required. Vide statute 26 & 29.[2]

11. Ordered that the schoole and schollers therein bee regulated according to the statute.[3]

12. Ordered that there be some, either almesmen, sexton or other person, appointed to keepe doggs out of the church, and that there be noe walking in the body of the church or cloysters in time of divine service, nor any boys or others playinge or idlinge in the churchyard on the Lord's day, and that they present the names of such as doe herein transgresse to the deane or subdeane or any of the prebendaries which shall be then resident.

13. Ordered that the porters attend in their office as they ought. Statute 27.

14. Ordered that all the surplices of the petty-cannons, singingmen and choristers be washed in one and the same weeke, except the surplices of those petty-cannons whose turne it is that weeke to doe the office of the church.

15. Ordered that the sub-deane or senior prebend present doe once in fifteene dayes cause the chaunter to give up the names of all those who have bene, and how often, absent from prayers within that time.

16. Item wee require that these our iniunctions be carefully registred and observed.
 Vera copia examinatur per[4] Willelmum Lambe, notarium publicum.
 [*A true copy to be checked by William Lamb, notary public.*]

---

[1] Cf. above, **136**.

[2] Cap. XXVI provides for four poor men to 'assist, as much as they are able, the sub-sacrists in lighting the candles and in tolling the bells'. Cap. XXIX specifies their outward garments 'as near as may be, of the same colour', the cloth to be supplied to them before Christmas 'that they may celebrate the birthday of our Lord Jesus Christ with new clothes and new souls', and that they should always 'wear on the left shoulder of their gowns a rose made of red silk'.

[3] Cap. XXV specified the necessary qualifications of the headmaster and the assistant master, and 'if they prove idle, negligent or not fit to teach, let them be expelled and deprived of their places, after a third admonition from the dean, or in his absence the sub-dean and chapter'.

[4] After 'per' the handwriting changes, Lamb's name being a signature.

222. [*fo. 112*]　　17 February 1670/1.　　　　　　　　Chapter House.
(Thomas Vyner, subdean; Thomas Washbourne; Anthony Andrewes.)

A Presentacion of Marlow Magna to Mr. Timothy Burrage.[1] Quibus die et loco, whereas the patronage and donacion of the vicaridge of Marlow Magna in the diocesse of Lincolne is the right of the deane & chapter of this church, and the same being now void by the death of Mr. John Fournesse, the last incumbent there, the abovenamed Mr. Vyner, Dr. Washbourne and Mr. Andrewes (beinge all that were resident at that time), assembled and mett together in the chapter howse the day abovemencioned for the passing of a presentacion to the vicaridge of Marlow Magna aforesaid. The said Mr. Vyner exhibited a proxie under the hand and seale of the right worshipfull Dr. William Brough, deane of Gloucester, bearinge date the tenth day of February instant, authorisinge and appointinge the said Mr. Vyner to give his voice and full consent to the passinge and sealinge of a presentacion of the said vicaridge of Marlow Magna to Tymothy Burrage, master of arts. And the said Mr. Vyner, Dr. Washbourne and Mr. Andrewes then likewise gave theire severall voices and consents to the passinge the said praesentacion of the vicaridge of Marlow Magna aforesaid to the said Timothy Burrage. And accordingly the said Mr. Timothy Burrage had a presentacion under the deane and chapter seale then presently granted and delivered unto him.

[*fo. 112v. blank*]

223.　[*fo. 113*]　　Sunday 23 July 1671.　　　　　　　　Chapter House.
(Thomas Washbourne, S.T.P.; William Lambe, notary public and registrar.)

Installatio venerabilis viri Thomae Vyner Decani Gloucestriae 1671. [*Installation of the venerable man Thomas Vyner as dean of Gloucester. Thomas Vyner, S.T.P., appeared in person and presented the king's letters patent, dated 11 July 1671, and he exhibited the royal mandate addressed to the chapter and canons to assign to the dean a stall in the choir and a place and a voice in the chapter, etc., as in* **100**, *above.*] Quibus die ac loco in propria persona sua comparuit venerabilis et discretus vir Thomas Vyner, sacrae theologiae professor, constitutus [*etc., as in* **100**, *above, but omitting reference to the oath to observe the cathedral's statutes and with minor verbal variations of which the most significant is the substitution of 'canons' for 'prebendaries' in two places. All this was done in the presence of Richard Parsons, Ll.B. and notary public, Edward Jackson, precentor, Abraham Gregory, M.A.,*[2] *Joseph Goodman, notary public, John Campion*[3] *and other servants of the said church*].
[*fo. 113v.*]
　　Ita testor Willelmus Lambe, notarius publicus et decano & capitulo registrarius.

---

[1] Perhaps the Timothy Burrage who matriculated as a sizar at Caius College, Cambridge, in 1656, graduating B.A. in 1660 and M.A. in 1663.

[2] Abraham Gregory, to be admitted in eight days' time to the prebend vacated by Vyner, was presumably attending in his capacity as assistant schoolmaster.

[3] For Campion, below, p. 162.

224.   [*fo. 114*]   29 July 1671.   Chapter House.
(Thomas Vyner, S.T.P., dean; Anthony Andrewes, treasurer; William Washbourne.)

Decanus Jurat. [*The dean takes the oath. As in* **2**, *above.*]
Tho[mas] Vyner, decan[us]; Antonius Andrewes; Will[elmus] Washbourne.
Ita testor Willelmus Lambe, notarius publicus.

225.   7 August 1671.   Chapter House.
Admissio Hypodidascali. Mr. Nath*[*aniel*] *Lyes. [1] [*Admission of the assistant schoolmaster. Nathaniel Lye, M.A., who had been chosen by the dean, was admitted by the dean, after he had taken the oath on the gospels, touched by him.*] Quibus die, loco et anno Nathaniell Lyes, in artibus magister, [*etc., as in* **50**, *above*].
Tho[mas] Vyner, deane.

226.   [*fo. 114v.*]   Thursday 31 July 1671.   Chapter House.
(Thomas Vyner, S.T.P., dean.)

Admissio Venerabilis Viri Abrahami Gregory. [*Admission of the venerable man Abraham Gregory. In the chapter house Abraham Gregory, M.A., exhibited the king's letters patent, dated 24 July instant, granting to him the prebend vacant by the preferment of Thomas Vyner to the deanery, and the royal mandate for his admission and installation; the dean admitted him, as in* **37**, *above. All this was done in the presence of James Davenant, Edward Jackson, precentor and minor canon, John Campion and other servants of the said church and of the writer, William Lamb, registrar.*] In domo capitulari dictae ecclesiae venerabilis vir Abrahamus Gregory, in artibus magister, exhibuit [*etc., as in* **107**, *above*].
Ita testor Guil[ielmus] Lambe, registrarius.

227.   [*fo. 115*]   Thursday the feast of St. Andrew the Apostle, 30 November 1671.
Chapter House.
(Thomas Vyner, S.T.P., dean; Thomas Washbourne, S.T.P.; Anthony Andrewes; Abraham Gregory.)

Electio Officiariorum 1671. [*Election of officers. The dean and prebendaries elected Anthony Andrews as subdean and Thomas Washbourne as receiver and treasurer. As in* **170**, *above, but including* hos *before* officiarios.]

Electio Precentoris. [*Election of the precentor. The dean chose Edward Jackson, one of the minor canons, who took the oath.*] Eodem die, loco et anno [*etc., as in* **219**, *above*].

Electio Sacristae. [*Election of the sacrist. The dean chose Edward Fidkin, one of the minor canons, who took the oath.*] Eodem die, loco et anno idem venerabilis decanus elegit in sacristam dictae ecclesiae Edvardum Fidkyn, unum minorum canonicorum ejusdem ecclesiae cathedralis &c., qui juramentum suscepit &c.
Ita testor Willelmus Lambe, notarius publicus.

---

[1] For Lye, below, p. 167.

228. [*fo. 115v.*]   30 November 1671.   Chapter House.

The Minor Canons, concerninge Marriages. Whereas severall differences and disputes have lately hapned betweene the minor cannons of this church about marriages had and to be had & solempnised therein (the praecentor for the time beinge challenginge that office as of right belonginge unto him),[1] to prevent the like, and to settle the same for the future, it is ordered and decreed, and the deane and chapter doe hereby order & decree, that the severall minor-canons shall have free liberty to marry in the cathedrall church, and that the minor canons soe marryinge there as aforesaid shall pay for every marriage soe by them severally had and solempnised unto the praecentor for the time beinge one shilling for registringe and entringe such marriages. And the sexton for the time beinge is to give notice to the praecentor of all such marriages that they may be registred accordingly.

> Tho[mas] Vyner, decan[us]; Antho[ny] Andrewes, subd[ecanus];
> Tho[mas] Washbourne, treas[urer]; Abraham Gregory.

229.   29 April 1672.   Chapter House.

Two Minor Canons to attend every Lord's Day. Whereas severall neglects have bene made by the minor cannons in attendinge at divine service on the Lord's day in the morninge[2] under pretence of servinge at theire severall cures, whereby the service of the church hath bene many times slenderly performed, it is therefore ordered that for the future two of the said cannons shall constantly attend the said service every Sunday morninge, and that the praecentor for the time beinge take care to have the same performed accordingly.

> Tho[mas] Vyner, deane; Anth[ony] Andrewes, subdean;
> Tho[mas] Washbourne treas[urer]; Abraham Gregory.

230. [*fo. 116*]   15 May 1672.   Chapter House.
(Thomas Vyner, S.T.P., dean; Anthony Andrewes, subdean; Thomas Washbourne, treasurer; William Washbourne; Abraham Gregory.)

Murrall to appear the twenty fourth of June. Quibus die, loco et anno Richard Murrall, one of the porters of this church, for non-attendance upon his said office according to the duty of his place, was discharged of the said office of porter unless he comes and gives his attendance here by the twenty fourth day of June next.

> Tho[mas] Vyner, decan[us]; Tho[mas] Washbourne.

Electio Sub-Sacristae. [*Election of the subsacrist. The dean chose as subsacrist John Campion the elder, who took the oath.*] Eodem die, loco et anno idem venerabilis decanus elegit in sub-sacristam dictae ecclesiae Johannem Campion seniorem, qui juramentum suscepit.

> Tho[mas] Vyner, decan[us].

---

[1] Cf. above, **221**, para. 2.
[2] The words 'in the morninge' are underlined in the MS.

231.   18 July 1672.   Chapter House.
(Thomas Vyner, S.T.P., dean; Thomas Washbourne, treasurer; William Washbourne; Abraham Gregory.)

Murrall's discharge of the Office of Porter. Whereas Richard Murrall, by an order of the fifteenth day of May last, was discharged of the office of porter of this church unless he came and gave his attendance by the twenty fourth day of June then next followinge, and whereas the said Richard Murrall did not appeare at the time aforesaid, it is therefore ordered and concluded that the said Richard Murrall be from henceforth discharged of the said office of porter, and is hereby declared to be discharged accordingly.

Eodem die, loco et anno, ordered that John Campion senior have a pattent of the sexton's place formerly granted to Berkly Wrenche, and that John Campion junior have the like patent which was formerly granted to Paule Bridger, both the said former patents being delivered up to the said deane and chapter, and a bond of fifty pounds to be given by the said John Campion senior to save the deane and chapter harmeles from the said former patents. The grant to be quam diu se bene gesserit [*as long as he shall behave himself well*]. The clause of distresse to be omitted.
          Ita testor Willelmus Lambe, registrarius.

232.   [*fo. 116v.*]   Tuesday 23 July 1672.   Chapter House.
(Thomas Vyner, S.T.P., dean.)

Admissio venerabilis viri Roberti Frampton. [*Admission of the venerable man Robert Frampton. In the chapter house Robert Frampton, M.A., exhibited the king's letters patent, dated 4 June last past, granting to him the prebend vacant by the death of Henry Savage, and the royal mandate for his admission and installation; the dean admitted him, as in* **37**, *above. All this was done in the presence of Thomas Pierce* (MS. *Peirce*), *gent., John Deighton, minor canon, George Evans, minor canon, John Campion and other servants of the said church and of the writer, William Lamb, registrar.*] In domo capitulari dictae ecclesiae venerabilis vir Robertus Frampton, in artibus magister, exhibuit [*etc., as in* **107**, *above*].
          Ita testor Willelmus Lambe, registrarius.

233.   [*fo. 117*]   29 July 1672.   Chapter House.

Quibus die, loco et anno, Mr. Deane declared Henry Payne of the citty of Gloucester, yeoman, to be porter in the place of Richard Murrall, lately discharged from the said office.
          Tho[mas] Vyner, deane.

234. *Dr. John Pritchett Recomended to be Bishop of Gloucester.* Charles R. Trusty and welbeloved, wee greete you well. Whereas the bishopricke of Gloucester is at this present void by the death of Dr. William Nicholson, late bishop there, wee let you weete that for certaine consideracions us at this present movinge of our princely disposicion and zeale, beinge desirous to present unto the same see a person meete thereunto, and consideringe the vertue, learning, wisedome, gravity and other the good guifts wherewith the reverend John Pritchett, doctor in divinity, is endued, wee have bene pleased by these our letters to name and recommend him unto you to be elected and chosen to the said bishopricke of

Gloucester. Wherefore wee require you upon the receipt hereof to proceed to your election accordinge to the lawes of this our realme and our Conge Deslire[1] herewith sent unto you, and the same election soe made to certifie unto us under your common seale. Given under our signett at our pallace of Westminster the 24th of September in the 24th yeare of our raigne, 1672.

To our trusty and welbeloved the deane & chapter
of our cathedrall church of Gloucester.   Sidney Bere.[2]

235. [*fo. 117v.*]

Le Congedeslire. [*The king's* congé d'élire, *dated at Westminster, 27 September 1672, to the dean and chapter, who, their church lacking a pastor through the death of William Nicholson, S.T.P., the last bishop, have asked for licence to elect a successor, which the king grants, asking them to elect a bishop useful and loyal to the king and the kingdom.*] Carolus Secundus, dei gracia Angliae, Scotiae, Franciae et Hiberniae rex, fidei defensor &c., dilectis nobis in Christo decano et capitulo ecclesiae nostrae cathedralis Gloucestriae, salutem. Ex parte vestra nobis est humiliter supplicatum ut, cum ecclesia predicta per mortem naturalem Gulielmi Nicholson, sacrae theologiae professoris, ultimi episcopi eiusdem, iam vacet et pastoris sit solacio destituta, alium vobis eligendi in episcopum et pastorem licentiam nostram fundatoriam vobis concedere dignaremur, nos, precibus vestris in hac parte favorabiliter inclinati, licentiam illam vobis tenore presencium duximus concedendam, rogantes ac in fide et dilectione quibus nobis tenemimi precipientes quod talem vobis eligatis in episcopum et pastorem qui deo devotus nobisque et regno nostro utilis et fidelis existat. In cujus rei testimonium has literas nostras fieri fecimus patentes. Teste me ipso apud Westmonasterium vicesimo septimo die Septembris anno regni nostri vicesimo quarto.

Grimston; Lowe.[3]

236.   Thursday 10 October 1672. between ten a.m. and noon.

Chapter House.
(Thomas Vyner S.T.P., dean, by his proxy Dr. Washbourne; Anthony Andrewes, subdean; Thomas Washbourne, S.T.P.; William Washbourne, M.A.; Abraham Gregory, MA.; William Lambe, registrar.)

Electio Episcopi, Dr. Pritchett. [*Election of the bishop, Dr. Pritchett. Richard Parsons, Ll.B. and notary public, exhibited the king's letters patent or* congé d'élire *under the Great Seal, dated 27 September 1672, for the election as bishop and pastor of the cathedral church of the episcopal see, vacant by the death of William Nicholson, S.T.P., the last bishop, of someone suitable, devout to God and useful and loyal to the king and his kingdom. He exhibited letters dated 10 November and signed by the king's hand nominating John Pritchett, S.T.P., as eligible by the dean and chapter, on the strength of*

---

[1] i.e. the *congé d'élire*, or permission to elect a bishop.
[2] Sidney Bere, Clerk of the Signet 1660–84.
[3] Sir Harbottle Grimston, Master of the Rolls 1660–85; George Lowe, Chancery clerk, clerk of the Petty Bag 1666–80.

which the dean and chapter elected John Pritchett and certified the king by a letter under the chapter seal dated 10 October. And on the same day they nominated Edmund Arnold and Thomas Swallow, notaries public of the Canterbury Court of Arches in London, jointly and severally, as their proctors to present their letter to the king and to do other things necessary.] Quibus die et loco constitutus personaliter Ricardus Parsons, legum baccalaureus et notarius publicus, cum [*etc., as in 54, above, as far as*] [*fo. 118*][1] et electionem hujusmodi eorum regiae majestati certificaverunt per literas sub sigillo eorum capitulari eodem decimo die Octobris datas. Eodemque die constituerunt et nominaverunt dilectos sibi in Christo Edmundum Arnold et [Thomam][2] Swallowe, almae curiae Cant. de Archubus London. notarios publicos conjunctim et divisim eorum procuratores &c. et exhibendum regiae majestati literas certificatorias et regalem suum assensum eleccionis predictae coram quocunque in ea parte potestatem habenti seu habituro usque ad finalem expeditionem ejusdem eorum nomine prosequendum ac confirmacionem in ea parte petendum &c. et generaliter omnia et singula facienda et exercenda quae in premissis necessaria fuerint &c.

237. [*fo. 118v.*]

Litera Certificatoria. [*Letter of certification. The dean and chapter, having received from Richard Parsons the king's letters patent for the election of a bishop to succeed William Nicholson and his letter of 24 September nominating John Pritchett, certify the king that on 10 October 1672, between the tenth and the twelfth hour before noon, being assembled in the chapter house they elected John Pritchett as bishop. Their letter was sealed on the same day.*] Illustrissimo in Christo principi ac domino nostro, Domino Carolo Secundo, dei gracia Angliae, Scociae, Franciae et Hiberniae regi, fidei defensori &c., vestri humiles et devoti Thomas Vyner, sacrae theologiae professor, decanus ecclesiae cathedralis Gloucestriensis, nec non Antonius Andrews, artis magister, ejusdem ecclesiae cathedralis Gloucestriae sub-decanus, Thomas Washbourne, S.T.P., Gulielmus Washbourne, artis magister, Abrahamus Gregory, artis magister, prebendarii in ecclesia cathedrali praedicta et ejusdem ecclesiae cathedralis capitulum, omnimodas submissionem et subjectionem debitas et condignas. Cum nos literas vestras patentes sive le Conge deslire, magno sigillo Angliae sigillatas, gerentes datum vicesimo septimo die Septembris anno regni vestri felicissimi vicesimo quarto, debita cum humilitate a Ricardo Parsons, legum bacolaureo et notario publico, nuper recepimus pro eleccione in episcopum et pastorem ecclesiae cathedralis Gloucestriae jam vacantem per mortem naturalem Gulielmi Nicolson, SS.T.P., ultimi episcopi et pastoris ibidem,[3] aliquem idoneum deo devotum vestraeque regiae majestati et regno vestro utilem et fidelem, una cum literis vestris missivis majestatis vestrae manu sacra signatis, gerentes datum vicesimo quarto Septembris anno praedicto, per quas venerabilis et egregius vir Johannes Pritchett, SS.T.P., in episcopum et pastorem ecclesiae cathedralis Gloucestriae praedictae per nos eligendus per easdem literas specialiter nominatus et commendatus existit; vestrae regiae celsitudini et majestati harum serie certificamus per presentes quod decimo die

---

[1] The word 'sigillo', the first of the folio, is also a catchword at the foot of fo. 117v.

[2] The MS. omits the forename, which may be deduced from **279** and **283**, below.

[3] The MS. has a closing bracket after the word 'ibidem' but no corresponding opening bracket.

Octobris anno domini 1672 et inter horas decimam et duodecimam antemeridiem ejusdem diei nos, decanus et capitulum ecclesiae cathedralis Gloucestriae praedictae, in domo capitulari ejusdem ecclesiae cathedralis solemniter et capitulariter congregati, eundem venerabilem et egregium virum Johannem Pritchett in episcopum et pastorem ecclesiae cathedralis Gloucestriae praedictae, juxta tenorem literarum vestrarum patentium et literarum vestrarum missivarum praedictarum, elegimus, pro ut per presentes eligimus. In quorum omnium et singulorum premissorum fidem et testimonium sigillum nostrum capitularem presentibus apponi fecimus. Datum quoad sigillacionem presentium decimo die Octobris anno supradicto.

Willelmus Lambe, notarius publicus et decano et capitulo registrarius.

238. [*fo. 119*]   Saturday the feast of St. Andrew the Apostle, 30 November 1672.

Chapter House.

(Thomas Vyner, S.T.P., dean; Thomas Washbourne, S.T.P.; Anthony Andrewes; Abraham Gregory.)

Electio Officiariorum 1672. [*Election of officers. The dean and chapter elected Anthony Andrewes as subdean and Abraham Gregory as receiver and treasurer.*[1] *As in* **170**, *above, but replacing* Idem decanus et iidem prebendarii prenominati elegerunt venerabiles viros in officiarios *with* Idem decanus et capitulum elegerunt[2] hos officiarios.]

Electio Praecentoris. [*Election of the precentor. The dean chose Edward Jackson, one of the minor canons, who took the oath.*] Eodem die, loco et anno [*etc., as in* **219**, *above*].

Electio Sacristae. [*Election of the sacrist. The dean chose John Deighton, one of the minor canons, who took the oath.*] Eodem die &c. idem venerabilis decanus elegit in sacristam dictae ecclesiae Johannem Dighton, unum minorum canonicorum ejusdem ecclesiae cathedralis &c., qui juramentum suscepit &c.

239.   Sunday[3] the feast of St. Andrew the Apostle, 30 November 1673.

Chapter House.

(Robert Frampton, S.T.P., dean; Thomas Washbourne, S.T.P.; William Washbourne; Abraham Gregory.)

Electio Officiariorum 1673. [*Election of officers. The dean and chapter elected Anthony Andrewes as subdean and Abraham Gregory as receiver and treasurer. As in* **238**, *above.*]

Electio Praecentoris. [*Election of the precentor. The dean chose Edward Jackson, one of the minor canons, who took the oath.*]. Eodem die, loco et anno [*etc., as in* **219**, *above*].

Electio Sacristae. [*Election of the sacrist. The dean chose John Deighton, one of the minor canons, who took the oath.*] Eodem die &c. [*etc., as in* **238**, *above*].

---

[1] It was evidently on his election as treasurer that Gregory began the register of which part is printed below, pp. 157–9.

[2] The MS. has 'eligerunt', which is correctly 'elegerunt' in later similar entries.

[3] The MS. has 'Die Sabati', but 30 Nov. 1673 was a Sunday.

240.   [*fo. 119v.*]   19 January 1673/4.   Chapter House.

Admissio Organistae. [*Admission of the organist. Charles Wren was admitted by the dean as organist and instructor of the choristers in the place of Daniel Henstridge, was installed in the choir by the precentor and took the oath on the gospels, touched by him.*] Quo die, loco et anno Carolus Wrenn admissus erat per decanum in locum organistae et choristarum instructoris huius ecclesiae in loco Danielis Henstridge et installatus in choro per praecentorem, qui quidem Carolus subiit juramenta respective ad sacrosancta dei evangelia per eum tacta &c.

[*fo. 120 and v. blank*]

241.   [*fo. 121*]   Tuesday 6 May 1673.   Chapter House.
(Thomas Washbourne, S.T.P.; William Lambe, notary public and registrar.)

Installatio venerabilis viri Roberti Frampton Decani Gloucestriae, 1673. [*Installation of the venerable man Robert Frampton as dean of Gloucester. Robert Frampton, M.A., appeared in person and presented the king's letters patent, dated 18 April 1673, and he exhibited the royal mandate addressed to the chapter and canons to assign to the dean a stall in the choir and a place and a voice in the chapter, etc., as in* **100**, *above.*] Quibus die ac loco in propria persona sua comparuit venerabilis et discretus vir Robertus Frampton, in artibus magister, constitutus [*etc., as in* **100**, *above, with minor verbal variations of which the most significant is the substitution of 'canons' for 'prebendaries' in two places. All this was done in the presence of Edward Jackson, precentor, George Evans, minor canon, John Campion, subsacrist, and other servants of the said church*].
[*fo. 121v.*] Ita testor Willelmus Lambe, notarius publicus decano et capitulo registrarius.

242.   [*fo. 122*]   6 May 1673.[1]   Chapter House.

Admissio Sub-Sacristae. Mr. Campion. [*Admission of the subsacrist.*] Quibus die, loco et anno &c., whereas upon a former treaty betweene the deane and chapter and Mr. William Wrenche about the surrender of a patent belonginge to Paule Bridger, sometime sub-sacrist of this church,[2] it was agreed that upon surrender of the said patent Mr. John Campion senior should be admitted in his place, but the said Mr. Wrenche refusinge then to deliver up the said patent, upon further debate of the said matter and upon surrender of the said patent into the hands of the deane and chapter, which was accordingly this day surrendred, it was fully concluded and agreed that the said Mr. Campion should be admitted sub-sacrist in the place of the said Paule Bridger, and the said Mr. Campion was thereupon admitted and sworne accordingly.

Mr. Wrench. Eodem die, loco et anno, Mr. William Wrenche produced a deputacon from his brother, Berkly Wrenche, for the place and office of sub-sacrist of this church, which

---

[1] This entry does not follow on from the record of the installation of Dean Frampton, having its own heading and being in a different hand (William Lamb's) on a new page. It is possible that **241** was inserted later.
[2] Cf. above, **231**.

said deputacon was read and allowed, and the said William Wrenche was thereupon admitted and sworne accordingly.

Ita testor Willelmus Lambe, notarius publicus.

243.   8 May 1673.   Chapter House.

Admissio Janitoris. [*Admission of a porter.*] Quibus die, loco et anno &c., whereas by an order of the eighteenth day of July (1672) Richard Murrall (for the reasons therein expressed) was discharged of the office of porter of this church,[1] and whereas afterwards (vizt.) the twenty ninth day of July followinge Henry Payne of the citty of Gloucester was by the then deane declared to be porter in the place of the said Richard Murrall, which said office the said Henry Payne refusinge to accept of, Mr. Deane elected into the office of porter of this church Walter Allard of Sainthurst in the county of Gloucester, yeoman, who was thereupon admitted and sworne accordingly.

Ita testor Willelmus Lambe, notarius publicus.

244.   [*fo. 122v.*]   26 May 1673.   Chapter House.

An Order Concerning King Edward's Gate belonginge to one of the Porters.[2] Quibus die, loco et anno &c., whereas the deane & chapter have heretofore leased the gatehouse comonly called Kinge Edward's Gate, belonginge to one of the porters of this church, for the terme of forty yeares, the interest of which lease is now vested in one Samuell Kinge of the citty of Gloucester, taylor, it is concluded and agreed (upon surrender of the said lease, which was accordingly done) that the said Samuell Kinge shall have a new lease of the said gatehouse for thirty yeares if the said Samuell Kinge and Mary his wife shall soe long live, under the yearely rent of twenty shillinges and other usuall covenants. Which said twenty shillinges the treasurer for the time beinge shall pay unto the porter for the time beinge untill the said lease shall fall into the churche's hands, and noe longer the same to be allowed upon the treasurer's accompt.

Ita testor Willelmus Lambe, registrarius.

Admissio Choristae. [*Admission of a chorister. John Sudeley was admitted by the dean in the place of an unnamed boy.*] Eodem die et loco &c. Johannes Sowdely admissus fuit per venerabilem decanum chorista in loco [. . .].[3]

Admissio Choristae. [*Admission of a chorister. An unnamed boy was admitted by the dean in the place of an unnamed boy.*] Eodem die [. . .][4] admissus fuit per venerabilem decanum chorista in loco [. . .].

---

[1] Cf. above, **230–1** and **233**.

[2] Cf. above, p. xix.

[3] The name of the chorister replaced was left blank; it seems from the chapter accounts that the only chorister who left in 1673 was Charles Twinninge.

[4] The name of the new chorister is left blank; apart from John Sudeley, it seems from the chapter accounts that the only boy to have joined the choir in 1673 was William George.

245. *[fo.* 123]   Tuesday 20 May 1673.   Chapter House.
(Robert Frampton, M.A., dean.)

Admissio venerabilis viri Nathanielis Hodges. *[Admission of the venerable man Nathaniel Hodges. In the chapter house Nathaniel Hodges, M.A., exhibited the king's letters patent, dated 4 May instant, granting to him the prebend or canonry vacant by the preferment of Robert Frampton to the deanery, and the royal mandate for his admission and installation; the dean admitted him, as in* **37**, *above. All this was done in the presence of Thomas Washbourne, William Washbourne, Abraham Gregory, prebendaries,[1] William Wrench and other servants of the said church and of the writer, William Lamb, registrar.]* In domo capitulari dictae ecclesiae venerabilis vir Nathanielis Hodges, in artibus magister, exhibuit [*etc., as in* **107**, *above*].

  Ita testor Willelmus Lambe, registrarius.

246. *[fo. 123v.]*

Mr. Hodges his Dispensation. Charles R. Trusty and welbeloved, wee greet you well. Whereas by the statutes or custome of that our cathedrall church of Gloucester the prebendarys residensiary of the same are to make theire residence there for the space of one and twenty days in a yeare, and whereas Nathaniell Hodges, master of arts, one of the prebendarys residensiary of our said church being domestique chaplaine to our right trusty and right welbeloved cousin & chancellor, Anthony, earle of Shaftsbury,[2] our high chancellor of England, is unable by reason of his constant attendance upon our said high chancellor to make the said residence of one and twenty days, wee have thought fitt and doe hereby dispense with him, the said Nathaniell Hodges, for the same; and it is accordingly our will and pleasure that you take noe advantage of him for or by reason of his not makinge the said residence of one and twenty days in a yeare (soe longe as he shall continue in the employment of chaplaine to our said high chancellor), butt suffer him notwithstandinge such his absence to receive and enjoy all the benefitts, profitts and emoluments of his place of prebendary residentiary of our said church of Gloucester in as full and ample manner as if he kept his residence according to the rules & statutes of the said church, and forsoe doinge this shall be your warrant; and soe wee bidd you farewell. Given at our court at Whitehall the two & twentith day of August 1673 in the five and twentieth yeare of our raigne.

  By his majestie's command.

  To our trusty & welbeloved the deane & chapter
  of our cathedrall churche of Gloucester.   Henry Coventry.[3]

---

  [1] Since the prebendaries are not named at the beginning of the entry as present it is possible that they were not present in the chapter house but only at the ceremony in the choir.
  [2] Anthony Ashley Cooper (1621–83), first earl of Shaftesbury, Lord Chancellor 1672–3.
  [3] Henry Coventry (1619–1686), Secretary of State 1672–80. He was the brother-in-law of Anthony Ashley Cooper, earl of Shaftesbury.

247. [*fo. 124*]   23 June 1674.   Chapter House.
(Robert Frampton, S.T.P., dean; Anthony Andrewes, subdean; Thomas Washbourne; William Washbourne; Abraham Gregory.)

James Evans his first Monition. At which day and place upon complaint made to Mr. Deane against James Evans, one of the beadesmen of this church, for neglectinge his duty and not cominge to divine prayers, Mr. Deane published his first monition or warninge to departe the church.
     Robert Frampton, dec[anus].

248.   27 June 1674.   Chapter House.

Paenalties on ye Quire men and other Officers. Whereas the severall members and officers of this church have of late very much neglected theire dutyes in frequentinge divine prayers, morninge and eveninge (contrary to the statutes of this church), occasioned partly thorough the smalenes of the paenalty inflicted on such offenders, it is ordered that for the future the paenalties to be inflicted for every absence at prayers shall be as followeth (that is to say)

		d.
A Minor-Cannon	——	iiii
The Organist	——	iiii
A Singing-man	——	ii
A Sexton	——	ii
A Porter	——	ii
A Beadesman	——	ii

And further that the chaunter for the time beinge shall every quarter bringe in his noate of the defaulters to the treasurer for the time being, which said treasurer is hereby impowred to deduct the same out of theire quarter pays, to be disposed of by the treasurer equally amongst those that have incurred noe paenalty.
     Robert Frampton, dec[anus]; Anthony Andrewes, subdec[anus]; Abra[ham] Gregory, thesau[rarius]; Tho[mas] Washbourne; Will[iam] Washbourne.[1]

249. [*fo. 124v.*] 29 June 1674.   Chapter House.

Admissio Archididascali. [*Admission of the schoolmaster. Oliver Gregory, M.A.,[2] who had been chosen by the dean, was admitted by the dean after he had taken the oath on the gospels, touched by him.*] Quibus die, loco et anno Oliverus Gregory, in artibus magister, qui in locum archididascali fuit electus per dominum decanum, infra collegium cathedralis Gloucestriae admissus fuit per venerabilem decanum antedictum, sumpto prius per eum iuramento[3] respective ad sacrosancta dei evangelia per eum tacta &c.

---

[1] The last two names have been squashed in on the left-hand side of the page as there was no space at the foot of the page.
[2] For Oliver Gregory, below, p. 164.
[3] MS. 'iuramenta'; cf. above, p. 29 n. 2.

250.   Monday the feast of St. Andrew the Apostle, 30 November 1674.

Chapter House.

(Robert Frampton, S.T.P., dean; Thomas Washbourne, S.T.P.; William Washbourne; Abraham Gregory.)

Electio Officiariorum 1674. [*Election of officers. The dean and chapter elected William Washbourne as subdean and Abraham Gregory as receiver and treasurer. As in* **238**, *above.*]

Electio Precentoris. [*Election of the precentor. The dean chose Edward Jackson, one of the minor canons, who took the oath.*] Eodem die, anno et loco [*etc., as in* **219**, *above*].

Electio Sacristae. [*Election of the sacrist. The dean chose John Deighton, one of the minor canons, who took the oath.*] Eodem die &c. [*etc., as in* **238**, *above*].
Ita testor Willelmus Lambe, notarius publicus.

251.   [*fo. 125*]   4 January 1674/5.   Chapter House.

Admissio Hypodidascali. Mr. Tho[*mas*] *Trippett.*[1] [*Admission of the assistant schoolmaster. Thomas Trippett, Ll.B., who had been chosen by the dean, was admitted by the dean after he had taken the oath on the gospels, touched by him.*] Quibus die, loco et anno Thomas Trippett, in legibus baccalaureus, [*etc., as in* **50**, *above*].
Ita testor Willelmus Lambe, notarius publicus.

252.   Tuesday the feast of St. Andrew the Apostle, 30 November 1675.

Chapter House.

(Robert Frampton, S.T.P., dean; Thomas Washbourne, S.T.P.; Hugh Naish by his proxy Abraham Gregory; Abraham Gregory.)

Electio Officiariorum 1675. [*Election of officers. The dean and chapter elected Thomas Washbourne as subdean and Abraham Gregory as receiver and treasurer. As in* **238**, *above.*]

Electio Praecentoris. [*Election of the precentor. The dean chose Edward Jackson, one of the minor canons, who took the oath.*] Eodem die, loco et anno [*etc., as in* **219**, *above*, *with* 'Edvarum' *instead of* 'Edvardum'].

[*fo. 125v.*]
Electio Sacristae. [*Election of the sacrist. The dean chose John Deighton, one of the minor canons, who took the oath.*] Eodem die &c. [*etc., as in* **238**, *above*].

The Markes granted to Dr. Gregory, Treasurer.[2] [*The dean and chapter resolved unanimously, on account of the work of Abraham Gregory in the office of treasurer*

---

[1] For Trippett, below, p. 169.

[2] The heading, evidently added after Abraham Gregory became a D.D. in 1677, is in the hand of William Lamb. The rest of the entry is in a hand different from all the others in the book, presumably that of Dean Frampton. Although the grant appears, from the way in which it is entered in the Act Book, to have been made at the meeting of 30 Nov. 1675, it was said four years later to have been made at that of 4 Jan. 1674/5: cf. below, **272**.

outstandingly accomplished over three years and the rents managed faithfully and wisely, that the marks of silver arising from seals in the previous year be given to Gregory out of gratitude, and that the same be done yearly so long as Gregory performs the same office with the same care.] Quibus die, loco et anno decanus et capitulum ob operam Domini Abraham Gregory in munere thesaurario per tres annos elapsos egregie navatam, reditusque ecclesiae fideliter et sagaciter administratos, marcas argenteas ex sigillis anni superioris prouenientes eidem Domino Gregory gratitudinis ergo dandas unanimiter decreverunt. Quod idem statuunt et decernunt quotannis faciendum, quamdiu dictus Dominus Gregory eodem officio eadem cum cura personaliter fungetur.

Robertus Frampton, decanus.

253.   24 July 1676.   Chapter House.

Mr. Fidkyn his first Admonition. Quibus die, loco et anno Mr. Subdeane pronounced against Edward Fidkyn, one of the minor canons, his first monition to depart this church for his frequent neglect of prayers and for his contempt towards some of the chapter and for other his abuses by him at severall times committed.

Ita testor Willelmus Lambe, registrarius.

254. [*fo. 126*]   Saturday 19 February 1675/6.   Chapter House.
(Robert Frampton, S.T.P., dean.)

Admissio Venerabilis viri Edwardi Fowler. [*Admission of the venerable man Edward Fowler. In the chapter house Edward Fowler, M.A., exhibited the king's letters patent, dated 4 February instant, granting to him the prebend vacant by the death of William Washbourne, and the royal mandate for his admission and installation; the dean admitted him, as in* **37**, *above. All this was done in the presence of Thomas Washbourne, Abraham Gregory, prebendaries,*[1] *John Campion, Walter Allard and other servants of the said church and of the writer, William Lamb, registrar.*] In domo capitulari dictae ecclesiae venerabilis vir Edvardus Fowler in artibus magister exhibuit [*etc., as in* **107**, *above*].

Ita testor Willelmus Lambe, registrarius.

255. [*fo. 126v.*] Saturday 1 April 1676.   Chapter House.
(Thomas Washbourne, S.T.P., subdean.)

Admissio Venerabilis Viri Asahel King. [*Admission of the venerable man Asahel King. In the chapter house Asahel King, M.A., exhibited the king's letters patent, dated 23 February last past, granting to him the prebend vacant by the death of Hugh Naish, and the royal mandate for his admission and installation; the subdean admitted him, as in* **37**, *above. All this was done in the presence of John Powell and Richard Parsons, notaries public, Edward Jackson, precentor, and the writer, William Lamb, registrar.*] In domo

---

[1] Cf. above, **245**, note.

capitulari dictae ecclesiae venerabilis vir Asahel King, in artibus magister, exhibuit [*etc.*, *as in* **107**, *above. Erroneously, Naish's name is followed by the words* ultimi professoris *instead of* ultimi possessoris].

[*fo. 127*] Ita testor Willelmus Lambe, registrarius.

256.   Saturday 25 May 1678.   Chapter House.
(Thomas Washbourne, S.T.P., subdean.)

Admissio venerabilis viri Radulphae[1] Cudworth. Vide postea fol. 129. [*Admission of the venerable man Ralph Cudworth. The entry is incomplete, breaking off at the foot of the page with the words* de agnoscendo dictum dominum nostrum. *The admission of Ralph Cudworth to a prebend is given in full two folios on: below,* **262**. *The incomplete entry repeats the erroneous* professoris *from* **255**, *above, a mistake which is not repeated in the complete entry.*]

257.   [*fo. 127v.*]   20 April 1676.   Chapter House.

Whereas John Wells, one of the lay-singingmen of this church, hath for severall weekes last past absented himself from the service of the said church without any leave asked or notice given of such his absence, it is this day ordered by Mr. Sub-Deane and the chapter that the said John Wells, according to the statutes of this church, be discharged of his said place or office of a singingman in this church from henceforth and is hereby discharged accordingly.[2]

Ita testor Willelmus Lambe, registrarius.

258.   [*fo. 128*]   Thursday the feast of St. Andrew the Apostle, 30 November 1676.

Chapter House.
(Robert Frampton, S.T.P., dean; Thomas Washbourne, S.T.P.; Abraham Gregory; Edward Fowler by his proxy Abraham Gregory.)

Electio Officiariorum 1676. [*Election of officers. The dean and chapter elected Thomas Washbourne as subdean and Abraham Gregory as receiver and treasurer. As in* **238**, *above.*]

Electio Praecentoris. [*Election of the precentor. The dean chose Edward Jackson, one of the minor canons, who took the oath.*] Eodem die, loco et anno [*etc., as in* **219**, *above*].

Electio Sacristae. [*Election of the sacrist. The dean chose John Deighton, one of the minor canons, who took the oath.*] Eodem die &c. [*etc., as in* **238**, *above*].

---

[1] *Sic* in MS.

[2] John Wells's dismissal was evidently reversed, for he continued to receive a salary as a lay singer until his death in 1703.

259. *[fo. 128v.]* Friday the feast of St. Andrew the Apostle, 30 November 1677.

Chapter House.

(Robert Frampton, S.T.P., dean; Thomas Washbourne, S.T.P.; Abraham Gregory; Edward Fowler by his proxy Abraham Gregory.)

Electio Officiariorum 1677. *[Election of officers. The dean and chapter elected Thomas Washbourne as subdean and Abraham Gregory as receiver and treasurer. As in* **238***, above.]*

Electio Praecentoris. *[Election of the precentor. The dean chose Edward Jackson, one of the minor canons, who took the oath.]* Eodem die, loco et anno *[etc., as in* **219***, above]*.

Electio Sacristae. *[Election of the sacrist. The dean chose John Deighton, one of the minor canons, who took the oath.]* Eodem die &c. *[etc., as in* **238***, above]*.

260. *[fo. 129]*   18 February 1677/8.   Chapter House.

Mr. Whittington*[1] *admitted a Minor-Canon. *[William Whittington, M.A., was admitted and assigned (a place) by the dean as a minor canon, and William took the oath on the gospels, touched by him.]* Quibus die, loco et anno Gulielmus Whittington, in artibus magister, admissus et assignatus erat per venerabilem decanum in locum unius minorum canonicorum infra ecclesiam cathedralem Gloucestriae, qui quidem Gulielmus subiit juramenta respective ad sacrosancta dei evangelia per eum tacta &c.

261.   7 April 1677.[2]   Chapter House.

Mr. Richard Parsons, Chancellor. Confirmacion of his Pattent. Quibus die, loco et anno the said [...][3] did give theire severall voices and full consents for the confirmacion of letters pattents or comission of the office and place of chancellor of the citty and dioces of Gloucester granted by the right reverend father in God, John, lord bishop of Gloucester, unto Richard Parsons, batchellor of lawes, and the same day the said pattent was confirmed under theire chapter seale accordingly.

262. *[fo. 129v.]* Saturday 25 May 1678.   Chapter House.
(Thomas Washbourne, S.T.P., subdean.)

Admissio venerabilis viri Radulphi Cudworth. *[Admission of the venerable man Ralph Cudworth. In the chapter house Ralph Cudworth, S.T.P., exhibited the king's letters patent, dated 1 April last past, granting to him the prebend vacant by the death of Asahel King, and the royal mandate for his admission and installation; the subdean admitted him, as in* **37***, above. All this was done in the presence of Edward Fowler, M.A., prebendary, Henry Fowler, alderman, John Campion and the writer, William Lamb, registrar.]* In domo capitulari dictae ecclesiae venerabilis vir Radulphus Cudworth, sacrae theologiae professor, exhibuit *[etc., as in* **107***, above]*.

[fo. 130] Ita testor Willelmus Lambe, registrarius.

---

[1] For Whittington, below, p. 170.

[2] The MS. omits the names of those attending the meeting after the date and in the gist of the entry, a gap being left for them in each place, and there are no signatures subscribing the entry.

[3] The MS. leaves two lines blank here.

263.   Wednesday 9 October 1678.   Chapter House.
(Robert Frampton, S.T.P., dean.)

Admissio venerabilis viri Georgii Bull. [*Admission of the venerable man George Bull. In the chapter house George Bull, M.A., exhibited the king's letters patent, dated 10 September last past, granting to him the prebend vacant by the death of Anthony Andrews, and the royal mandate for his admission and installation; the subdean admitted him, as in* **37**, *above. All this was done in the presence of Thomas Washbourne, Abraham Gregory, prebendaries, and other servants of the said church and in the presence of the writer, William Lamb, registrar.*] In domo capitulari dictae ecclesiae venerabilis vir Georgius Bull, in artibus magister, exhibit [*etc., as in* **107**, *above*].
    [*f. 130v.*] Ita testor Guilielmus Lambe, notarius publicus.

264.   [*fo. 131*]   Saturday the feast of St. Andrew the Apostle, 30 November 1678.
                                                                                        Chapter House.
(Robert Frampton, S.T.P., dean; Thomas Washbourne, S.T.P.; Abraham Gregory, S.T.P.; Edward Fowler by his proxy Abraham Gregory; Ralph Cudworth, S.T.P., by his proxy Thomas Washbourne; George Bull.)

Electio Officiariorum 1678. [*Election of officers. The dean and chapter elected Thomas Washbourne as subdean and Abraham Gregory as receiver and treasurer. As in* **238**, *above.*]

Electio Praecentoris. [*Election of the precentor. The dean chose John Deighton, one of the minor canons, who took the oath.*] Eodem die, loco et anno [*etc., as in* **219**, *above*].

Electio Sacristae. [*Election of the sacrist. The dean chose George Evans, one of the minor canons, who took the oath.*] Eodem die &c. [*etc., as in* **238**, *above*].
    Ita testor Guilielmus Lambe, notarius publicus.

265.   [*fo. 131v.*]   [. . .]¹ December 1678.   Chapter House.

Quibus die, loco et anno Mr. Deane pronounced against Edward Fidkin, one of the minor canons, his second monition to depart this church for his frequent tipling and debauching himself and especially for coming and reading of praiers in that disguise.
    Robert Frampton, decan[us]; Abra[ham] Gregory, thesaur[arius];
    Geo[rge] Bull, canon.

266. [*Mandate from John Pritchett, bishop of Gloucester, dated at London 10 December 1678, to the dean and chapter to assign to Thomas Hyde, M.A., whom the bishop has admitted to the archdeaconry of Gloucester with the rectory of Dursley, vacant by the death of John Gregory,² a stall in the choir and to install him.*] Johannes, providencia

---

¹ The MS. has space for the day of the month to be added, which was never done.
² John Gregory had died on the day of the date of the letter: below, p. 164.

divina Gloucestriae episcopus, dilectis nobis in Christo venerabilibus & egregiis viris domino decano ecclesiae cathedralis Gloucestriae etiamque ejusdem ecclesiae capitulo, salutem in domino sempiternam. Cum nos dilectum nobis in Christo Thomam Hyde, clericum, in artibus magistrum, ad archidiaconatum Gloucestriae cum rectoria de Dursley, jam per mortem venerabilis viri Johannis Gregory, clerici, ultimi archidiaconis & rectoris ibidem, vacantem, et ad nostra donacionem et collacionem pleno jure (ratione episcopatus Gloucestriae) spectantem admiserimus ipsumque archidiaconum dicti archidiaconatus Gloucestriae et rectorem rectoriae de Dursley cum suis iuribus, membris & pertinentiis universis canonice instituendo conferimus & conferendo instituimus & investimus (uti per alias literas nostras sibi inde factas plenius liquet et appareat), vobis igitur coniunctim et divisim committimus ac firmiter injungendo mandamus quod sine dilacione locum et stallum in choro dictae cathedralis ecclesiae Gloucestriae prefato Thomae Hyde legitime assignatis vel assignari faciatis ac prefatum archidiaconum installatis seu installari faciatis cum effectu, et quod in premissis feceritis nos debite certificetis unacum presentibus. In cuius rei testimonium sigillum episcopale nostrum presentibus apposui fecimus. Datum London. decimo die mensis Decembris anno domini 1678 ac nostrae consecracionis anno septimo.

Jo[hannes] Gloucestrensis.

267. [*Memorandum that on 11 January 1678/9 Thomas Washbourne, subdean, assigned a stall and a place in the choir to Thomas Hyde, in accordance with the mandate, in the presence of Abraham Gregory, prebendary, John Deighton, precentor, and William Lamb.*] Memorandum quod undecimo die Januarii anno intrascripto venerabilis vir Thomas Washbourne, S.T.P., subdecanus ecclesiae cathedralis Gloucestriae, stallum et locum in choro intranominato Thomae Hyde, clerico, secundum tenorem hujus mandati assignavit, in presentia Abrahami Gregory, praebendarii, Johannis Deighton, praecentoris, meique Willelmi Lambe, registrarii.

Ita testor Gulielmus Lambe, notarius publicus et decano et capitulo registrarius.

268. [*fo. 132*]   26 March 1679.   Chapter House.
(Robert Frampton, S.T.P., dean; Thomas Washbourne, S.T.P., subdean; Abraham Gregory, S.T.P.; George Bull.)

Dr. Gregory, Clerk for the Convocation. Quibus die et loco &c. the said Mr. Deane, Dr. Washbourn, Dr. Gregory & Mr. George Bull gave their severall voices unto the said Dr. Gregory to be clerk for the convocacion house for the chapter of this church at this present parliament. By reason whereof the said Dr. Gregory was elected and chosen clerk of the convocacion to serve for the body of the chapter of this church. And it was then also decreed that an instrument for the performance thereof should be made under the chapter seale unto him the said Dr. Gregory. The tenor whereof followeth in these words vizt. Pateat [*etc., as in* **64**, *above, with the correct cross-reference to fo. 32*].

Ita testor Willelmus Lambe, registrarius.

269. [*fo. 132v.*]   10 April 1679.   Chapter House.

This day Dr. Washbourn, sub-deane of this church, gave Mr. Rosingrave,[1] organist, his first admonition for beating and wounding of John Payn, one of the singingmen of this church.

> Tho[mas] Washbourne, subd[ean].
> Ita testor Willelmus Lambe, notarius publicus.

270. Memorandum that upon the 23rd of June 1679, at a chapter where were present Dr. Washburn, sub dean, having the dean's proxy, Dr. Abraham Gregory, treasurer, Nathaniel Hodges, Edward Fowler, Dr. Cudworth, prebends of the cathedrall church of Gloucester, it was ordered by a majority, every one consenting then present (Dr. Gregory only excepted),[2] that a certain scandalous picture of the Holy Trinity being in the west window of the quire of the said church, should be removed, & other glasse put in to the place.

> Tho[mas] Washbourne; Nath[aniel] Hodges.

271. [*An entry comprising the last twenty-two lines of fo. 132v. and the first twenty-eight of fo. 133 in the hand of Abraham Gregory has, together with his signature at the end, been so thoroughly crossed out that it is largely illegible. It gives Gregory's version of the scandalous affair of the breaking of the west window of the choir. Because his version in the Act Book had been deleted, Gregory wrote his account of the events in the Register of Leases, of which as treasurer he had control. His account is printed below as Appendix I, pp. 157–9.*]

272. [*fo. 133*] **The Twenty Markes taken off.** Whereas the deane and chapter by an act bearing date the fourth day of January 1674[3] (for the good service done and to be done by the then treasurer, Mr. Abraham Gregory) did give and grant unto the said treasurer the severall markes payable to the deane and chapter upon sealing any lease, to continue to him so long as he should be treasurer, the said deane and chapter having since made choice of Mr. Nathaniell Hodges to be treasurer[4] in the place of the said Mr. (now Dr.) Gregory, it is now upon the motion and desire of the said Mr. Hodges ordered that the said markes be not continued to him or to any other treasurer for the future but to be disposed of as formerly.

> Ita testor Willelmus Lambe, registrarius.

[*fo. 133v. blank*]

---

[1] Daniel Roseingrave, for whom see below, p. 168.

[2] The words 'every one consenting then present (Dr. Gregory only excepted)' have been crossed out so thoroughly that they are illegible. They are supplied from another MS.: below, p. 157.

[3] i.e. 1675 according to the modern calendar. Cf. above, **252,** where the grant appears to have been made at the meeting of 30 Nov. 1675.

[4] At the meeting of 30 Nov. 1679: below, **274.**

273.   *[fo. 134]*   4 October 1679.   Chapter House.
(Robert Frampton, S.T.P., dean; Thomas Washbourne, S.T.P., subdean; Abraham Gregory, S.T.P.; Nathaniel Hodges.)

Clerke of the Convocation. Dr. Cudworth. Quibus die et loco &c. the said Mr. Deane, Dr. Washbourne, Dr. Gregory & Mr. Nathaniel Hodges gave their severall voyces unto Ralph Cudworth, doctor in divinity, to be clerk for the convocacion house for the chapter of this church at the ensuing parliament, by reason whereof the said Dr. Cudworth was elected and chosen clerk of the convocacion to serve for the body of the chapter of this church. And it was then also decreed that an instrument for the performance thereof should be made under the chapter seale unto him, the said Dr. Cudworth, the tenor whereof followeth in these words (vizt.) Pateat [*etc., as in* **64**, *above, with the correct cross-reference to fo. 32*].

Ita testor Willelmus Lambe, notarius publicus.

274.   *[fo. 134v.]*   Saturday the feast of St Andrew the Apostle, 30 November 1679.
Chapter House.
(Robert Frampton, S.T.P., dean; Thomas Washbourne, S.T.P.; Nathaniel Hodges; George Bull.)

Electio Officiariorum 1679. [*Election of officers. The dean and chapter elected Thomas Washbourne as subdean and Nathaniel Hodges as receiver and treasurer. As in* **238**, *above.*]

Electio Praecentoris. [*Election of the precentor. The dean chose John Deighton, one of the minor canons, who took the oath.*] Eodem die et anno [*etc., as in* **219**, *above*].

Electio Sacristae. [*Election of the sacrist. The dean chose George Evans, one of the minor canons, who took the oath.*] Eodem die &c. [*etc., as in* **238**, *above*].

Ita testor Guilielmus Lambe, notarius publicus.

275.   *[fo. 135]*   12 April 1680.   Chapter House.

It is ordered that Mr. Treasurer doe pay unto Mr. Chancellor[1] such and soe much money as was agreed to be paid him, and to take an acquittance for the same.

Eight pounds per Annum towards the Repaire of St. Paul's for 5 yeares.[2] It is likewise ordered and agreed that the treasurer for the time being shall yearely pay towards the repaire of St. Paul's church in London the summe of eight pounds, the first payment to begin at Michaelmas next and soe to continue for the space of five yeares and noe longer.

---

[1] The order may relate to an entry in the accounts on 21 July of a payment to 'Mr. Chancellor' of £7 'by order of D : C for a gratuity'.

[2] The order resulted from a brief to raise money for the building of the new St. Paul's cathedral following the Great Fire in 1666. On 23 Nov. 1681 the chapter duly paid £16 'towards the building of St. Paul's', and on 2 May 1687 £24 'Given to St. Pauls, for the 3 last years' subscription'.

Forty shillings for Keeping the Library.[1] It is then likewise ordered that the treasurer for the time being shall yearely pay unto Walter Allard, one of the porters of this church, the summe of forty shillings for keeping and attending the library, the first payment to begin at Xmas next.

Ita testor Willelmus Lambe, registrarius.

276.   [*fo. 135v.*]   Tuesday the feast of St. Andrew the Apostle, 30 November 1680.

Chapter House.

(Robert Frampton, S.T.P., dean; Thomas Washbourne, S.T.P.; Nathaniel Hodges; George Bull.)

Electio Officiariorum 1680. [*Election of officers. The dean and chapter elected Thomas Washbourne as subdean and Nathaniel Hodges as receiver and treasurer. As in* **238**, *above.*]

Electio Praecentoris. [*Election of the precentor. The dean chose John Deighton, one of the minor canons, who took the oath.*] Eodem die et anno [*etc., as in* **219**, *above*].

Electio Sacristae. [*Election of the sacrist. The dean chose George Evans, one of the minor canons, who took the oath.*] Eodem die &c. [*etc., as in* **238**, *above, erroneously omitting the word* 'canonicorum'].

Ita testor Willelmus Lambe, registrarius.

277.   [*fo. 136*]

Robertus Frampton, S.T.P.[2] Charles R. Trusty & welbeloved, we greet you well. Whereas the bishopricke of Gloucester is at present void by the death of Dr. John Pritchett, late bishopp there, we lett you weet that, for certaine considerations us at this present moveing, we out of our princely disposicion and zeale, being desirous to preferre unto the same see a person meet thereunto, and considering the vertue, learning, wisdome, gravity and other good guifts wherewith the reverend Robert Frampton, doctor in divinity, one of our chaplains in ordinary and deane of our cathedrall church of Gloucester aforesaid, is indued, wee have been pleased by these our letters to recomend him unto you to be elected and chosen to the said bishopricke of Gloucester. Wherefore we require you upon receipt hereof to proceed to your eleccion according to the lawes of this our realme and our Conge d'eslire herewith sent unto you, and the same eleccion soe made to certifye unto us under your common seale. Given under our signett at our pallace of Westminster the fourteenth day of January in the two and thirtyeth yeare of our reigne [1681].

> To our trusty and welbeloved the
> deane and chapter of our
> cathedrall church of Gloucester.

Sidney Bere.

---

[1] Cf. above, p. xxiv.
[2] The letters 'S.T.P.' seem to have been added alongside his name as an afterthought.

278. [*The king's* congé d'élire, *dated at Westminster, 14 January 1680/1, to the dean and chapter, who, their church lacking a pastor through the death of John Pritchett, S.T.P., the last bishop, have asked for licence to elect a successor, which the king grants, asking them to elect a bishop useful and loyal to the king and the kingdom.*] Carolus Secundus, [*etc., as in* **235**, *above*].

Grimston; Pengry.[1]

279. [*fo. 136v.*]   Friday 28 January 1680/1, between three and five p.m. Chapter House. (Thomas Washbourne, S.T.P., subdean; Abraham Gregory, S.T.P.; Nathaniel Hodges, M.A.; Ralph Cudworth, S.T.P., by his proxy Nathaniel Hodges; George Bull, M.A., by the same proxy.)[2]

Electio Episcopi, Dr. Frampton. [*Election of the bishop, Robert Frampton. Richard Parsons, Ll.B., notary public and chancellor of the diocese, exhibited the king's letters patent or* congé d'élire *under the Great Seal dated 14 January 1681, for the election as bishop and pastor of the cathedral church of the episcopal see, vacant by the death of John Pritchett, S.T.P., the last bishop, of someone suitable, devout to God and useful and loyal to the king and his kingdom. He exhibited letters dated 14 January aforesaid and signed by the king's hand nominating Robert Frampton, S.T.P., dean of Gloucester, as eligible by the subdean and chapter, on the strength of which the subdean and chapter elected Robert Frampton and certified the king by a letter under the chapter seal dated 28 January. And on the same day they nominated Edmund Shaw and Thomas Swallow, notaries public, jointly and severally, as their proctors to present their letter to the king and to do other things necessary.*] Quibus die et loco constitutus personaliter venerabilis vir Richardus Parsons, legum baccalaureus, notarius publicus et cancellarius diocesoes Gloucestriae, cum [*etc., as in* **54**, *above, as far as*] et electionem huiusmodi eorum regiae majestati certificaverunt per literas sub sigillo eorum capitulari eodem vicesimo octavo die Januarii datas. Eodemque die constituerunt et nominaverunt dilectos sibi in Christo Edmundum Shaw et Thomam Swallow notarios publicos coniunctim et divisim eorum procuratores &c. et exhibendum regiae majestati literas certificatorias et regalem suum assensum eleccionis predictae coram quocunque in ea parte potestatem habente seu habituro usque ad finalem expedicionem ejusdem eorum nomine prosequendi ac confirmacionem in ea parte petendi &c. et generaliter omnia et singula facienda et exercenda quae in premissis necessaria fuerint &c.

280. [*fo. 137*]

[*The subdean and chapter, having received from Richard Parsons the king's letters patent for the election of a bishop to succeed John Pritchett, certify the king that on 28 January 1681, between the third and the fifth hour after noon, being assembled in the*

---

[1] Sir Harbottle Grimston, Master of the Rolls 1660–85; Aaron Pengry, Chancery clerk, clerk of the Petty Bag 1678–97.

[2] The preamble to the entry has 'In presentia mei', presumably meaning William Lamb, the registrar, who, however, is not named.

chapter house they elected Robert Frampton as bishop. Dated 28 January the said year.]
Illustrissimo in Christo principi ac domino nostro, Domino Carolo Secundo, dei gratia
Angliae, Scotiae, Franciae et Hiberniae regi, fidei defensori &c., vestri humiles et devoti
Thomas Washbourne, sacrae theologiae professor, ecclesiae cathe[d]ralis Sanctae et
Individuae Trinitatis Gloucestrensis subdecanus, et capitulum ejusdem ecclesiae
omnimodas submissionem et subjectionem debitas et condignas. Cum nos [*etc., as in* 237,
above, as far as] In quorum omnium et singulorum premissorum fidem et testimonium
sigillum nostrum commune presentibus apponi fecimus. Datum in domo nostra capitulari
vicesimo octavo die Januarii predicti et anno predicto.

281.   [fo. 137v.]

[*The subdean and chapter's letter to the archbishop of Canterbury,*[1] *dated 28 January
1680/1, informing him that they have elected Robert Frampton as bishop and asking him
to confirm the election.*] Reverendissimo in Christo patri et domino Guilielmo providentia
divina Cantuariensi archiepiscopo totius Angliae primati et metropolitano, nos Thomas
Washbourne, sacrae theologiae professor, ecclesiae cathedralis Sanctae et Individuae
Trinitatis Gloucestriae subdecanus, et capitulum ejusdem ecclesiae vestrae
reverendissimae paternitati tenore presentium innotescimus et significamus quod, vacante
nuper sede episcopali Gloucestrensis per obitum reverendi in Christo patris Domini
Johannis Pritchett, ultimi episcopi et pastoris ibidem,[2] nos subdecanus et capitulum
antedicti, vigore et authoritate serenissimae regiae majestatis licentiae de alio nobis et
ecclesiae cathedralis predictae eligendo in episcopum et pastorem factae et concessae, in
domo nostra capitulari die dati presentium capitulariter congregati capitulum ibidem
facientes, servatis per nos de jure ac regni Angliae statutis et ecclesiae cathedralis
predictae ordinationibus et consuetudinibus approbatis in ea parte servandis, habitoque
inter nos diligenti tractatu de persona idonea in ea parte eligenda, tandem in reverendum
in Christo patrem ac dominum, Dominum Robertum Frampton, sacrae theologiae
professorem, vota nostra direximus ipsumque in nostrum et dictae ecclesiae cathedralis
Gloucestrensis predictae episcopum et pastorem unanimiter et concorditer nullo
contradicente vel reclamante elegimus, vestrae reverentiae humiliter supplicantes
quatenus huiusmodi electioni sic per nos de persona prefati reverendi patris factae et
celebratae ea omnia et singula, quae iuxta formam statutorum huius incliti regni Angliae
in ea parte edita sunt et provisa, vestra reverentia facere et perimplere dignaretur, ut deo
optimo maximo bonorum omnium largitore favente et cooperante dictam electionem et
confirmationem nobis proesse valeat utiliter et prodesse ac ut nos sub uno et eius
regimine bene possimus deo dicta ecclesia militari, sicque deus optimus maximus vestram
reverendissimam paternitatem ad ecclesiae suae solamen et utilitatem diu conservet in
prosperis. In quorum omnium et singulorum fidem et testimonium sigillum nostrum
commune presentibus apponi fecimus. Datum in domo nostra capitulari vicesimo octavo
die Januarii anno regni domini nostri Caroli Secundi, dei gratia Angliae, Scotiae, Franciae
et Hiberniae regis, fidei defensoris &c., tricesimo secundo annoque domini 1680.

---

[1] William Sancroft, consecrated archbishop 27 Jan. 1678, deprived as a nonjuror 1 Feb. 1690.

[2] As in **237** the MS. has a closing bracket after the word 'ibidem' but no corresponding opening
bracket.

282. [*fo. 138*]

[*The subdean and chapter's letter to Robert Frampton, dated 28 January 1680/1, informing him, in similar words to those in* **281**, *above, that they have elected him as bishop and asking him to consent to the election.*] Reverendo in Christo patri et domino, Domino Roberto Frampton, sacrae theologiae professori, nos Thomas Washbourne, sacrae theologiae professor, ecclesiae cathedralis Sanctae et Individuae Trinitatis Gloucestrensis subdecanus, et capitulum ejusdem ecclesiae, reverentiam debitam et salutem in omnium salvatore. Vestrae reverentiae tenore presentium innotessimus et significamus quod vacante nuper sede episcopali Gloucestrensis (per obitum reverendi in Christo patris Domini Johannis Pritchett, ultimi episcopi et pastoris ibidem) nos subdecanus et capitulum antedicti in domo nostra capitulari die dati presentium, vigore et authoritate licentiae serenissimi in Christo principis et domini nostri, Domini Caroli Secundi, dei gratia Angliae, Scotiae, Franciae et Hiberniae regis, fidei defensoris &c., nobis in hac parte factae et concessae, ad effectum eligendi novum episcopum et pastorem ecclesiae cathedralis predictae capitulariter congregati et capitulum ibidem facientes, servatis de jure et consuetudine ac statutis hujus regni Angliae de jure in hac parte servandis, habitoque inter nos tractatu diligenti de persona idonea in ea parte eligenda tandem in vos, prefatum reverendum patrem, vota nostra direximus ac vos, prefatum reverendum patrem per regiam majestatem nobis nominatum et commendatum, in nostrum et dictae ecclesiae cathedralis Gloucestrensis predictae episcopum et pastorem unanimiter eligimus, et dictam electionem huiusmodi dicto serenissimo nostro domino regi per literas nostras certificatorias sigillo nostro communi sigillatas significavimus et notum fecimus, quocirca vestram reverendam paternitatem humiliter et obnixe rogamus quatenus huiusmodi electioni de persona vestra sic (ut prefertur) per nos factae et celebratae consentire ac consensum et assensum vestros eidem prebere gratiose dignemini. In quorum omnium et singulorum fidem et testimonium sigillum nostrum commune presentibus apponi fecimus. Datum in domo nostra capitulari vicesimo octavo die Januarii anno regni domini nostri Caroli Secundi, dei gratia Angliae, Scotiae, Franciae et Hiberniae regis, fidei defensoris &c., tricesimo secundo annoque domini 1680.

283. [*fo. 138v.*]

[*The subdean and chapter's letter, dated 28 January 1680/1, declaring in a very formal way that they have made Edward Shaw and Thomas Swallow, notaries public, their proctors, jointly and severally with the fullest possible powers, to complete the necessary stages in the appointment of Robert Frampton as bishop with Frampton himself, the king and the archbishop.*] Pateat universis per presentes quod nos Thomas Washbourne, sacrae theologiae professor, ecclesiae cathedralis Sanctae et Individuae Trinitatis Gloucestrensis subdecanus, et capitulum ejusdem ecclesiae dilectos nobis in Christo Edvardum Shaw et Thomam Swallow, notarios publicos, coniunctim et divisim, ita quod non sit conditio melior primitus occupantium nec deterior subsequentium sed quod unus eorum incipit id ipsorum quilibet libere prosequi valeat mediate pariter et finire, nostros veros, certos, legitimos et indubitatos procuratores, actores, factores negotiorumque nostrorum gestores et nuntios speciales et generales ad infrascripta omnia et singula nominamus, ordinamus, facimus et constituimus per presentes, damusque pariter et concedimus eisdem procuratoribus nostris coniunctim et eorum cuilibet per se divisim potestatem generalem et mandatum speciale pro nobis ac vice, loco et nomine nostris coram reverendo in Christo patre ac domino, Domino Roberto Frampton, sacrae theologiae professore, ecclesiae cathedralis Sanctae et Individuae Trinitatis Gloucestrensis nuper decano, nunc vero episcopo predictae ecclesiae electo, comparendi, interessendi literasque certificatorias sive decretum de et super electione sua huiusmodi per nos factas et confectas sigilloque nostro communi sigillatas eidem reverendo patri exhibendi et ostendendi ipsumque suppliciter et cum instantia (quoties et quando ei seu eorum alicui visum fuerit expediri) quod ipse electioni de se factae consentire et consensium suum eidem expresse prebere dignetur rogandi et requirendi, electionemque sive certificatorium super electione huiusmodi predicta serenissimo domino nostro Carolo Secundo, dei gratia Angliae, Scotiae, Franciae et Hiberniae regi, fidei defensori &c., dictae ecclesiae cathedralis patrono et fundatori, significandi et intimandi, necnon negotium confirmationis electionis predictae coram reverendissimo in Christo patre ac domino, Domino Guilielmo, providentia divina Cantuariensi archiepiscopo, totius Angliae primate et metropolitano, ejusve vicario in spiritualibus generali sive commissario quocumque in hac parte, necnon instrumentum totius processus predicti exhibendi usque ad finalem expeditionem ejusdem nomine nostro prosequendi ac confirmationem in ea parte petendi et obtinendi, provocandi et appellandi ac provocationes et appellationes huiusmodi notificandi et intimandi, alium insuper seu alios procuratorem sive procuratores loco suo et eorum cujuslibet substituendi ac substitutum vel substitutos huiusmodi revocandi procuratorisque officium in se et eorum quemlibet reassumendi [*fo. 139*] quoties et quando id eis seu eorum alicui melius videbitur expediri, et generaliter omnia et singula alia faciendi, exercendi et expediendi usque ad finalem expeditionem negotii confirmationis huiusmodi quae in premissis aut circa ea necessaria fuerint seu quomodolibet opportuna, licet mandatum de se exigat magis speciale quam superius est expressum, promittentes et promittimus nos ratum, gratum et firmum perpetuo habituros totum et quidquid procuratores nostri predicti aut eorum aliquis fecerint seu fecerit in premissis vel eorum aliquo sub hypotheca et obligatione omnium et singulorum bonorum nostrorum tam presentium quam futurorum et in ea parte cautionem exponimus per presentes. In cujus rei testimonium sigillum nostrum commune presentibus apponi fecimus. Datum in domo nostra capitulari vicesimo octavo die Januarii anno regni domini nostri Caroli Secundi, dei gratia Angliae, Scotiae, Franciae et Hiberniae regis, fidei defensoris &c., tricesimo secundo annoque domini 1680.

284.   [*fo. 139v.*]   2 March 1680/1.   Chapter House.

Upon consideracion had of the granting and renewing such leases for lives as are now in being and not as yet renewed, it is this day concluded and agreed upon that all such persons as have any such leases for lives unrenewed shall and may from henceforth renew the same for lives as formerly, or otherwise for yeares as may be thought most fitt and convenient.

Ita testor Willelmus Lambe, registrarius.

285. [*fo. 140*]   15 March 1680/1.   Chapter House.
(Robert Frampton, S.T.P., dean;[1] Thomas Washbourne, S.T.P., subdean; Abraham Gregory, S.T.P.; Nathaniel Hodges.)

Choice of a Clerk for the Convocation House. Dr. Cudworth.[2] Quibus die et loco &c. the said Mr. Deane, Dr. Washbourne, Dr. Gregory and Mr. Nathaniel Hodges gave their severall voyces unto Ralph Cudworth, doctor in divinity, to be clerk for the convocacion house for the chapter of this church at the ensuing parliament. By reason whereof the said Dr. Cudworth was elected and chosen clerk of the convocacion to serve for the body of the chapter of this church. And it was then also decreed that an instrument for the performance thereof should be made under the chapter seale unto him the said Dr. Cudworth, the tenor whereof followeth in these words (vizt.) Pateat [*etc., as in* **64**, *above, with the correct cross-reference to fo. 32*].
        Ita Testor Willelmus Lambe, registrarius.

286. [*fo. 140v.*]   Saturday 30 April 1681.   Chapter House.
(Abraham Gregory, S.T.P., prebendary; William Lambe, notary public and registrar.)

Installatio venerabilis viri Thomae Marshall Decani Gloucestriae 1681. [*Installation of the venerable man Thomas Marshall as dean of Gloucester. Thomas Marshall, S.T.P., appeared in person and presented the king's letters patent, dated 15 April 1681, and he exhibited the royal mandate addressed to the chapter and canons to assign to the dean a stall in the choir and a place and a voice in the chapter, etc., as in* **100**, *above.*] Quibus die ac loco in propria persona sua comparuit venerabilis et discretus vir Thomas Marshall, sacrae theologiae professor, constitutus [*etc., as in* **100**, *above, with minor verbal variations of which the most significant is the substitution of 'canons' for 'prebendaries' in two places. All this was done in the presence of John Deighton, precentor, George Evans, minor canon, John Campion, subsacrist, and other servants of the said church*].
        [*fo. 141*] Ita testor Willelmus Lambe, registrarius.

287. [*fo. 141v.*]   Wednesday the feast of St. Andrew the Apostle, 30 November 1681.
                                                                          Chapter House.
(Thomas Marshall, S.T.P., dean; Thomas Washbourne, S.T.P.; Abraham Gregory, S.T.P.; Nathaniel Hodges; George Bull.)

Electio Offici*[*ari*]*orum 1681. [*Election of officers. The dean and chapter elected Thomas*

---

    [1] Robert Frampton remained as dean: although elected as bishop of Gloucester on 28 Jan. he was not consecrated until 27 March.
    [2] The heading is written not in the margin, as usual, but at the end of the entry, alongside William Lamb's signature, in a different hand.

Washbourne as subdean and Nathaniel Hodges as treasurer. As in 238, *omitting* et receptorem.[1]]

> Tho[mas] Marshal, decanus; Tho[mas] Washbourne; Nath[aniel] Hodges;
> Abra[ham] Gregory; Geo[rge] Bull.[2]

[*The dean chose as precentor John Deighton, one of the minor canons, who took the oath.*] Eodem die et anno [*etc., as in* **219**, *above*].[3]

> Tho[mas] Marshal, decanus.

[*The dean chose as sacrist George Evans, one of the minor canons, who took the oath.*] Eodem die &c. [*etc., as in* **238**, *above*].

> Tho[mas] Marshal, decanus.

288. [*fo. 142*]   17 May 1682.   Chapter House.

[*Stephen Jefferies*[4] *was admitted by the dean as organist and instructor of the choristers in the place of Charles Wren,*[5] *deceased, was installed in the choir by the precentor and took the oath on the gospels, touched by him.*] Quibus die et anno Stephanus Jefferies admissus erat per decanum in locum organistae et choristarum instructoris hujus ecclesiae in loco Caroli Wren mortui, et installatus in choro per cantatorem. Qui quidem Stephanus subiit juramenta respective ad sacrosancta dei evangelia per eum tacta &c.

> Tho[mas] Marshal, decanus.

289. [*fo. 142v.*]   Thursday the feast of St. Andrew the Apostle, 30 November 1682.
                                                                     Chapter House.

(Thomas Marshall, S.T.P., dean; Abraham Gregory, S.T.P.; Nathaniel Hodges; George Bull.)

Electio Officiariorum 1682. [*Election of officers. The dean and chapter elected Thomas Washbourne, S.T.P., as subdean and Nathaniel Hodges as receiver and treasurer. As in* **238**, *above.*]

> Tho[mas] Marshal, decanus; Abra[ham] Gregory;
> Nath[aniel] Hodges; Geo[rge] Bull.

---

[1] Although Hodges is said to have been elected as treasurer only and not as receiver and treasurer, the accounts for the year have the heading 'Computus Magistri Nath. Hodges Receptoris gen. sive Thesaurarii'.

[2] These signatures, in a blacker ink than that of the entry which they follow, are squashed, those of Abraham Gregory and George Bull being written on the left-hand side of the page; they were presumably added after the next paragraph was entered in the book.

[3] The MS. has no heading for the election of either the precentor or the sacrist.

[4] For Jefferies, below, pp. 165–6.

[5] Wren was buried on 5 Dec. 1678 and Jefferies in fact succeeded not Wren but Daniel Roseingrave: below, pp. 168, 171.

Electio Praecentoris. [*Election of the precentor. The dean chose John Deighton, one of the minor canons, who took the oath.*] Eodem die, loco et anno [*etc., as in* **219**, *above*].

Tho[mas] Marshal, decanus.

Electio Sacristae. [*Election of the sacrist. The dean chose George Evans, one of the minor canons, who took the oath.*] Eodem die &c. [*etc., as in* **238**, *above*].

Tho[mas] Marshal, decanus.

Ita testor Johannes Bicknell, notarius publicus 1682.

290.   [*fo.* 143]   Friday the feast of St. Andrew the Apostle, 30 November 1683.[1]

Chapter House.

(Thomas Marshall, S.T.P., dean, by his proxy Dr. Washbourne; Thomas Washbourne, S.T.P.; Abraham Gregory, S.T.P.; Nathaniel Hodges; George Bull.)

Electio Officiariorum 1683. [*Election of officers. The dean and chapter elected Thomas Washbourne, S.T.P., as subdean and Nathaniel Hodges as receiver and treasurer. As in* **238**, *above.*]

Tho[mas] Washbourne, subd[ean]; Abra[ham] Gregory;
Nath[aniel] Hodges; Geo[rge] Bull.

Electio Praecentoris. [*Election of the precentor. The subdean chose John Deighton, one of the minor canons, who took the oath.*] Eodem die, loco et anno idem venerabilis subdecanus elegit in praecentorem [*etc., as in* **219**, *above*].

Tho[mas] Washbourne, subd[ean]; Abra[ham] Gregory;
Nath[aniel] Hodges; Geo[rge] Bull.

Electio Sacristae. [*Election of the sacrist. The subdean chose George Evans, one of the minor canons, who took the oath.*] Eodem die &c. Idem venerabilis subdecanus elegit in sacristam [*etc., as in* **238**, *above*].

Tho[mas] Washbourne, subd[ean]; Abra[ham] Gregory;
Nath[aniel] Hodges; Geo[rge] Bull.

291. [*fo. 143v.*]

Mr. Machell's Dispensation.[2] Charles R. Trusty and welbeloved, we greet you well. Whereas our trusty and welbeloved John Machell, esquire, hath by his humble peticion informed us that he and those under whom he claymes have been long tenants unto your church for the rectory of Chiping Norton in our county of Oxon. by grant for lives,[3] and being now desirous to renew the same for three lives, hath humbly prayed us to dispense in his behalfe with the locall statutes of the said church and a letter[4] sent you by our late royall father, which we are informed restraine you from granting leases of your lands for any other terme then for one and twenty yeares, we, taking into our royall consideracion

---

[1] The entry is chronologically out of order.
[2] The heading is written not in the margin, as usual, but at the end of the entry.
[3] The accounts show that Machell paid an annual rent of £18 in 1680–1 and until 1700 or later.
[4] Above, **123**.

the good services of the said John Machell, have thought fitt to condescend to his request, and accordingly in pursuance of the power reserved unto us therein we doe by these presents dispense with the said locall statutes and letter in behalfe of the said John Machell. And we doe authorize and impower you to renew his lease of the said rectory of Chiping Norton for three lives (which we are graciously pleased to recommend to you), any thing in the said locall statutes or letter to the contrary notwithstanding. And so we bid you farewell. Given at our court at Windsor the 19th day of June 1683 in the five and thirtieth yeare of our reigne.

By his majestie's command.   Sunderland.[1]

292.   [*fo. 144*]   23 June 1683.   Chapter House.

[*William Randall and William Cowles were admitted by the dean* (*as choristers*) *in the places of two unnamed boys.*] Quibus die, loco et anno Gulielmus Randall et Gulielmus Cowles admissi fuerunt per venerabilem decanum choristae in loco &c.[2]

Tho[mas] Marshal, decanus.

293.   25 June 1683.   Chapter House.

Terriers of Lands to be brought in before renewall.[3] Whereas severall inconveniencies have and may arise between the deane and chapter and theire tennants for want of terriers of theire severall lands, which have bene unhappily omitted to be made and given in, the doing whereof (wee conceive) will be the onely meanes to preserve the churche's rights and the peace and quiett of theire tennants for the future, be it therefore ordered, and it is hereby ordered and declared, that from henceforth no leases of any lands belonging to the church shall be granted or renewed to any person or persons without first bringing in a terrier or particular of theire severall lands, exactly butted and bounded, and the severall tennants to have as timely notice of this order as possibly may be, that when they come to renew they may not pretend ignorance thereof.

Tho[mas] Marshal, dean; Tho[mas] Washbourne, subd[ean];
Nath[aniel] Hodges; Ra[lph] Cudworth; Geo[rge] Bull.

294.   [*fo. 144v.*]

Mr. Trinder's Dispensation.[4] Charles R. Trusty and welbeloved, we greet you well. Whereas our trusty & welbeloved John Trinder, esquire, hath by his humble petition informed us that he & his ancestors have long been tenants unto your church for the Mannor of Eastleach Martin in our county of Gloucester[5] by demise for lives; and being

---

[1] Robert Spencer, earl of Sunderland, Secretary of State 1679–81 and 1683–88.

[2] William Randall had been receiving payment as a chorister since 1681, and William Cowles since 1682, presumably both as probationers.

[3] The heading is written not in the margin, as usual, but at the end of the entry.

[4] The heading is written not in the margin, as usual, but at the end of the entry.

[5] The accounts show that for 1683–4 and earlier years Jane Trinder, widow, paid an annual rent of £10 16*s.* for the manor of Eastleach Martin.

now desirous to renew the same for three lives hath humbly prayed us to dispense in his behalfe with the locall statutes of the said church and a letter[1] sent you by our late royall father, which we are informed restraine you from granting leases of the said lands for any other terme then one & twenty yeares, we, taking into our royall consideracion the great loyalty of the said John Trinder to our selfe and our royall father of blessed memory, and being informed of some good services he performed to you in the late rebellion, have thought fit to condescend to his request, and accordingly in pursuance of the power reserved unto us therein we doe by these presents dispense with the said locall statutes and letter in behalfe of the said John Trinder, and we doe authorize & impower you to renew his said lease of the said mannor of Eastleach Martin for three lives (which we are graciously pleased to recommend to you), any thing in the said locall statutes or letter to the contrary notwithstanding. And soe we bid you farewell. Given at our court at Newmarkett the 7th day of March 1683/4 in the six & thirtieth yeare of our reigne.

By his majestie's command.   Sunderland.

[fo. 145 blank]

295. *[fo. 145v.]*   11 September 1684.   Deanery.

[Maurice Wheeler, M.A.,[2] was admitted by the dean as schoolmaster, having taken the oath on the gospels, touched by him.] Quibus die, loco et anno Mauritius Wheeler, artium magister, admissus fuit per dominum decanum in locum archididasculi, sumpto prius per eum juramento[3] respective ad sacrosancta dei evangelia per eum tacta &c.

296. *[fo. 146]*   18 September 1684.   Chapter House.

Memorandum[4] that this following clause was agreed upon by the dean & chapter, on the said day, and in the said place, to be inserted for the time to come in every lease of tenements within the precincts of this church, mutatis mutandis, viz.

'And furthermore it is covenanted & agreed by and between the said parties to these presents, and the said Clement Dowle[5] for himself, his executors, administrators and assignes, & for every of them, doth covenant, promise & graunt to and with the said dean & chapter, & their successors, that neither he the said Clement Dowle, his executors, administrators or assignes, nor any under-tenant or under-tenants, or any person whatsoever clayming from, by or under him, them or any of them shall or may have, hold, execute or enjoy any office of or belonging to the city of Gloucester, during the

---

[1] Above, **123**.

[2] For Wheeler, below, p. 170.

[3] MS. 'juramenta'; cf. above, p. 29 n. 2.

[4] At the foot of the page in the margin is written the word 'Vacated', as though it was the title to the entry.

[5] Clement Dowle of the city of Gloucester, mercer, was lessee in the Commonwealth period of the ground on which no. 19 College Green was to be built and presumably built the house there. He continued as lessee until 1684 when the lease was granted to Job Dowle, also a mercer.

time of his or their abode or dwelling in the said demised premisses or any part thereof, but shall and will at all times remove from the said premisses, and out of the precincts of the said church, during his or their holding, exercising or enjoying any such office, unless he or they, shall first obtain leav[e] under the common seal of the said dean & chapter, for his, or their, continuance or abode there. And furthermore that the said Clement Dowle, his executors, administrators and assignes, and all and every tenant or tenants, or other person whatsoever, clayming from, by or under him, them or any of them, shall & will from time to time, at all times during his & their dwelling or inhabiting in the said premisses or any part thereof, make their ingress, egress & regress to & from the said premisses at such due & laudable times & hours, as the statutes of the said church do require.'

[*fo. 146v.*] It was also agreed by the same persons at the same time & place, that a power of reentry shall be reserved to the dean & chapter, upon every lease hereafter to be graunted, upon the breach of any covenant, as well as upon non payment of rent.

> Tho[mas] Marshal, dean; Tho[mas] Washbourne, subd[ean]; Abra[ham] Gregory; Nath[aniel] Hodges; Edw[ard] Fowler.

297.   The feast of St. Andrew the Apostle, 30 November 1684.

Chapter House.

(Thomas Marshall, S.Th.P., dean, by his proxy George Bull; Thomas Washbourn, S.T.P., subdean; Abraham Gregory, S.T.P.; Nathaniel Hodges; George Bull.)

Electio Officiariorum 1684. [*Election of officers. The dean and chapter elected Abraham Gregory as subdean and Nathaniel Hodges as receiver and treasurer. As in* **238**, *above.*]

> Tho[mas] Washbourne; Abra[ham] Gregory; Nath[aniel] Hodges; Geo[rge] Bull.

[*fo. 147*]

Electio Praecentoris. [*Election of the precentor. The subdean and chapter, with the dean's consent, elected as precentor John Deighton, one of the minor canons, who took the oath.*] Eodem die, anno et loco idem venerabilis vir sub-decanus et capitulum elegerunt (cum consensu decani)[1] in praecentorem dictae ecclesiae Johannem Deighton, unum minorum canonicorum eiusdem ecclesiae cathedralis &c., qui iuramentum suscepit &c.

> Tho[mas] Washbourne; Abra[ham] Gregory; Nath[aniel] Hodges; Geo[rge] Bull.

Electio Sacristae. [*Election of the sacrist. The subdean and chapter, with the dean's consent, elected as sacrist George Evans, one of the minor canons, who took the oath.*] Eodem die &c. idem venerabilis subdecanus et capitulum (cum consensu decani) elegerunt in sacristam dictae ecclesiae Georgium Evans, unum minorum canonicorum eiusdem ecclesiae cathedralis &c. qui iuramentum suscepit.

> Tho[mas] Washbourne; Abra[ham] Gregory; Nath[aniel] Hodges; Geo[rge] Bull.

---

[1] The words 'cum consensu decani' are inserted, apparently as an afterthought, above the line in the record of both the precentor's and the sacrist's appointments.

298. 15 January 1684/5. Chapter House.
(Abraham Gregory, subdean; Nathaniel Hodges, treasurer.)

Admissio Minoris Canonici. Mr. Thache.[1] [*Admission of a minor canon. Thomas Thache, A.M., who had been chosen by the dean, was admitted by the subdean, after he had taken the oath on the gospels, touched by him.*] Quibus die, loco et anno Thomas Thatch, A.M., qui in locum minoris canonici infra collegium ecclesiae cathedralis Gloucestriae per dominum decanum electus fuit, per Magistrum Sub Decanum fuit admissus, sumpto prius per eum iuramento respective ad sacro-sancta dei evangelia per eum tacta &c.

Abra[ham] Gregory, subdec[anus]; Nath[aniel] Hodges, thesaur[arius].

299. 31 January 1684/5. Chapter House.
(Abraham Gregory, subdean; Thomas Washbourn.)

Mr. Jefferies' first Admonition. At which time and place Mr. Subdean pronounced to Mr. Stephen Jefferies organist of this church his first admonition to depart this church for his manifold neglects and unreasonable abscences from the church without any leave desiered or obtaind.

Abra[ham] Gregory, subdec[anus]; Tho[mas] Washbourne.

300. [*fo. 147v.*] 20 April 1685. Chapter House.
(Abraham Gregory, subdean; Nathaniel Hodges, treasurer.)

Admissio Minoris Canonici. Mr. Jenninges.[2] [*Admission of a minor canon. Henry Jennings, A.M., who had been chosen by the dean, was admitted by the subdean, after he had taken the oath on the gospels, touched by him.*] Quibus die, loco et anno Henricus Jennings, A.M., [*etc., as in* **298**, *above*].[3]

Abra[ham] Gregory, subdec[anus]; Nath[aniel] Hodges, thesaur[arius].

301. Saturday 6 June 1685. Chapter House.
(Abraham Gregory, S.T.P., subdean; Thomas Washbourne, S.T.P.; Nathaniel Hodges, A.M.; John Bicknell, notary public.)

Installatio venerabilis viri Gulielmi Jane Decani Gloucestriae 1685. [*Installation of the venerable man William Jane as dean of Gloucester. William Jane, S.T.P., appeared in person and presented the king's letters patent, dated 15 May 1685, with the king's mandate included for his admission etc., as in* **100**, *above, but with a different form at the beginning of the entry.*] Quibus die, anno et loco in propria persona sua comparuit venerabilis et discretus vir Gulielmus Jane, sacrae theologiae professor, constitutus et ordinatus in decanum ecclesiae cathedralis Sanctae et Individuae Trinitatis Gloucestriae,

---

[1] The name 'Mr. Thache' has been added in a hand that is different from that of the rest of the heading. The rest of the entry and the two that follow are in the hand of Abraham Gregory. For Thache, below, p. 169.

[2] The name 'Mr. Jenninges' has been added in a hand that is different from that of the rest of the heading. For Jennings, below, p. 163.

[3] Unusually, the order of the words 'sumpto prius per eum' is changed to 'sumpto per eum prius'.

et ex parte sua subdecano et prebendariis praedictis praesentavit literas patentes illustrissimi in Christo principis ac domini nostri, Domini Jacobi Secundi, dei gratia Angliae, Scotiae, Franciae et Hiberniae regis, fidei defensoris &c., gerentes datas decimo quinto die Maii anno regni sui primo, cum mandato regis incluso pro admissione, institucione et investicione dicti Gulielmi Jane in decanatum ecclesiae cathedralis Gloucestriae praedictae cum omnibus et singulis suis juribus, membris et pertinentiis universis uti moris est. Ac insuper dictus venerabilis decanus ordinatus et constitutus, virtute literarum patentium praedictarum, ex parte sua et pro se petiit et requisivit a subdecano et prebendariis praedictis stallum in [*etc., as in* **100**, *above, with minor verbal variations, adding* 'in presentia prebendariorum predictorum' *in the reference to the subdean's accepting the letters patent, and ending, on fo. 148*[1]] in presentia Johannis Deighton, praecentoris, Edvardi Fidkin, Thomae Thatch, minorum canonicorum duorum, Johannis Campion, subsacristae, aliorumque dictae ecclesiae ministrorum.

Ita testor Johannes Bicknell, notarius publicus.

Admissio Laici Cantatoris. Edward Tyler.[2] [*Admission of a lay singer. Edward Tyler was admitted by the dean in the place of Richard Elliott,*[3] *was installed in the choir by the precentor and took the oaths on the gospels, touched by him.*] Eodem die et anno Edvardus Tyler admissus fuit per dominum decanum antedictum in locum unius laicorum cantatorum infra ecclesiam cathedralem Gloucestriae in loco Richardi Elliott, et installatus in choro per cantatorem, qui quidem Edvardus subiit juramenta respective ad sacrosancta dei evangelia per eum tacta &c.

302.   [*fo. 148v.*]   1 October 1685.[4]   Chapter House.
(Abraham Gregory, subdean; Thomas Washbourne, S.T.P.; George Bull by his proxy the subdean.)

Mr. John Deighton's first admonition. At which time and place Mr. Sub-Dean pronounced to Mr. John Deighton, minor canon and chaunter of this church, his first admonition to depart this church for his manifold repeated neglects and unreasonable abscences from the choire and divine service there, without any leave obtain or desired, notwithstanding many well known orders of the chapter, and warnings privately given in the chapter house.

Abra[ham] Gregory, sub-decanus.

Mr. Ed[ward] Fidkin referd to Mr. Dean. The same day it appeared to Mr. Sub-Dean that Edward Fidkin, another minor canon of this church, had very scandalously neglected his duty, and almost dayly absented himselfe from the service of this church, without any leave for abscence obtained or desiered. Whereupon Mr. Sub-Dean summoned the said

---

[1] The word 'repugnarint', the first of the folio, is also a catchword at the foot of fo. 147v.

[2] The name 'Edward Tyler' has been added in a hand that is different from that of the rest of the heading. Tyler had been a chorister from 1667 (**203**) to 1672, and remained a lay singer until 1720 or later.

[3] Richard Elliott or Elliotts had been a lay singer since 1660, and previously a chorister from 1636 (**133**) to 1641.

[4] The entry is in the hand of Abraham Gregory.

Edward Fidkin into the chapter house, and severely admonishing him of his fault told him hee highly deservd an admonition, but, in regard hee found two admonitions formerly published against him, hee did reserve him and his cause to Mr. Dean's consideration.

  Abra[ham] Gregory, sub-decanus.

303.   Thursday the feast of St. Andrew the Apostle, 30 November 1685.

                       Chapter House.

(William Jane, S.T.P., dean; Abraham Gregory, S.T.P.; Nathaniel Ho[d]ges; Ralph Cudworth; George Bull.)

Electio Officiariorum 1685. [*Election of officers. The dean and chapter elected Abraham Gregory as subdean and Nathaniel Hodges as receiver and treasurer. As in* **238**, *above.*]

  Guil[ielmus] Jane, dec[anus].

[*fo. 149*]

Electio Praecentoris. [*Election of the precentor. The dean chose John Deighton, who took the oath.*] Eodem die, loco et anno [*etc., as in* **219**, *above*].

  Guil[ielmus] Jane, dec[anus].

Electio Sacristae. [*Election of the sacrist. The dean chose Thomas Thache, one of the minor canons, who took the oath.*] Eodem die &c. [*etc., as in* **238**, *above*].[1]

304.   13 February 1685/6.   Chapter House.

(Abraham Gregory, S.T.P., subdean; Thomas Washbourne, S.T.P.)

Mr. Hilton Hipodidascalus. [*Admission of the assistant schoolmaster. John Hilton, M.A., who had been chosen by the dean, was admitted by Dr. Abraham Gregory, subdean, after he had taken the oath on the gospels, touched by him.*] Quibus die, loco et anno Johannes Hilton, in artibus magister, qui in locum hipodidascali [*etc., as in* **50**, *above*].

305. [*fo. 149v.*] 28 September 1686.   Chapter House.

(Abraham Gregory, S.T.P., subdean; Thomas Washbourne, S.T.P.; George Bull, S.T.P.)

Orders Concerninge the College Schoole. Quo die et loco, It was ordered by Mr. Sub-Deane and the chapter, with Mr. Deane's concurrence signified by his letter, that, whereas there hath lately arisen a dispute concerning the removing of children out of the lower into the upper schoole betweene the master and usher of the schoole belonginge to this church, that for the future the antient custome shall constantly be observed, (that is) That noe child shall for the future be removed out of the lower schoole, nor admitted de novo into the upper schoole, untill he be so well grounded by the usher[2] in the rudiments of the Latine tongue as that he shall be able to make for his exercise five or six lines of plaine true Latine, and shall understand the scanning, and proving of verses, and the making of two verses for one night's exercise.

  Abra[ham] Gregory, subdec[anus]; Tho[mas] Washbourne; Geo[rge] Bull.

---

[1] This entry is not subscribed by the dean.

[2] The words 'by the usher' have been inserted above the line in Abraham Gregory's handwriting, although the passage itself is not in his hand.

306. [*fo. 150*]   Tuesday the feast of St. Andrew the Apostle, 30 November 1686.

Chapter House.

(Abraham Gregory, S.T.P., subdean; Thomas Washbourne, S.T.P.; Nathaniel Hodges, treasurer; Edward Fowler, S.T.P., by his proxy Mr. Hodges; George Bull.)

Electio Officiariorum 1686. [*Election of officers. The subdean and chapter elected Thomas Washbourne, S.T.P., as subdean and Abraham Gregory as receiver and treasurer.*] Idem sub-decanus et capitulum elegerunt hos officiarios (viz.) Thomam Washborne, S.T.P., praedictae ecclesiae prebendarium [*etc., as in* **170**, *above*].

Electio Praecentoris. [*Election of the precentor. The subdean chose John Deighton, who took the oath.*] Eodem die, loco et anno idem venerabilis subdecanus elegit in praecentorem [*etc., as in* **219**, *above*].

Electio Sacristae.[1] [*Election of the sacrist. The subdean chose Thomas Thache, one of the minor canons, who took the oath.*] Eodem die &c. idem venerabilis subdecanus elegit [*etc., as in* **238**, *above*].

It is ordered that James Sayer senior[2] be and is hereby admitted sacrist [*recte* subsacrist] as deputy to Mr. Berkly Wrench, he [*sc.* Sayer] giving such security for such materialls which shall come to his hands as Mr. Deane (when present) shall approve of.

Eodem die &c. It is ordered that a release be given to Mr. Nathaniel Hodges, late treasurer, under the seale of the deane & chapter.[3]

307. [*fo. 150v.*]   Wednesday 3 February 1686/7.   Chapter House.
(Thomas Washbourne, S.T.P., subdean; Abraham Gregory, S.T.P., treasurer.)

Admissio Elemozinarii. Robertus Stagg. [*Admission of an almsman. Robert Stagg*[4] *appeared and sought to be admitted in place of James Bevan,*[5] *lately deceased, by virtue of letters patent granted to him and addressed to the dean and chapter, and registered in their registry, whereupon the subdean admitted him, to have the emoluments belonging to the place from Michaelmas last past.*] Comparuit quidam Robertus Stagg et petiit admitti in locum elemozinarii dictae ecclesiae in loco cujusdam Jacobi Bevan nuper defuncti virtute literarum patentium sibi in ea parte concessarum, decano et capitulo dictae ecclesiae directarum et apud registrarium eorundem decani et capituli registratarum. Unde dictus venerabilis sub-decanus dictum Robertum Stagg in elemozinarium admisit, habere et percipere omnia emolumenta et proficua ad locum elemozinarium spectantia a festo Sancti Michaelis Archangeli ultimo preterito.

---

[1] While the heading is written as usual boldly in the margin, the rest of the entry is squashed in.

[2] The abbreviated word 'senior' has been added above the line, presumably as an afterthought. Sayer was on 29 June 1693 granted the place of almsman vacant by the death of Robert Stagg.

[3] Why the outgoing treasurer needed a release (or acquittance) is not apparent.

[4] Robert Stagg remained an almsman until 1693: cf. above, this page, n. 2.

[5] In 1682 he was referred to in the cathedral accounts as Edward, not James Bevan.

308. [*fo. 151*]   Saturday 21 May 1687.   Chapter House.
(William Jane, S.T.P., dean.)

Admissio venerabilis viri Lucae Beaulieu. [*Admission of the venerable man Luke Beaulieu. In the chapter house Luke Beaulieu, S.T.B., exhibited the king's letters patent, dated 10 May instant, granting to him the prebend vacant by the death of Thomas Washbourne, and the royal mandate for his admission and installation; the dean admitted him, as in* **37**, *above. All this was done in the presence of William Jane, dean, Abraham Gregory, prebendary, and other servants of the said church and of the writer, William Lamb, registrar.*] In domo capitulari dictae ecclesiae venerabilis vir Lucas Beaulieu sacrae theologiae baccalaureus exhibuit [*etc., as in* **107**, *above*].
        Ita testor Willelmus Lambe, registrarius.

309. [*fo. 151v.*]   18 August 1687.   Chapter House.
(William Jane, S.T.P., dean; Abraham Gregory, S.T.P., treasurer, by his proxy the dean; Edward Fowler, S.T.P.; Ralph Cudworth, S.T.P.)

Dr. Cudworth Sub-Deane. Quo die et loco, whereas Dr. Washbourn, late sub-deane of this church, is lately deceased and his place or office of sub-deane is thereby become void, it is ordered and agreed that Dr. Ralph Cudworth be chosen and elected sub-deane for the remainder of the yeare ensuing. And the said Dr. Cudworth is hereby chosen and elected sub-deane accordingly.
        Ita testor Wilhelmus Lambe, notarius publicus.

310.   1 September 1687.   Chapter House.

For paling in some part of the Upper Church-yard for securing the graves. Whereas severall inconveniencies have hapned in the upper churchyard by coaches, carts and drays passing over the graves there, and severall complaints havinge bene made by the persons concernd, for preventing the same for the future it is ordered that the old pale now standinge be removed, and soe placed that the buriall place aforesaid may be secured from all such inconveniencies, and is hereby ordered to remove the same accordingly.
        Willhelmus Jane, decanus, per Doctor[em] Cudworth procur[atorem] suum; Radulphus Cudworth sub-dec[anus]; Abra[ham] Gregory, thesaur[arius]; Edvardus Fowler[1] per procur[atorem] suum R. Cudworth.

311. [*fo. 152*]   Wednesday the feast of St. Andrew the Apostle, 30 November 1687.
                                            Chapter House.
(William Jane, S.T.P., dean; Ralph Cudworth, S.T.P., subdean, by his proxy Dr. Bull; Abraham Gregory, S.T.P., treasurer; Nathaniel Hodges; Edward Fowler, S.T.P., by his proxy Mr. Hodges; George Bull.)

[1] Fowler's name has been added below that of 'Georgius Bull,' which has been crossed out.

Electio officiariorum 1687. [*Election of officers. The dean and chapter elected Nathaniel Hodges as subdean and Abraham Gregory as receiver and treasurer. As in* **306**, *above.*]

Electio Praecentoris. [*Election of the precentor. The dean chose John Deighton, who took the oath.*] Eodem die, loco et anno [*etc., as in* **219**, *above*].

Electio Sacristae. [*Election of the sacrist. The dean chose Thomas Thache, one of the minor canons, who took the oath.*] Eodem die &c. idem venerabilis decanus elegit [*etc., as in* **238**, *above*].

Organs repaire. £70. Eodem die et loco &c. It was ordered by Mr. Deane and chapter that seaventy pounds remayning due to Mr. Barnard Smith for repaire of the organs shall be paid by Dr. Gregory, now chosen treasurer for the next yeare, out of the first moneys that shall come to his hands.[1]

> W. Jane, dean; Nath[aniel] Hodges, sub-d[ecanus];
> Abra[ham] Gregory, thesaur[arius].

[*fo. 152v. blank*]

312. [*fo. 153*] ***An Inventory of all and singuler the Goods and Utensills belonging to the Cathedrall of Gloucester, Taken the Thirtieth day of November 1681.***[2]

> In the custody of Mr. Hodges, treasurer.

Two large silver guilt flagons.
Two large silver guilt bowles with covers.
Two silver guilt challices with covers [*crossed out*; *in the margin:*] Mistake [*with a cross at each end of the entry*].
Two large silver guilt candlesticks.
One iron chest, and one haire trunck plated.

> In the custody of Mr. Campion.

One silver guilt bason.
One crimsom velvett cloth fring'd, one cushion of the same.
One other crimson velvett pullpit cloth fringed, with one cushion of the same.
One other old cushion of the same.
One Bible, one Comon Praier Book covered with crimson velvett, and silver guilt bosses.
One diaper table cloth, one damask table cloth.
Two damask napkyns.
One piece of arras for the altar.
One piece of crimson damask with Jehovah imbroidered in the middle.
One table cloth of redd and blew tissue.
One green table cloth, one old blew one.
Twenty large blew cushions with tassells.

---

[1] The £70 was paid to Bernard Smith in Dec. 1687; he had already been paid £80 at the end of 1686. He was to be paid an annual salary of £8 for the next five years.

[2] The inventory was written on a separate sheet of paper which has been pasted into the book.

Eightene small cushions. Three seat clothes.

Two old imbroidered copes.

Five large green cushions.

Two brass branches.

Purple curtaines & valens in the arch deacon's seat.

Two silver guilt claspes broken off.

    In the Library.

One table board: one greene carpett.

Three leather chaires, and two formes.

313. [*fo. 153v.*] Charles R. [*etc., a repetition, with a few insignificant differences in spelling and punctuation, of* 'Mr. Machell's Dispensation', *entered on fo. 143v.* (*above,* **291**)].

[*fo. 154 and v. blank*]

314. [*fo. 155*] ***The names of the Bishops, Deanes & Prebends of Gloucester contayned in this Booke and the time of theire severall Installacions & Admissions.***[1]

Bishops:	fol:		fol:
Dr. Goodman	39	Dr. Pritchett	117: 118
Dr. Nicolson		Dr. Frampton	136: 137: 138: 139
Deanes:			
Dr. Lawde	3	Dr. Brough	77
Dr. Senhouse	33	Dr. Vyner	113
Dr. Wynniffe	38	Dr. Frampton	121[2]
Dr. Warburton	56	Dr. Marshall	140
Dr. Frewen	57	Dr. Jane	147
Canons or Prebends:[3]			
Mr. Thomas Bayly	20[4]	Mr. Jacob	[100]
Dr. Isles	34	Mr. Vyner D.D.	101
Mr. John Wood	43	Mr. Andrewes	102
Mr. George Palmer	58	Dr. Savage	103 [*recte* 102v.]
Dr. Sheldon	60	Mr. Washbourne	103
Dr. English	62	Mr. Gregory D.D.	115[5]
Mr. Osborne	74	Mr. Frampton D.D.	117[6]
Dr. Washbourne	96	Mr. Hodges	123
Dr. Warmistry	97	Mr. Fowler D.D.	126

[1] In the MS. the names are arranged in a single column.

[2] The number could be 121 or 122; Frampton's installation as dean (**241**) is recorded on fo. 121.

[3] The MS. repeats the heading on the verso simply as 'Canons', without 'or Prebends'.

[4] Changed from 22. The documents relating to Bayly's appointment to a prebend (**4**) are on fos. 20–1, but he never became a canon of Gloucester.

[5] Changed from 114. Abraham Gregory's admission (**226**) is recorded on fo. 114v.

[6] Changed from 116. Robert Frampton's admission as a canon (**232**) is recorded on folio 116v.

[*fo. 155v.*]

Dr. Blandford	98	Mr. Kinge	126
Mr. Hugh Naish	99	Dr. Cudworth	129
Mr. Harris	99	Dr.[1] Bull	130
Dr. Harwood	100	Mr. Beauliew B.D.	151

315. [*fo. 156*]

An Abstract of the most memorable Acts and Orders contayned in this Booke.

A	fol:
Audit Allowances	55
Arch-Deacon Mr. Hugh Robinson	62: 64: 131
Admissio Archididascali	23
Admissio Hypodidascali	25: 33: 51
Admissio Elemozynarii	27
Admissio Laici Cantatoris	29
Admissio Choristae	29
Admissio Organistae	30: 75
B	
Blackleach: for the Backdoore	45
Bishop Lawde's Orders	68
Bishop Nicolson's Orders	111
C	
Comunion Table	4
Clerk for the Convocation	31: 75: 42: 140
Chancellors: Patents Confirmation	36: 49: 109: 129
Councill to the D. & Ch. John Robins Esq. & Thomas Williams Esq.	86
Chapter-Clarke: William Lambe	83:[2] 49: 66
D	
Dispensation for Audit	23: 61: 78
Dispensation for Dr. Loe &c.	27: 48: 79: 80: 123
E	
Electio Praecentoris	25
Electio Officiariorum	28
Electio Sacristae & Subsacristae	119: 122
Electio Janitoris	122
F	
G	
H	
Hanslape Francis his Suspention	106

---

[1] 'Mr.' has been changed in the MS. to 'Dr.'.

[2] William Lamb's appointment is in fact recorded on fo. 81v. (above, **170**).

---

[1] The entry is written over the capital 'L' for the next alphabetical section, the capital letters having been written before the index entries were made.

[2] At the lower right-hand corner of the page are written the letters GHF; cf. above, p. xxix.

[*fos. 157v.–160 blank*]

316. [*fo. 160v.*] ***Bookes Relating onely to the Dean and Chapter's Concern.***

One book of King Henry the Eight's charter of the Colledge, fairly written.[1]

One book called the Chapter Book for registring all acts of chapter.[2]

Six leiger bookes for entring all leases and other publick writings successively from Henry the Eight's time to King Charles the Second.[3]

One old book for keeping of courts for the severall mannors belonging to the Colledge in Henry the Eight's time.[4]

---

[1] Probably the grant of endowment to the dean and chapter, dated 4 Sept. 1541, which is in the cathedral library.

[2] That is, the Act Book itself.

[3] The six earliest registers of leases are in fact dated thus: *c.* 1550–1616, 1617–43, 1660–7, 1667–77, 1677–87, 1687–98. Possibly when the note was written there was an earlier Henrician register in existence, making six books up to the time of Charles II.

[4] The book has not been identified.

APPENDIX I:
THE BREAKING OF THE WEST WINDOW OF THE CHOIR

[Among the archives of the dean and chapter is an interesting book (catalogue number D 936 E 16) much of which is in the hand of Dr. Abraham Gregory, which he probably began as an aide-memoire during the years that he was treasurer. The book contains much information about people to whom the dean and chapter leased property, including such personal details as, for example, the books those people gave to the cathedral library. After Gregory's account of the breaking of the west window of the choir had been obliterated in the Chapter Act Book[1] he rewrote it in this book.[2]]

[Title:] **A Register of the Dean and Chapter of Gloucester beginning at Michaelmas 1672: and containing the severall leases set by the Church since that time, with the severall Fines paid, the years expired in the Old leases surrendred, the value of the severall estates as then accounted, the reasons of Favour in the better bargains, and the names of such tenants as by any unworthy Carriage have iustly Forfeited future Kindnesse.**

[*page 14*] **An impartiall account of Mr. Fowler's breaking the West Window of the Quire, as appears by Mr. Hodges's Memorandum in the Chapter book, and Dr. Gregory's answear.**

Mr. Hodge's Memorandum.

Memorandum That upon the 23d of June 1679, at a Chapter, where were present Dr. Washbourn, Subdean (having the Dean's proxy), Dr. Abraham Gregory, Treasurour, Nathaniel Hodges, Edward Fowler, Dr. Cudworth, prebends of the Cathedrall church of Gloucester, it was ordered by a maiority, every one consenting then present (Dr. Gregory only excepted) that a certain scandalous picture of the holy Trinity, being in the west window of the quire of the said church, should be removed, and other glasse put into the place.

Tho[mas] Washbourn;
Nath[aniel] Hodges.

Dr. Gregory's answear immediately subioynd to the memorandum.

Since by the memorandum above written by Mr. Hodges his private hand (contrary to all the praecedents of this book) Dr. Gregory thinks himself expos'd, by the expressing his negative vote, against all example, for the vindicating his reputation from all unworthy reflections, hee desires a few particulars which follow may also bee remembred.

1. That the order above mentioned neither is, nor could bee a legall act of Chapter, since every such act requires the presence of the Dean, or the Chapter Clarke, by one of whose hands it ought to bee entred and subscribd; but at the making this order, the Dean was absent, and the Chapter Clarke (against all former practise) was turned out of the Chapter house, nor was any proxie from the Dean exhibited, as in such case ought to bee done.

---

[1] Above, **270** and **271**.

[2] See S. J. A. Evans and S. Eward, 'Dr. Abraham Gregory, a Seventeenth-Century Prebendary of Gloucester Cathedral', *Trans. B.G.A.S.* xcv (1978), 59–67, which also gives Fowler's view of the affair.

Here 2 notes are added not entred into the Chapter book, as neither the notes following.

First that the Dean was wont to leave his proxies limited to such perticulars as hee foresaw might happen, and in such case, if Dr. Washbourn had any proxie it could not warrant any thinge which was not mentioned therein, as it is evident by the Dean's great displeasure this was not.

Secondly that the memorandum was not entred till long after the thinge done, and till Mr. Fowler earnestly by leter upon leter prest it, doubting his being questioned, and at last was entred by Mr. Hodges, Mr. Lamb the Chapter Clarke absolutely refusing it, as against his oath and duty. Whereas Chapter acts are alwayes written down in the Chapter house by the Chapter Clarke as soon as they are made.

2. That the supposd act (had it been legall) appointed only the removall of the glasse, but under pretence thereof it was immediately broken down by a violent hand, which was not ordered, To the begetting a greater scandall, than that it designed to remove.

Note, that the order in truth was, that the Treasurour should remove it, but because hee would not promise to do it, Mr. Fowler said, 'I will go and do it presently my selfe', and so did. The next Sunday the Conventicle-preacher[1] urgd, that now it was evident the establisht Church needed a more thorough reformation, since its own members confest the dreggs of popery were remaining in it.

3. That Dr. Gregory did not consent to the removall or breaking of the glasse at that time, for reasons which were not then answeared, and therefore hee desires by posterity may bee considered.

[page 15]   1. That the glasse obiected against had stood the reformation of the Church of England and of the Church of Scotland; that is neither any of their praedecessors in that church since H. the 8th nor any of the Scotch souldiers (that did much mischeife to the windowes in the church and cloysters) during the late wars, had been angry at or scandalis'd with it. And therefore hee thought it too high a gratification of the fanaticall party, out of a sudden zeal to beat it down, without some publick censure or order from their superiours.

Note, the Triennial visitation of the D. & Chap. was then approaching.

2. That hee understood not any such representation in the glasse (and scandall by it) as was complaind of; and if any private person would interpret it according to his own fancy, the fault was in him, not in the window. It was a scandall rather taken, than given.

3. That if there were any such representation understood in it, yet this glasse was up so high, and stood in so private a place, that not one in a thousand that came into the church either did, or easily could, see it; and that hee had livd a member of that church well nigh 20 years, but never knew one person offended with it before. Though hee himselfe had taken notice of it.

---

[1] i.e. James Forbes, for whom see below, p. 163.

4. That whatever the repraesentation was, it was nothing otherwise but the very same with the common seal of the said Cathedrall church; that if in conscience they thought themselves bound to break the window, they must bee bound to break their seal also; nay rather to break their seal; since the window being under the locks and keyes of the church, no body could come to adore it, but the impression put to every lease and writing that passeth the seal, goes abroad into many hands, and at their pleasure may bee worshipt by them.

Here it was obiected, that if they brake the seal they could passe no more leases, but Dr. Gregory answeared, that interest had no consideration in a case of conscience, as they pretended this to bee; and that, if it really were their duty to break the one, they ought to destroy the other. If it were not their duty, hee could not thinke it their prudence (in such a iuncture) to meddle with either.

1. Note Scotland was then in rebellion.

2. Mr. Fowler was the man (not the Subdean who ought) that proposd. Hee it was that earnestly perswaded it. Hee it was that with a long pole dasht it to peices, in the sight of many, and some strangers of quality then in the church.

3. All this is entred here, because blotted out of the Chapter book.

APPENDIX II:
CHARLES II'S LETTER FOR THE PROVISION OF VICARS AND CURATES

[The original letter below, stained at the top left corner where it once bore a seal, has been pasted into the book between fos. 87 and 88.]

Charles R. Whereas formerly due care hath not been taken by you or your Predecessors to provide sufficient maintenance for the Vicars or Curates which officiate in the parochiall churches appropriated to the Dean and Chapter of that Church, Our will is that forthwith provision be made for the Augmentation of all such Vicaridges and Cures where the Tythes and profitts are appropriated to you and your Successors in such manner that they who immediately attend upon the performance of Ministeriall Offices in every parish may have a competent portion out of every Rectory impropriated to your Use. And to this end Our further Will is that no lease be granted of any Rectories or Parsonages belonging to your Corporation by you or your Successors, untill you shall provide that the respective Vicaridges or Curates' places (where are no Vicaridges endowed) have so much revenue in Glebe, Tythes or other emoluments as commonly will amount to £80 per Annum or more if it will beare it, and in good forme of law established upon them and their Successors. And where the Rectories are of small value and cannot admitt of such portion to the Vicar or Curate Our Will is that one half of the profitts of such Rectory be reserved for the maintenance of the Vicar or Curate. And if any leases or Grants of such fore-named Rectories have been made by you since the first day of June last past, and you did not ordain Competent Augmentations of the Vicaridges or Cures in the respective places, Our Will is that out of the Fynes which you have received or are to receive you do adde such increase to the Vicars and Curates as is agreeable to the rates and proportions above mentioned. And Wee do Declare Our Will and pleasure in all the particulars fore-recited to be that if you or your Successors, or any Person, holding any Dignity, office, Benefice or Prebend in that Our Church doe or shall refuse or omitt to observe these our Commands we shall judge them unworthy of our future favour whensoever any preferrment Ecclesiasticall may be expected by them from Us. Given at Our Court at Whitehall this 9th August 1660, in the 12th yeare of Our Reigne [1660].

By his Majestie's Command.   Edward Nicholas.

    To Our trusty and welbeloved the Deane and Chapter of Our
    Cathedrall Church of Gloucester and to their Successors.

APPENDIX III: BIOGRAPHICAL NOTES

Biographical notes of cathedral dignitaries and of others who require more than a line or two have been collected below. People whose biographies are included in *O.D.N.B.* are treated more briefly than the others. Dates between 1 January and 24 March are given according to the modern reckoning of the beginning of the year. Where not otherwise stated information about academic careers is taken from *Alumni Cantab.* and *Alumni Oxon.* Information about bishops, deans, archdeacons and prebendaries of Gloucester is taken or corroborated from *Fasti*.

AISGILL, HENRY. Matriculated 22 Dec. 1576 at Queen's College, Oxford, aged 17, B.A. 1579, M.A. 1584. Held the sixth prebend from 1597; rector of Llawhaden (Pembs.), 1606, chancellor of St. David's, 1605, vicar of Down Hatherley, where he was buried. Died 18 June 1622. Cf. *Parsons*, 371.

ALLIBOND, JOHN. See *O.D.N.B.* Hugh Robinson's proxy for his installation as archdeacon (**118**). Rector of St. Mary de Crypt 1634–8, perpetual curate of St. Nicholas, Gloucester, 1635–48, rector of Broadwell 1636–58. In a satirical letter which he wrote in 1639 to the Laudian divine and historian Dr. Peter Heylyn, a friend of William Laud, he was very critical of the puritan party in Gloucester. Died 1658. The chapter made a grant to his widow Margaret in 1661 (**185**).

ANDREWS, ANTHONY. Matriculated 26 Oct. 1621 at Trinity College, Oxford, aged 17, B.A. 1625, M.A. 1629. Vicar of Burford (Oxon.), 1634, rector of Great Stambridge (Essex), 1635–41, vicar of North Shoebury (Essex), 1637–40. Admitted 20 Nov. 1665 to the prebend vacant by the resignation of Thomas Vyner (**197**). Died 4 Sept. 1678: *Fasti*; *Alumni Oxon.*

ANGELL, JOHN. Of Gloucester, graduated B.A. from Magdalen Hall, Oxford, 1614, M.A. 1616. Admitted as assistant schoolmaster 4 Feb. 1624 (**50**). In 1628 he was appointed by the mayor and aldermen of Leicester as the town preacher. He suffered from some mental affliction, and was described as 'a painful preacher' (*Alumni Oxon.*), being often in trouble. He later became lecturer at Grantham (Lincs.), where he was buried 6 June 1655. Cf. Wood, *Athenae*, iii. 397.

ANGELL, JOHN. Son of Abel Angel, was cathedral porter from 1636 or earlier until the Commonwealth period, and then at the Restoration until his death in 1665 (**174**). An earlier John Angell was porter in 1615 and was succeeded in the office by Abel Angell.

ANYAN, THOMAS. See *O.D.N.B.* Held the fourth prebend from *c.* 1612 until his death. President of Corpus Christi College, Oxford, 1614–29. His drinking was regarded as scandalous. Died 1632 or 1633 and was buried in Canterbury cathedral, where also he was a canon.

BABER, FRANCIS. Matriculated 13 Dec. 1616 at Trinity College, Oxford, aged 17, B.A. 1620, M.A. 1622, B.C.L. 1624, D.C.L. 1628. Chancellor of Gloucester diocese, 1630, having been granted a patent for the office in 1627 (**78**), until his death, 17 June 1669. Lessee of two tenements in Millers Green on the site of which the later Deanery was built. He gave £15 towards the cost of the new organ of 1665, as well as a number of law books to the cathedral library. He died in 1669 and was buried in the cathedral, where his monument is on the west wall of the Seabroke Chapel: cf. *Parsons*, 415.

BAYLY, THOMAS. A patent for his preferment to a prebend was registered 11 April 1617 (**4**), but he was never installed as a canon. Perhaps the same as Thomas Baylie (died 1663; see *O.D.N.B.*), a fellow of Magdalen College, Oxford, 1610–15, and rector of Manningford Bruce (Wilts.), 1621, and of Mildenhall (Wilts.), who became a member of the Westminster assembly of divines.

BEAULIEU, LUKE. See *O.D.N.B.* Admitted 21 May 1687 to the prebend vacant by the death of Thomas Washbourne (**308**). Educated at the university of Saumur, he left France for religious reasons and in 1667 sought refuge in England where he became known for his learning. Died 1723.

BLANDFORD, WALTER. See *O.D.N.B.* Admitted 22 Aug. 1660 to a prebend (**191**). Consecrated 3 Dec. 1665 as bishop of Oxford and translated 14 June 1671 to the see of Worcester. Died July 1675.

BRETT, HENRY. The Henry Brett who witnessed the admission of Walter Blandford to a prebend in 1660 (**191**) was probably either the landowner, an alderman of Gloucester from 1672, who died 31 March 1674 aged 87, or his elder son, of Ashleworth manor, who died unmarried in 1672. Henry the father and his grandson, another Henry, with his sisters Margaret and Joyce (Jocosa), gave books to the cathedral library.

BRIDGER, LAURENCE. Fellow of Magdalen College, Oxford, 1658, B.A. 1570, M.A. 1574. Presented by Queen Elizabeth 2 Nov. 1580 to the third prebend, which he resigned in 1625 (**60**). He had served as treasurer and as subdean. Died 18 Oct. 1625.

BRODGATE, RICHARD. Various members of the Brodgate family, who lived in Babylon and the infirmary, filled positions for many years until the Commonwealth period as choristers (**5**), as lay singers, and from 1622, with Richard, as a minor canon (**38**). A Richard Brodgate had appeared as a lay singer at the bishop's visitation in 1616, and together with Thomas Tully was in trouble with the chapter on 16 Nov. 1621 (**34**). As there is no record of that Richard having left the cathedral, he was presumably the same as the Richard admitted in 1622 as a minor canon. He was paid as a minor canon until 1637, when the accounts show payments to 'Mistress Bradgate and her familye beeing shutt upp of the Infection of the plague and for buryall of the people that dyed in the house for the wardesmens attendance &c.', and her 'remoovall out of her house.' Richard may have been one of those who then perished. Another Richard Brodgate was admitted a chorister in 1618 (**13**), apparently being replaced as late as 1630 (**97**), and as a lay singer in May 1639 (**146**), in which function he continued at the Restoration (**172**, **194**). He was dead by 24 June 1667, when his place as a lay singer was filled (**203**).

BROOKE, PETER. Presented by the dean and chapter to the vicarage of St. Mary de Lode in March 1627 (**72**), he had been a lay clerk since 1605 or earlier: he was mentioned in the records variously as a lay clerk and a minor canon before Nov. 1640, being only then formally admitted as a minor canon (**156**). He seems not to have been a graduate of either Oxford or Cambridge. He was presumably dead by 1661, when Francis Hanslape was vicar of St. Mary de Lode.

BROUGH, WILLIAM. See *O.D.N.B.* Chaplain to King Charles I and from 1 Feb. 1639 a canon of Windsor (where the archives retain his book of memoranda concerning the customs of the chapter of Windsor), he suffered much during the wars. Nominated dean of Gloucester 17 Aug. 1643 (**159**) and installed (by proxy) 20 Nov. 1644 (**171**). Died 5 July 1671.

BULL, GEORGE. See *O.D.N.B.* Admitted 9 Oct. 1678 to the prebend vacant by the death of Anthony Andrews (**263**). Consecrated bishop of St. David's, 1705. Died 1710.

CAMPION, JOHN. A talented local painter who did much painting for the dean and chapter in the 1660s and 1670s, including the coats of arms and decorations on the organ made in 1665 by Thomas Harris, besides gilding and painting the effigy and tomb-chest of Robert, duke of Normandy, in the choir. He witnessed the admission of Abraham Gregory to a prebend 31 July 1671 (**226**). In 1672 he and John Campion the younger, presumably his son, were granted the sextons' places previously held by Barkeley Wrench and Paul Bridger (**231**), and one of them remained sexton until 1688.

COVERT, ISABELLA. The dean and chapter's tenant for the parsonage of Chipping Norton (Oxon.) in 1666 (**200**). Daughter of Sir John Leigh, of Longborough 8 miles west of Chipping Norton, and wife of Sir John Covert, of Slaugham (Sussex), who was created a baronet in 1660 and died 11 March 1679, when the baronetcy became extinct.

CUDWORTH, RALPH. See *O.D.N.B.* Admitted 25 May 1678 to the prebend vacant by the death of Asahel King (**256**). Cudworth was one of the Cambridge Platonists, centred on Emmanuel College, Cambridge. Died 1688. Among his published works was *The True Intellectual System of the Universe* (1678), a copy of which he gave to Gloucester cathedral library.

DEIGHTON, JOHN. Presumably he who matriculated 26 Oct. 1660 at Trinity College, Oxford, he was admitted as a minor canon in 1667 (**204**), was chosen by the dean as sacrist in 1672 (**238**) and as precentor in 1678 (**264**), continuing in that office until 1695 notwithstanding his being admonished in 1685 for his 'manifold repeated neglects' and unreasonable absences from divine service (**302**).

ELBRIDGE, WILLIAM. Son of John Elbridge of Bentham (Glos.), he matriculated 30 Oct. 1635 at Balliol College, Oxford, aged 17, B.A 1639. Admitted as assistant master of the college school 21 May 1639 (**146**), he was ordained by the bishop of Gloucester on 19 Sept. 1641, and later obtained various livings in the diocese of Gloucester.

ENGLISH, JOHN. Matriculated 16 June 1610 at Balliol College, Oxford, aged 17, B.A. 1612, M.A. 1615, B.D. 1624, D.D. 1630. Held livings in Lincs. and Hants.; rector of Rudford 1634 and served the cure of Cheltenham 1646: *Alumni Oxon*. Admittted to the second prebend 22 April 1634 (**117**). He lived in Little Cloister House, rooms adjoining which were leased in 1665 to his daughter Bridget (**202**), widow of John Vaulx (below). Dead by 26 Nov. 1647 and buried at Cheltenham: *Fasti*; *Walker Revised*, 172–3.

FIDKIN, EDWARD. Of Hartlebury (Worcs.), matriculated 17 July 1663 at Balliol College, Oxford, aged 18. Elected as a minor canon in Dec. 1666 (**181**), presented as rector or vicar of Matson 29 April 1669 (**212**), and chosen as sacrist 30 Nov. 1671 (**227**), he caused the dean and chapter much trouble by his neglect of prayers and demeanour (**253**), his drinking (**265**), and his absence from service (**302**).

FORBES, JAMES. The 'conventicle preacher' mentioned in Abraham Gregory's account of the breaking of the west window of the choir (above, p. 158), he was descended from an old Scottish family and was educated at Aberdeen university and at Oxford, where he became M.A. in 1654. During the Commonwealth period he preached for six years at the cathedral, his life often being in danger. He was several times imprisoned for private preaching. Dean Frampton tried in vain to persuade him to conform. At his death in May 1712, aged 83, he was buried under his own communion-table in the Unitarian chapel in Barton Street, Gloucester. When the chapel was demolished in 1966 his remains were cremated and they were reburied in the south walk of the cathedral cloisters on 21 Dec. 1966. About that time also his valuable library was scandalously dispersed and sold.

FOWLER, EDWARD. See *O.D.N.B.* Admitted 19 Feb. 1676 to the prebend vacant by the death of William Washbourne (**254**). Nominated as bishop of Gloucester 22 April 1691, consecrated 5 July. Died 1714. Cf. above, p. 157.

FRAMPTON, ROBERT. See *O.D.N.B.* Admitted 23 July 1672 to the prebend vacant by the death of Henry Savage (**232**). Installed as dean of Gloucester 6 May 1673 (**241**). Nominated as bishop of Gloucester 1 Jan. 1681, consecrated 27 March, deprived 1 Feb. 1690. Died 25 May 1708.

FREWEN, ACCEPTED. See *O.D.N.B.* Installed as dean of Gloucester in Sept. 1631 (**101**). Nominated as bishop of Coventry and Lichfield (**159**) 17 Aug. 1643, consecrated 28 April 1644; translated to the archbishopric of York 4 Oct. 1660. Died 28 March 1664.

GOODMAN, GODFREY. See *O.D.N.B.* Elected as bishop of Gloucester 26 Nov. 1624 (**54**), consecrated 6 March 1625, deprived, 1640. Died 19 Jan. 1656.

GRAYLE or GRAILE, EZRA. Admitted as assistant master of the college school 14 June 1632 (**106**). Son of Edmund Graile of Wotton under Edge, he matriculated 31 Oct. 1623 at Magdalen Hall, Oxford, aged 14, graduating B.A. from Balliol College 1627, M.A. 1633. He became rector of Lassington (Glos.) in 1633, following the death of Elias Wrench, and was buried there in Feb. 1649: *Parsons*, 231.

GRAYLE or GRAILE, JOHN. See *O.D.N.B.* Son of John Graile of Stow on the Wold, he became assistant master of the college school 25 Oct. 1634 (**120**), the day after he graduated B.A. from Magdalen Hall, Oxford, aged 20 or 21. He vacated the position a year later and became a puritanical preacher. Died early in 1654.

GREGORY, ABRAHAM. Matriculated 7 Dec. 1660 at Oriel College, Oxford, aged 17, M.A. (Cantab.) 1665, D.D. 1677. From Nov. 1660, before matriculating, he was assistant master of the college school, and it was presumably in that capacity that on 23 July 1671 he witnessed the installation as dean of Thomas Vyner (**223**), being admitted eight days later to the prebend vacated by Vyner's promotion (**226**), subscribing on the same day to the Act of Uniformity before the bishop of Gloucester at Bishop's Cleeve. The Act Book contains no record of his appointment as minor canon or assistant master, or of his performing their duties, but the Account Book shows payment to him for both. Vicar of Sandhurst 1664–76, rector of Cowley 1670–3, vicar of Churcham 1673–90, rector of St. Mary de Crypt, Gloucester, 1675, rector of Cromhall, 1679; canon and precentor of Llandaff, 1679. He was the younger brother of John (below). When the brothers both subscribed to the Act of Uniformity on 13 Aug. 1662 Abraham was living in the common kitchen (later no. 3 Millers Green) and John at the schoolmaster's house (later no. 4). Elected receiver and treasurer in Nov. 1672, Abraham was rewarded in 1675 with an honorarium for his performance as receiver and treasurer (**252**), an office which he held from 1672 (**238**) until 1679 (**272**, **274**) and again in 1686, 1687 (**306**, **311**), 1688 and 1689. He died 29 July 1690 and was buried in the cathedral cloister: *Parsons*, 426. In the cathedral library is a fine portrait of him, given to the dean and chapter by Mr. Manning Watts in April 1931. Cf. above, p. 157.

GREGORY, JOHN. Elder brother of Abraham (above), he graduated B.A. from Pembroke Hall, Cambridge, 1667, M.A. 1672. He was headmaster of the college school 1660–73. He was also rector of Hempsted, on the south-west edge of Gloucester, from 1669 and rector of Dursley (Glos.) and archdeacon of Gloucester from 1671. He died 10 Dec. 1678: *Fasti*.

GREGORY, OLIVER. Nephew of Abraham and John Gregory (above), matriculated 3 March 1665 at St. Edmund Hall, Oxford, aged 16, B.A. from Queen's College, Oxford, 1668, M.A. 1671. He succeeded his uncle John as headmaster of the college school, being admitted on 29 June 1674 (**249**).

HANBURY, JOHN. M.P. for the city of Gloucester (to which he gave a piece of plate) in 1628–9. He gave a bible to the dean and chapter in 1660 and later gave an unusual clock to the college school, where he had been a pupil: *V.C.H. Glos.* iv. 371; Bonnor, *Gloucester Cathedral*, 18.

HANSLAPE, FRANCIS. Matriculated 18 April 1637 at Oriel College, Oxford, aged 15. One of the minor canons, though there seems to be no record of his appointment; his house was among those which at the Restoration needed to be reglazed. In 1661 he was elected precentor (**166**), an office which he held in Oct. 1667 when his drunken behaviour following the mayor's feast caused the dean to suspend him, and by Feb. 1668 he had resigned the vicarage of St. Mary de Lode, Gloucester (**207**), which he had held since 1661. He was perhaps rector of Littleton upon Severn *c*. 1670: *Alumni Oxon*.

HARRIS, ROBERT. Perhaps one of three of the name who graduated B.A. at Oxford 1617–24, he was admitted to a prebend on 24 Sept. 1660, but the only record of his admission in the Act Book is a marginal heading before an unfilled space (**193**). He subscribed to the Act of Uniformity on 9 July 1662, in the presence of Edward Williams, clerk. Dead by 12 Nov. 1662.

HARWOOD or HARWARD, RICHARD. Matriculated (age not given) 27 Jan. 1632 at Magdalen Hall, Oxford, B.A. 1634, M.A. 1637, B.D. 1646, D.D. 1660. Admitted 11 Nov. 1660 to the fourth prebend (**194**). Rector of Stow on the Wold. Dead by 23 April 1669, when he was buried in St. Michael's church, Gloucester.

HAYES, CHRISTOPHER. Admitted as a lay singer 13 March 1620 (**22**), he was admonished 19 Oct. 1620 for negligence and failure to improve his singing (**27**). He received a salary as a lay singer until 1641 (cathedral accounts) but was again told in June 1626 to try to improve his singing (**66**). He was living during the Commonwealth period in the infirmary and Babylon: 'Oliver's Survey'. He died 25 Jan. 1655 and was buried in the cathedral: *Parsons*, 417.

HENSTRIDGE, DANIEL. Admitted in Dec. 1666 as master of the choristers and organist (**181**). He retained the position until the end of 1673, Charles Wren being admitted as his successor 19 Jan. 1674 (**240**). The dean and chapter have among their music manuscripts a morning service, an evening service and three anthems composed by Henstridge.

HOARE, JOHN. Headmaster of the college school in 1616 at the bishop's visitation. Perhaps the John Hore who matriculated 16 June 1610 at Magdalen Hall, Oxford, aged 17, B.A. 1611, M.A. 1614, rector of Oddington, 1616.

HODGES, NATHANIEL. Matriculated (age not given) at Christ Church, Oxford, 21 March 1651, B.A. 26 May 1654, M.A. 9 April 1657; Whyte's professor of moral philosophy 1668–73. Admitted 20 May 1673 to the prebend vacant by the preferment of Robert Frampton as dean (**245**). Also canon of Norwich, 1673. Died 28 Aug. 1700.

HOSIER, PHILIP. Admitted as organist and instructor of the choristers 19 Oct. 1620 (**28**). He seems to have been the only organist of the cathedral to be ordained. The diocesan records show that on 23 Sept. 1621, at an ordination in the cathedral, 'Philip Hosyer organist' was ordained 'to exercise the office of deacon within the said Cathedral or under any sufficient minister within the city or dioces of Gloucester & not otherwise nor in any other manner.' From 1628 to 1632 he was curate of St. Mary de Crypt and All Saints, Gloucester, and from 1634 to 1642 incumbent of St. John the Baptist.

HOSIER, WILLIAM. Admitted as a chorister 10 Oct. 1627 (**74**), and replaced 12 Feb. 1631 (**99**). A chorister at Magdalen College, Oxford, 1630–7, B.A. from New College 1638. Admitted as a minor canon 11 June 1639 (**147**).

HULETT, WILLIAM. Matriculated Easter 1632 as a sizar at Clare College, Cambridge. Admitted as a minor canon 10 Oct. 1627 (**74**). Admonished 1631 for speaking 'insolently and unmannerly' to the dean (**103**). Perhaps curate of St. Ewen and St. Mary de Grace, Gloucester, 1635; curate of Frocester in 1661.

ILES, THOMAS. Matriculated 23 Nov. 1604 at Christ Church, Oxford, aged 16, B.A. 1608, M.A. 1611, D.D. 1619. Rector of Lasborough, 1609, of Todenham, 1618. Admitted 13 July 1622 to the sixth prebend (**37**). Died 20 June 1649. Cf. *Walker Revised*, 175.

JACKSON, EDWARD. Matriculated 19 July 1659 at St. John's College, Oxford, B.A. 1663. A minor canon from 1664 (**188**) to 1677, elected as sacrist 6 Dec. 1666 (**180**, the earliest record in the Act Book of the election of a sacrist), and as precentor 26 Oct. 1667 (**206**), in which office he presumably began the cathedral's first register of marriages, baptisms, and burials (the earliest entries being made retrospectively) in accordance with Bishop Nicholson's order at his visitation of 1669 (**221**). He was presented to the rectory of Rudford 29 April 1669 (**212**). Died 3 Jan. 1677 and was buried in the cathedral: *Parsons*, 416 (giving his age as 33 though he was probably older).

JACOB, FRANCIS. Sizar, 30 March 1638, at St. John's College, Cambridge, aged 16, B.A. 1641, M.A. 1647. Subscribed to the Act of Uniformity 17 Dec. 1662, when he was 'now to be admitted into a prebend of Gloucester', but the only record of his admission in the Act Book is a marginal heading before an unfilled space (**195**). He had been presented by the king on 12 Nov. 1662 to the prebend vacant by the death of Robert Harris, but had apparently been present as a prebendary at the visitation of the cathedral in 1661. He had resigned by 13 June 1665.

JANE, WILLIAM. Matriculated 5 Dec. 1660 at Christ Church, Oxford, aged 16, B.A. 1664, M.A. 1667, B.D. 1674, D.D. 1679, canon of Christ Church, 1578, regius professor of divinity 1680–1707. Installed 6 June 1685 as dean of Gloucester (**301**). Died 22 Feb. 1707.

JEFFERIES, STEPHEN. Admitted 17 May 1682 as organist and instructor of the choristers (**288**). A chorister at Salisbury cathedral, in Nov. 1674 he became a lay vicar there, where he occasionally acted as deputy to the organist Michael Wise. At Gloucester in Jan. 1685 he was admonished for his manifold neglects and unreasonable absences (**299**). Some of his many compositions survive in the cathedral library. He died while still organist and was buried in the cathedral cloister in Jan. 1712. He was staunchly Protestant. The second Chapter Act Book records that he received a further monition: at the end of morning service on 18 Feb. 1689, the day appointed by parliament for thanksgiving 'for making the Prince of Orange the instrument of the kingdom's delivery from Popery and arbitrary government', as soon as the blessing was given, he played 'over upon the organ a Comon Ballad in the hearing of fiftene hundred or two thousand people to the great scandall of religion, prophanation of the Church, and greivous offence of all good Christians'. Though very strongly reprimanded, after evening prayer Jefferies did 'assoone as the last Amen was ended, in the presence and hearing of all the congregation, fall upon the same straine, and on the organ plaid over the same common ballad againe: insomuch that the young gentlewomen invited one another to dance, the strangers cryed it were better that the organs were pull'd downe then that they should be so used: and all sorts declared, that the D. and Chapter could never remove the scandall, if they did not imediately turne away so insolent & prophane a person out of the Church'. The ballad was probably 'Lilliburlero', the haunting tune of which had danced King James II out of three kingdoms.

JENNINGS, HENRY. Matriculated 18 March 1678 at Magdalen Hall, Oxford, aged 16, B.A. 1681, clerk, Magdalen College, 1682–5, M.A. 1684. Chosen by the dean as a minor canon and admitted 20 April 1685 (**300**).

JONES, JOHN. An alderman of the city of Gloucester, he was named as witness to ceremonies (**35, 52**). He served as registrar to eight successive bishops of Gloucester (**54** etc.). He leased from the dean and chapter the 'old void and ruinous house commonly called the Old Workhouse and Old Schoolhouse' (now known as the Parliament Room) at an annual rent of 20*s*. At his death in 1630 he left his rights and title to the house to his son Henry.

KING, ASAHEL. Admitted 3 July 1665 at Queens' College, Cambridge, aged 17, matriculated 1667, B.A. 1669, M.A. 1672. Admitted 1 April 1676 to the prebend vacant by the death of Hugh Naish (**255**), and rector of Doynton 1677–8, he had died by 25 April 1678 and was buried at St. Andrew, Holborn (Middx.).

LAMB, WILLIAM. Appointed as chapter clerk or registrar at the annual audit in 1665 (**170**) and remained as such until June 1705. An alderman of Gloucester from 1682 until he resigned that office in 1691. He died 21 Oct. 1705, aged 82, and was buried in the cathedral cloister.

LANGLEY, JOHN. See *O.D.N.B.* Assistant master of the college school from 1616. Appointed 'archididascalus' or headmaster 9 March 1618 (**9**), resigned 24 Dec. 1627, readmitted 11 Aug. 1628 (**83**). A puritan, in 1635 he refused to take the oath which was binding on all schoolmasters to be loyal to the Church of England and to obey the bishops, and was suspended by Sir Nathaniel Brent, vicar general of the province of Canterbury, at the metropolitan visitation. In 1640 he became high master of St. Paul's School, London, where one of his pupils was to be Samuel Pepys. In June 1644 he gave evidence in the cause of Archbishop Laud, and testified to various innovations introduced by Laud in the liturgy at Gloucester cathedral during his time as dean there. Died 13 Sept. 1657.

LAUD, WILLIAM. See *O.D.N.B.* Installed as dean of Gloucester 20 Dec. 1616 (**1**). He recorded in his diary that the king had said that he well knew that the Gloucester deanery 'was a shell without a kernel': *Laud's Troubles and Tryal*, p. 4. On 29 June 1621 the king nominated him to the bishopric of St. David's, allowing him to hold the presidentship of St. John's College, Oxford, *in commendam*. His last signature in the Act Book as dean of Gloucester was 8 Oct. 1621 (**33**). He was consecrated 18 Nov. 1621, being translated to Bath and Wells 18 Sept. 1626, to London 15 July 1628 and to Canterbury 19 Sept. 1633. Died on the scaffold 10 Jan. 1645. The dean and chapter of Gloucester own his backgammon board and pieces.

LOE, THOMAS. Admitted as cathedral organist 8 Aug. 1665 (**172**), in succession to Robert Webb, who had died in poverty. In June 1665 the chapter had paid £10 to 'Mr. Low the Organist for & towards his charge in removing from Salisbury'. He was to remain at Gloucester only one year, and may possibly have returned to Salisbury, where in 1674 a lay vicar named Thomas Lowe taught the choristers as deputy to Salisbury cathedral's organist, the composer Michael Wise.

LOE or LEO, WILLIAM. See *O.D.N.B.* Held the fifth prebend from 1602, having been vicar of Churcham from 1598 and headmaster of the college school from 1600. Rector of Rudford from 1633 (**116**). In 1618, following differences with Dean Laud about the moving of the high altar, he accepted the position of pastor to the Merchant Adventurers in Hamburg (**16, 19**), but had returned to Gloucester by Oct. 1620 (**26–7**). He later became vicar of Wandsworth (Surrey), and was buried in Westminster Abbey 21 Sept. 1645.

LOE, WILLIAM. Son of Canon William Loe (above), he graduated from Trinity College, Cambridge, 1626. Before 1632 he held leases of the gatehouse over King Edward's Gate and of part of the Miskin ground in the Lower College churchyard. In 1632 he was apparently living in Gloucester. Vicar of Kirkby Masham (Yorks.), 1639. Died 1679.

LOVELL, RICHARD. Son of Richard Lovell of Oxford, he matriculated 13 Nov. 1635 at Magdalen College, Oxford, aged 16, B.A. 1637, M.A. 1640. Admitted as assistant master of the college school 7 March 1638 (**141**). Later ordained, he became rector of St. Peter, Sandwich (Kent), 1639. He may have been the Richard Lovel who in 1655 was described as being tutor to the duke of Gloucester, and who in 1657 was included, as chaplain, among the duke's servants.

LYE, NATHANIEL. Son of Giles Lye, of Gloucester, he matriculated 18 March 1665 at Brasenose College, Oxford, aged 16, B.A. 1668, M.A. 1671; D.D. from Jesus College, Cambridge, 1692. Admitted as assistant master of the college school 7 Aug. 1671 (**225**), he became rector of Cowley in 1673, rector of Kemerton in 1675, a canon of Bristol in 1691, archdeacon of Gloucester and rector of Dursley in 1714 and a canon of Gloucester in 1723. Died 29 Oct. 1737.

MARBURY, THOMAS and GEORGE. A grant of 5 Sept. 1604 was made to Thomas and Lawrence Marbury to write all presentations to the Great Seal of England, for life; and one of 10 July 1608 was made to George Marbury, in reversion after Thomas Marbury, of the office of engrossing letters patent of donation, presentations etc. to ecclesiastical preferments, for life, Lawrence evidently having died. Thomas was still alive on 10 Aug. 1611: *Calendar of State Papers Domestic, 1603–10.*

MARSHALL, THOMAS. See *O.D.N.B.* Installed 30 April 1681 as dean (**286**). Died 18 April 1685.

MARWOOD, RICHARD. Admitted as a minor canon 16 Oct. 1617 (**6**); the implication is that he was then admitted for the first time, yet a Richard Marwood had received a stipend as one of the four minor canons in 1609–10 and appeared at the bishop's visitation in 1616. Admonished 1 Dec. 1623 for beating a child undeservedly (**48**). Elected as precentor 30 Nov. 1625 (**63**) and in successive years up to and including 1640 (**156**).

MASON, WILLIAM. Deputy sexton, admonished for his behaviour towards the subdean 19 Oct. 1620 (**28**); he was also deputy porter and he received a salary as clerk of works (*supervisor operum*) from 1610 or earlier until 1641. In 1615 and 1626 he took a lease of the college mill, later no. 2 Millers Green.

NAISH or NASHE, HUGH. Matriculated 11 July 1636 at Oriel College, Oxford, aged 15, B.A. 1640, perhaps M.A. 1642. Admitted to a prebend 10 Sept. 1660 in succession to Thomas Washbourne, but the only record of his admission in the Act Book is a marginal heading before an unfilled space (**192**). He subscribed to the Act of Uniformity 18 Aug. 1662 in the presence of William Peirson, notary public, John Vaulx, and others. He had died by 7 Feb. 1676 and was buried at Harlaxton (Leics.), where he was rector.

NICHOLSON, JOHN. Matriculated 23 June 1621 at Magdalen Hall, Oxford, aged 15, B.A. from Magdalen College 1625, M.A. 1627, B. & D.C.L. 1639. His son John was also a lawyer. His patent for the office of chancellor of the diocese was granted by Bishop William Nicholson (**215**), whose cousin and executor he was: *O.D.N.B.* s.v. Nicholson, William.

NICHOLSON, WILLIAM. See *O.D.N.B.* Elected as bishop of Gloucester 26 Nov. 1660, consecrated 6 Jan. 1661. Died 5 Feb. 1672.

OKEOVER, JOHN. See *O.D.N.B.* Organist and master of the choristers from 1640 (**153**). Described as 'late organist' in 1654 when, as John Oker, he was admitted by gift as a freeman of Gloucester: *Freemen of Gloucester*, 12. He was an almsman in 1660, but was replaced in 1661. Died ? 1663.

OSBORNE, GILBERT. Matriculated 7 Dec. 1621 at Broadgate Hall, Oxford, aged 19, B.A. from Pembroke College 1624, M.A. 1627. Admitted 10 March 1640 to the third prebend (**151**). He died 16 Feb. 1657 at Withington (Glos.), where he was rector from 1634: Bigland, *Glos.* iv. 1495, 1502; *Walker Revised*, 175; cf. *Parsons*, 396.

PALMER, GEORGE. Matriculated 5 May 1615 at Lincoln College, Oxford, aged 18, B.A. 1615, M.A. from Magdalen College 1618, B.D. from Exeter College 1626. Admitted 25 Oct. 1632 to the first prebend (**107**). Dead by 28 Sept. 1658.

PARSONS, RICHARD. See *O.D.N.B.* Chancellor of the diocese from 1677 (**261**) and rector of Driffield from 1674. He lived in the common kitchen, later no. 3 Millers Green. The order of 12 April 1680 (**275**) that money be paid to him may be linked to an entry in the accounts of 21 July of a payment to Mr. Chancellor of £7 'by order of d[ean and] c[hapter] for a gratuity'. *Parsons*, pp. xiii sqq.

PRIOR, CHRISTOPHER. Presumably a son of Canon Thomas Prior (below), he graduated B.A. from Balliol College, Oxford, 1633, M.A. 1636, B.D. 1643. Admitted assistant master of the college school 13 Nov. 1635 (**128**). Later ordained, he became a canon of Salisbury cathedral in 1641, of Wells cathedral in 1643, and principal of New Inn Hall, Oxford, also in 1643. Died 1659.

PRIOR, THOMAS. Matriculated 20 Jan. 1604 at Broadgate Hall, Oxford, aged 18, B.A. 1607, M.A. 1612. Admitted to the first prebend in 1612, he had died by 25 Sept. 1632. In March 1633 the Gloucester city corporation ordered that because his 'extraordinary bountie to the poore & other workes of pietie and charities' resulted in his estate at his death being much impoverished, £10 should be given to his widow 'towards the maynetenaunce and support of her & her children'.

PRITCHETT, JOHN. Bishop of Gloucester, elected 10 Oct. (**236**), consecrated 3 Nov. 1672. He seems not to have been a graduate of either Oxford or Cambridge. Died 1 Jan. 1681.

ROBINS, JOHN. On 22 Oct. 1666 he surrendered the office of counsel to the dean and chapter (**183**), for which he had been paid an annual fee of £2, as requested by the dean because he lived too far from Gloucester. The cathedral accounts show that Thomas Williams was thereafter paid as counsel to the dean and chapter, but Robins continued to collect and pay to the chapter its rents from the manor of Matson and the tithes of Tredworth. For some years before the Commonwealth period the rents had been collected and paid by a Henry Robins.

ROBINSON, ANTHONY. Matriculated 14 Oct. 1597 at St. Albans Hall, Oxford, aged 15; student of Middle Temple, 1601. Clerk and registrar to the dean and chapter from *c.* 1613 (**77**). M.P. for Gloucester 1621–2, 1624–5; mayor 1629. Died 1641: *V.C.H. Glos.* iv. 377.

ROBINSON, ANTHONY. Son of the registrar of the same name, he graduated from Corpus Christi College, Oxford, 1632, M.A. 1635. Later ordained, he was vicar of Down Hatherley from 1640 and rector of Oddington from 1660.

ROBINSON, HUGH. See *O.D.N.B.* Installed as archdeacon of Gloucester 8 July 1634 (**118**). Rector of Dursley 1625–47. Died 30 March 1655.

ROSEINGRAVE, DANIEL. See *O.D.N.B.* Cathedral organist 1679–81, as shown in the accounts; his admission not recorded in the Act Book. Admonished 10 April 1679 for beating and wounding one of the lay singers (**269**).

SANDY, JOHN. He appeared as a minor canon at the bishop's visitation, 1613, even though he does not seem to have been in holy orders. In the bishop's visitations of 1594, 1610 and 1616, he was described as a lay clerk. The accounts show that he received a salary as a minor canon from 1609 or earlier until 1641. He was admonished on 15 May 1620 for leaving before the end of services and for talking and 'jangling' during prayers (**24**). On 10 Sept. 1641 a licence was granted for the marriage of 'John Sandy of Gloucester College' and Julian (sc. Gillian) Tyther of St. Bartholomew's. Another John Sandy was admitted as an almsman in 1639 (**145**).

SAVAGE, HENRY. Matriculated 11 March 1625 at Balliol College, Oxford, aged 20, B.A. 1625, M.A. 1630, B.D. 1637, D.D. 1651; master of the college 1651. Chaplain in ordinary to Charles II. Admitted 12 Jan.1666 to the prebend vacant by the preferment of Walter Blandford to the bishopric of Oxford (**198**). Died 6 June 1672.

SENHOUSE, RICHARD. See *O.D.N.B.* Installed 13 Dec. 1621 as dean (**35**). Consecrated as bishop of Carlisle 26 Sept. 1624. Died 6 May 1626.

SHELDON, GILBERT. See *O.D.N.B.* Admitted 26 Feb. 1633 to the fourth prebend, he was appointed dean of the Chapel Royal at the Restoration and in Oct. 1660 was elected bishop of London and nominated archbishop of Canterbury in June 1663. In 1667, on the resignation of the earl of Clarendon, he was elected (though never installed) chancellor of Oxford University, and at his own expense built the Sheldonian Theatre at Oxford which was named after him. Died 9 Nov. 1677.

SMITH (or SCHMIDT), BERNARD (1635?–1708). See *O.D.N.B.* The German organ-builder known as Father Smith, employed to work on the organ in the 1680s. He was paid £80 at the end of 1686 and £70 in Dec. 1687 (**311**). It is not known why the dean and chapter employed Smith rather than their usual organ-builder, Renatus Harris, Thomas Harris's son.

THACHE (THATCH), THOMAS. Son of Thomas, rector of Sapperton, matriculated 29 March 1677 at New College, Oxford, aged 19, B.A. 1680, M.A. 1683. Chosen by the dean as a minor canon and admitted 15 Jan. 1685 (**298**). Rector of Rudford, 1685; vicar of Churcham, 1697.

THEYER, JOHN. See *O.D.N.B.* He acted as chapter clerk at the Restoration; the Act Book contains no record of his appointment. In 1661 he was granted the offices of attorney and steward to the chapter and was also their collector of rents in the city of Gloucester. William Lamb was chosen to succeed him 30 Nov. 1665 (**170**). The chapter told the bishop in 1666 that Theyer 'for not giving a satisfactorie account of his trust hath beene layd aside.' He died at Cooper's Hill, Brockworth, 25 Aug. 1673. He was an antiquary, and Charles II bought 312 items from his collection of manuscripts.

THOMAS, GRIFFITH. One of the cathedral's almsmen from 1660, he had a patent for the office of sexton and was appointed in 1665 as deputy to Richard Murrall, the porter (**174**). His son Edward died in June 1667 while a chorister (**203**). After Griffith's death at the end of 1668 the chapter had difficulty in recovering the keys to the cathedral from his widow, who had apparently caused trouble earlier, for two lay singers had asked the bishop at his visitation in 1663 to disregard a complaint 'by reason the mallice comes from soe malitious a wooman as the sexton's wife is.'

TOMKINS, THOMAS. A minor canon from 1594 or earlier, he was precentor by 1609 and was elected as such annually 1617–24. He was also vicar of St. Mary de Lode, Gloucester, which was in the gift of the dean and chapter, and had died by 28 March 1627 (**72**). The dean and chapter paid his widow £1 10*s.* on condition that she left the house where she lived. He was father of the composer Thomas Tomkins, organist of Worcester cathedral, for whom see *O.D.N.B.*

TRIPPETT, THOMAS. Son of Thomas Trippett, of Gloucester, he matriculated 21 May 1669 at Merton College, Oxford, aged 17, B.C.L. 1677. On 3 Oct. 1673 he became assistant master of the Crypt School, Gloucester, and was admitted assistant master of the college school 4 Jan. 1675 (**251**).

VAULX, BRIDGET. Daughter of the prebendary Dr. John English (above) and wife of John Vaulx, a notary public who was 'proregistrar' to the bishop of Gloucester and was buried in the cathedral in Dec. 1663, where Bridget (d. 14 Feb. 1670) was also buried: *Parsons*, 409. In 1665 she was granted a lease of rooms 'over the little cloister leading into the great cloister', adjoining the prebendal house where her father had lived, and in 1667 was granted instead a lease of the Innsworth tithes (**202**).

VYNER or VINER, THOMAS. B.A. 1650 from Catharine Hall, Cambridge, M.A. 1653, B.D. Oxford 1662, D.D. 1671. Rector of Staunton from 1652. Admitted 9 Aug. 1665 to the prebend vacant by the resignation of Francis Jacob (173), having been presented 13 June and subscribed to the Act of Uniformity 20 July. He resigned that prebend on being presented on 10 Nov. to the prebend vacant by the death of Thomas Warmestry, to which he was admitted 20 Nov. 1665 (196). On 23 July 1671 he was installed as dean of Gloucester, having subscribed to the Act of Uniformity on 22 July before the bishop at Bishop's Cleeve in the presence of Richard Parsons. He died 11 April 1673 and was buried in the cathedral: *Parsons*, 408. His brother Sir Robert Viner, goldsmith, lord mayor of London, and friend of Samuel Pepys, gave books to Gloucester cathedral library; for him see *O.D.N.B.*

WARBURTON, GEORGE. Matriculated 28 March 1595 at Brasenose College, Oxford, aged 15, B.A. 1598, M.A. 1603, D.D. 1636. Installed as dean of Gloucester on 11 June 1631 (100); less than two months later, on 3 Aug., he was presented to the deanery of Wells, being instituted to that deanery on 20 Aug. and installed on 25 Aug. Died Dec. 1641.

WARMESTRY, Thomas. See *O.D.N.B.* Admitted to a prebend 19 Aug. 1660 (190). Dean of Worcester from 1661. Died 30 Oct. 1665.

WASHBOURNE, THOMAS. See *O.D.N.B.* Rector of Dumbleton from 1641. Admitted 7 Aug. 1660 to the third prebend (189); he had earlier been granted a prebend in 1643. He served as subdean from 1661 (166), subscribing to the Act of Uniformity on both 11 and 15 Aug. 1662. Vicar of St. Mary de Lode, Gloucester, 1668–70. He was the author of *Divine Poems* (1654). He died 6 May 1687, aged 80, and was buried in Gloucester cathedral: cf. *Parsons*, 410.

WASHBOURNE, WILLIAM. Younger brother of Thomas (above). Matriculated 15 June 1632 at Balliol College, Oxford, aged 15, B.A. 1634, M.A. 1639; fellow of Oriel College. Admitted 8 May 1669 to the prebend vacant by the death of Richard Harwood (199), and on the same day subscribed to the Act of Uniformity. He died 28 Nov. 1675, aged 60, and was buried in Gloucester cathedral: cf. *Parsons*, 410.

WHEELER, MAURICE. See *O.D.N.B.*; Bonnor, *Gloucester Cathedral*, 18–19. Admitted 11 Sept. 1684 as headmaster of the college school, where he remained until his resignation in 1712, beginning a register of alumni (in which for the first time it was called the King's School), encouraging the boys in a monthly 'combat of the pen' (the winners copying their exercises in their best handwriting into a special book kept for the purpose), founding a school library and encouraging gifts to the library. From 1709 until his departure from Gloucester he was also the cathedral librarian. Died 6 Oct. 1727.

WHITTINGTON, WILLIAM. Matriculated 6 May 1670 at Brasenose College, Oxford, aged 18, B.A. from Hart Hall 1674, M.A. 1676. Admitted 18 Feb. 1678 as a minor canon (260), and acted as cathedral librarian from 1682. He gave some books to the library. Rector, 1680, of St. Mary de Crypt, Gloucester, where he was buried, having died 12 Dec. 1684: *Parsons*, 206, where he is said to have been in his 30th year, though he was evidently older. Also rector of Rudford.

WIDDOWES, THOMAS. Brother of the divine Giles Widdowes (for whom see *O.D.N.B.*), he matriculated in April 1627 at Gloucester Hall, Oxford, aged 14, was a demy of Magdalen College 1630–6, and graduated B.A. 1631, M.A. 1633. Admitted headmaster of the college school Nov. 1635 (124), he had his stipend increased just one year later (135). He was ejected during the Commonwealth period, but became minister of Woodstock (Oxon.) and master of the school there, and later also at Northleach, where he died in June 1655.

WILLIAMS, DANIEL. Son of a Warwickshire parson, matriculated 30 June 1615 at St. John's College, Oxford, aged 18, B.A. 1619, M.A. from Gloucester Hall 1628. Admitted 14 Oct. 1618 as assistant master of the college school (12). Ordained deacon by the bishop of Gloucester, 1619, and priest in June 1620.

WINNIFFE, THOMAS. See *O.D.N.B.* Installed 10 Nov. 1624 as dean (**52**); resigned 1631 on appointment as dean of St. Paul's, London. Consecrated 6 Feb. 1642 as bishop of Lincoln. Died 19 Sept. 1654.

WOOD, JOHN. Admitted 23 Nov. 1625 to the third prebend (**60**). Presumably one of the four or more of the same name in *Alumni Oxon.* Dead by 15 Feb. 1640.

WORKMAN, GILES. Matriculated 27 June 1623 at Magdalen Hall, Oxford, aged 18, B.A. 1626, M.A 1629. Admitted 23 June 1628 as assistant master of the college school (**82**), which he left in 1632 to become vicar of Walford (Herefs.). In 1646 he acted temporarily as headmaster of the college school at Gloucester, but in the same year was appointed to preach the word of God in the parish church of St. Nicholas, Gloucester, the register of which contains the entry Αιγιδιου Ουρκμαν Λειτοργουντος [i.e. 'Giles Workman, minister'] and is in his writing for two years. He died in 1665 as rector of Alderley, to which he had been presented by Sir Matthew Hale, afterwards Lord Chief Justice. Anthony à Wood described him as a 'quiet and peaceable puritan' in distinction from his more fiery puritan brother John.

WREN, CHARLES. Admitted 19 Jan. 1674 as cathedral organist and instructor of the choristers (**240**). The cathedral register records his burial on 5 Dec. 1678, with a note of an affidavit of the same sworn on 10 Dec. 1678 by Joanna Whiting of the college before Thomas Washbourne, S.T.P., in the presence of John Paine (perhaps the lay singer of that name) and Thomas Aldridge.

WRENCH, BARKELEY. One of seven sons of Canon Elias Wrench (below), he was a chorister from 1621 (**32**) to 1629 (**87**). In 1617 Barkeley held the patent of the sexton's office, probably bought for him soon after his birth. In 1629, when the duties were performed by a deputy, William Mason, he tried to resign the patent (**87**). He was paid as a subsacrist of the cathedral 1616–41 and 1660–91; his deputy in that office was admitted in Nov. 1686 (**306**). Appointed organist of Ludlow church (Mon.) in March 1636, from Nov. 1638 he was for a short time the cathedral organist and master of the choristers (**144**), perhaps given the position only because the chapter remembered his father with affection; he seems to have been incapable, for some unspecified reason, of performing his duties, and had left by Nov. 1639 (**149**), being replaced by John Okeover in April 1640 (**153**).

WRENCH, ELIAS. Matriculated Easter 1578 as a sizar of Trinity College, Cambridge, B.A. 1583, M.A. 1586. Headmaster of the college school, Gloucester, 1588, and still in 1594. Presented 16 March 1599 to the second prebend. Rector of Lassington 1606–33 and of Rudford until 1633. He had seven sons, of whom Barkeley, Simeon (or Simon) and William are mentioned in the Act Book and Elias was vicar of Trent (Dorset) 1644–80; the others were Henry, John and Joshua. His daughters Radagond and Joan in 1628 received a lease of a dwelling in the infirmary, where they lived until 1649. He died 4 Oct. 1633, aged 71, and was buried in the cathedral choir in front of the stall later belonging to the canon-in-residence. Parsons records his grave, 'just before the sub-dean's seat': *Parsons*, 415. Fosbrooke says that the stone was removed to the west cloister walk, but Rudder records it as being in the south transept. On 20 Oct. 1634 Wrench's widow Mary took leases of the college mill and the common kitchen (later nos. 2 and 3 Millers Green) and kept them until she was turned out by the Parliamentarians in 1649. The cathedral accounts show that she was afterwards in need, for in 1660–1 the chapter paid 5*s.* to 'Mr. Wrenche's poore widow by Mr. Deane's order.'

WRENCH, SIMEON (or SIMON). One of seven sons of Canon Elias Wrench (above), he matriculated 28 Nov. 1623 at Corpus Christi College, Oxford, aged 15, B.A. 1627, M.A. 1630. He held the patent of the janitor's or porter's office by 1616, aged no more than 8, and from 1620 jointly with his brother William. They kept joint possession until 1641, so their resignation in June 1629 (**87**) was not effective. The brothers did not perform the duties themselves, but took the salary and paid a smaller amount to a deputy, William Mason. Simeon had a lease of the common kitchen from 1612, when he was only four, and from 1618 to 1622 jointly with his brother John. He was vicar of Llangammarch (Brec.) from 1631.

WRENCH, WILLIAM. One of seven sons of Canon Elias Wrench (above), he held the office of janitor or porter from 1620 until 1641 jointly with his brother Simeon (above). In 1639 William took a lease of the house that became no. 20 College Green, from which he was turned out in the Commonwealth period. A lawyer by profession, he was reappointed in 1662 as porter, with custody of all keys, but on 13 Dec. 1665 received from the dean a first monition to depart the church, for his 'unpeaceable demeanour' and his contempt of the dean and chapter's authority (**176**), and on 19 Aug. 1669 a second monition, for his uncivil demeanour to the dean and chapter but especially for his contempt of the bishop's authority (**214**). After some dispute about succession to the office (**242**), he was paid as a sexton or subsacrist from 1673 until *c.* 1679. He was buried in July 1693.

INDEX OF PERSONS AND PLACES

References that are not in italic and prefixed with '*p.*' are to entry-numbers, not pages. Places other than major cities are in Gloucestershire unless otherwise identified.

Abbot, George, archbishop of Canterbury, 23, 30, 54, 56
Aberdeen, university, *p. 163*
Abload, *see* Sandhurst
Addams close, in St. Mary de Lode parish, Gloucester, 128
Aisgill, Henry, *p. 161*; canon, *pp. xxvi, xxxii, 1*; 1–2, 4, 6, 14–15, 20, 27, 32, 35 *n*, 37, 126, 132; subdean, 6–7, 12; treasurer, 12
Alderley, rector, *p. 171*
Aldridge, Thomas, *p. 171*
All Saints' church, Gloucester, curate, *p. 165*
Allard, Walter, *p. xix*; 243, 254, 275
Allibond (Alleband, Allebond), John, 118, 122, 185, *p. 161*
— Margaret, wife of John, 185; *p. 161*
Andrews (Andrewes), Anthony, *pp. 161–2*; canon, *p. xxxii*; 170, 179, 201–2, 206–11, 213, 215, 219–20, 222, 227, 238, 263; admitted, 197, 314; subdean, 227–30, 236–9, 247–8; treasurer, 220, 224
Angell, Abel, *p. 161*
— John (fl. 1615), *p. 161*
— John (d. 1655), 50, 52; *p. 161*
— John (d. 1665), 174; *p. 161*
Anslip, *see* Hanslape
Anyan, Thomas, *p. 161*; canon, *pp. xxxii, 1*; 11, 30, 80, 101, 111; dispensed for absence, 18, 75
Archdeacon's Meadow, Gloucester, *p. xxii*
Arlington, earl of, *see* Bennet, Henry
Arnold, Edmund, 236
Ashleworth, manor, *p. 162*

Baber, Francis, 78; *p. 161*
Babylon, in the cathedral precinct, *pp. xvi, xxi, 162, 164*
Bacon, Sir Francis, 4
Badgeworth, *see* Bentham
Baldwyn, Mr., 187 *n*
Balliol College, Oxford, 101; *pp. 163, 168–70*
Bannester, William, 52
Barber, Thomas, 127
Barksdale, Clement, vicar of Naunton, *p. xxiv*

Barnwood (Barnewood), 165; manor, *p. xxii*; 143, 186, 217 *n*; rectory, *p. xxii*
Barton Street, Gloucester, 93 *n*; Unitarian chapel, *p. 163*
Bath and Wells, bishop, *p. 166*
Bath, earl of, *see* Bourchier, Henry
Baylis, John, 151
Bayly, Thomas, 4, 314; *p. 161*
Baynham, Samuel, 60
Beale, Mr., 187 *n*
Beames, John, *p. xv*; 31, 86, 92
Beaulieu, Luke, *p. 161*; canon, *p. xxxii*; admitted, 308, 314
Bennet, Henry, earl of Arlington, 163
Bentham, in Badgeworth, *p. 163*
Bere, Sidney, 234, 277
Bermis, Philip, 13, 22
Bertie, Montagu, earl of Lindsey, *p. xvii*
Bevan, Edward, 307 *n*
— James, 307
Bicknell, John, 289, 301
Birdwood (Birdewood), in Churcham, 206
Bishopp, Nathaniel, 93
Blackleech (Blackleach, Blackleeche), Abraham, *pp. xv, xix*; 67, 315
— Gertrude, 67 *n*
— William, *p. xix*; 67 *n*
Blandford, Walter, *p. 162*; canon, *pp. xxxii, 169*; 163–6, 198; admitted, 191, 314; bishop of Oxford, 164, 198, 200; *p. 169*
Bondholt (Bondhoult) tithes, *see* Upton St. Leonards
Bourchier, Henry, earl of Bath, *p. xvii*
Boyle, Elianor (née Jones), 216
Bradgate, *see* Brodgate
Bradshawe, James, vicar of Brookthorpe, 11
Brasenose College, Oxford, *pp. 167, 170*
Brent, Sir Nathaniel, 136; *p. 166*
Brett, Henry, 191; (three such), *p. 162*
— Joyce, *p. 162*
— Margaret, *p. 162*
Brice, Stephen, 151
Bridgeman, George, 109
— Sir John, 109

SELECTIVE INDEX OF SUBJECTS

References that are not in italic and prefixed with '*p.*' are to entry-numbers, not pages.